# The Lost Adventures of
# SHERLOCK HOLMES

# The Lost Adventures of
# SHERLOCK HOLMES

## based on the original radio plays by
## Dennis Green
## and
## Anthony Boucher

## Written by
## Ken Greenwald

**MALLARD PRESS**
An imprint of BDD Promotional Book Company, Inc.
666 Fifth Avenue
New York, N.Y. 10103

*To DENIS GREEN and ANTHONY BOUCHER*

Though gone, still with us through
their creativity and work. Their
original writing on the Sherlock Holmes
radio series made this book possible.


*Special Thanks to:*

## MARY GREEN
## PHYLLIS WHITE (née BOUCHER)
## GLENHALL TAYLOR

Their patience, understanding and
help made this book a reality.

The Sherlock Holmes short stories in this book were based on the following radio plays by Denis Green and Anthony Boucher:

*The Second Generation*
Broadcast on December 17, 1945
(based on an incident in *A Scandal in Bohemia*)

*The April Fool Adventure*
Broadcast on April 1, 1946
(based on an incident in *A Study in Scarlet*)

*The Amateur Mendicant Society*
Broadcast on April 2, 1945
(based on an incident in *The Five Orange Pips*)

*The Out-Of-Date Murder*
Broadcast on September 9, 1945
(based on an incident in *Wisteria Lodge*)

*The Demon Barber*
Broadcast on January 28, 1946
(based on an incident in *The Yellow Face*)

*Murder Beyond the Mountains*
Broadcast on January 15, 1946
(based on an incident in *The Empty House*)

*The Uneasy Easychair*
Broadcast on May 13, 1946
(based on an incident in *The Musgrove Ritual*)

*The Baconian Cipher*
Broadcast on May 27, 1946
(based on an incident in *The Sign of Four*)

*The Headless Monk*
Broadcast on April 15, 1946
(based on an incident in *The Devil's Foot*)

*The Camberwell Poisoners*
Broadcast on February 18, 1946
(based on an incident in *The Five Orange Pips*)

*The Iron Box*
Broadcast on December 31, 1945
(based on an incident in *Silver Blaze*)

*The Girl with the Gazelle*
Broadcast on March 25, 1946
(based on an incident in *The Final Problem*)

*The Notorious Canary Trainer*
Broadcast on April 23, 1945
(based on an incident in *Wisteria Lodge*)

# Contents

Foreword 7

Introduction 11

1. The Adventure of the Second Generation 15
2. The April Fool's Adventure 31
3. The Case of the Amateur Mendicants 45
4. The Adventure of the Out-of-Date Murder 59
5. The Case of the Demon Barber 73
6. Murder Beyond the Mountains 87
7. The Case of the Uneasy Easy Chair 101
8. The Case of the Baconian Cipher 115
9. The Adventure of the Headless Monk 129
10. The Case of the Camberwell Poisoners 145
11. The Adventure of the Iron Box 159
12. The Adventure of the Notorious Canary Trainer 173
13. The Case of the Girl with the Gazelle 191

# FOREWORD

*by*

## KEN GREENWALD

IT is early October in 1945. I'm only a month into my tenth year. School has just let out and I am walking home with my best friend Jerry as we joke and talk until we reach the corner where we part to go our separate ways. It's Monday, and the beginning of the week for all the kids serials on the radio. I want to get home as soon as I can to hear Superman, Terry and the Pirates, and Jack Armstrong. As I wave goodbye to Jerry, I walk the two long blocks to my house and notice that almost all the windows in every house are closed. That's because a cool breeze is in the air and we are heading towards winter. Only three weeks ago, in September, it was extremely hot. Everyone's window was open because air conditioning for the average home was unheard of in those days. I mention this because I can remember vividly walking down the street one hot summer evening while people were listening to Al Jolson on the Kraft Music Hall radio show. He was so popular that everyone, yes, everyone listened to him. That's why, as I walked that evening, I could hear the show coming from every window. I never missed a joke, a line, or a word of the broadcast! That was one of the great joys of radio. You didn't have to stay in one place and look at a screen to see and understand what was going on. Women often sewed, ironed clothes or prepared food for the coming meal, while men would be fixing something, working on a crossword puzzle or helping their children as the radio was playing in the background, never once missing a beat on what was being presented.

When I got home from school, I tossed my books and homework on my bed and went right to the radio to catch up on what was happening to Superman and all the other adventure heroes. But what I really was waiting for, as I did every week for thirty-nine weeks a year, was to turn the radio dial to KHJ, the Mutual Network radio station in Los Angeles, so I could listen to THE NEW ADVENTURES OF SHERLOCK HOLMES, starring Basil Rathbone and Nigel Bruce. By that time, my mother had gotten me ready for bed, making me put on my pajamas, brush my teeth and wash my face, all of which I was loath to do as a kid. She would give me a kiss, then tuck me under the covers and close the door to my room, while I lay there totally and miserably wide awake. I never wanted to go to sleep that early. I wanted to listen to all the adult radio shows, just like my mom and dad were doing. When I was sure my parents were busy in the other room, I would quietly turn on the radio, which was located next to my bed on the desk. It was a tiny four-tube Arvin with no dial light. By the way, I still own that radio. When I turned it on, the tubes would light up bright for a second, casting their iridescence against the wall, then dim down as they warmed up. It was dark in my room, but as my eyes because accustomed, the dim light from the glowing tubes cast a gentle reddish glow on everything so that I could see clearly. I knew exactly where each important radio station was on the dial by touch and position. It was easy for me to find KHJ. I would keep the volume very low so my mother would not know I was listening, then tune in Sherlock Holmes. Once I heard the Mutual Network cue, I knew the show would start. And sure enough, there came the familiar theme music, which always sent a chill up my spine. I would pull the covers tight around me and push my pillow and head as close to the radio as I could to catch every word, every action, every deed that Sherlock Holmes and Dr. Watson went through. I was never disappointed. It was one of my favorite radio shows as a child. For some reason, I never remembered the stories for more than a week, each new story taking over when the next Sherlock Holmes show as broadcast. But I never forgot the music or those wonderfully familiar voices of Basil Rathbone and Nigel Bruce.

Before I knew it, all of that disappeared, as I grew up and entered the world of reality. As an adult I often hummed the theme music to the radio show or thought about Rathbone and Bruce in their roles as Holmes and Watson. Yes, I had watched the films many times (they are still playing them over and over on television), but it wasn't the same. How can sitting in a movie theatre or sitting on a couch before my t.v. duplicate the wonderful times I had when I was tucked safely in bed with the lights out listening to a small radio present me with drama, fantasy, comedy and variety, all for free, and all of it dancing beautifully in my imagination, day by month by year? There has never been anything quite like it and, sadly, I must say there will never be anything like it again.

That's what radio, Sherlock Holmes, and the nineteen forties meant to me. Now, in the late nineteen eighties the world is totally different. Yet, what listening to radio did for me was to open the door to the world of imagination and entertainment. And that's where I stayed. I have, and am now working in the entertainment industry, as a writer, producer and director of short films, and as one member of a team of archivists for Pacific Pioneer Broadcasters, an important Los Angeles radio museum. Out of my contacts with people from my work in the archives, the world of Sherlock Holmes on radio came to life again!

I had never imagined I would once again hear that familiar opening theme on the show. When I did, that same kind of exciting chill I had as a child again ran up my spine. I was home. And I was determined to do something about it. It was by sheer accident that our small group of radio devotees learned of a long run of missing Sherlock Holmes radio shows from 1945. Our excitement grew even greater for we knew it had to be Rathbone and Bruce as the famous detective and his loyal companion. We managed to track the shows down and collect them. It was a true gold mine of Sherlock Holmes radio shows! But what to do with them? Often the most commonplace events and daily doings lead to deeds and actions that would ordinarily not even be considered. I and the small group of friends who had rescued the

Holmes radio shows were sitting in, of all places, a hamburger joint, discussing this amazing find, when one of us said:

"Why don't we release a couple of the shows on a record?"

We looked at each other for a moment in quiet curiosity, then we burst forth with talk and plans. One year later the record album was released. Six months after the release everyone turned to me and said:

"Ken, you're a writer, why don't we put out a book of Sherlock Holmes short stories based on the radio plays?"

Incredible! This thing was snowballing and everyone was delighted and excited by it all. Before long, we signed a contract with Simon and Schuster to have them release the entire 1945 Holmes radio season with Basil Rathbone and Nigel Bruce as the stars!

I was more than half way through writing the book of short stories when this happened. As I helped produce the cassettes and write the book, the greatest excitement of all was that I could listen to and relive the stories of Holmes and Watson on the radio as I had done those long years ago in 1945.

Before I started writing this book, I had to ask myself an important question: How do I try and top the writing of Denis Green and Anthony Boucher? I decided it was silly to try. Denis Green and Anthony Boucher were wonderful writers and I had no intention of trying to best them. Instead, I wanted to augment them, to add to their writing with my own. What I have done is to take a long lost medium of writing, radio plays, and turn them into the short story form. Not an easy task. There is much in the radio play format that doesn't work well in the short story format. I had to change these things and add dialogue where necessary. Musical bridges that were used in the radio shows to show passage of time I had to turn into Watson's narrative describing what Holmes and he were doing. Scene shifts and broken actions in the radio plays that were easily accepted by the listening audience as a natural progression had to be translated into the written form for the reader to comprehend.

What we have then is a book of stories that is a combination of the writings of Denis Green, Anthony Boucher and Ken Greenwald. I retained as much of the original as possible, changing or adding only where necessary. Most of the narrative scenes and descriptions are my own. If you really want to see the differences, just pick up some of the Simon and Schuster radio cassettes in your local bookstore and compare what I have done to what Green and Boucher did originally.

An important factor is that I have not tried to write as Sir Arthur Conan Doyle wrote. It would be unfair to him. I am not trying to imitate Conan Doyle's style, but rather to be true to the writings of Green and Boucher, using the style of Victorian English as the structure on which to unfold the stories. This approach has allowed me to honor Sir Arthur Conan Doyle's characters, retain the feel of Victorian England, and to utilize as much of the Green and Boucher material as possible.

I would like to emphasize a very important point as you read these stories. There have been many actors portraying Sherlock Holmes and Dr. Watson. To me, and to thousands of others,

Basil Rathbone and Nigel Bruce are, and will always be, Sherlock Holmes and Dr. Watson. It doesn't matter that their performances often do not fit Sir Arthur Conan Doyle's actual descriptions of the characters and how they were in his original works. It simply seems to be the accepted way most people identify Basil Rathbone with Sherlock Holmes and Nigel Bruce with Dr. Watson. Therefore, please be aware I wrote these stories with Rathbone and Bruce in mind, just as Green and Boucher did for the radio series. As you read, do think of Rathbone and Bruce in the roles of the great detective and his companion, won't you?

KEN GREENWALD
Los Angeles, California
September 8, 1988

# INTRODUCTION

### by

### Dr. John H. Watson

IT has been a very long time since I retired from my medical practice, as well as my writing stories about the exploits of my good friend Sherlock Holmes. I am sure it may surprise most of you to learn that, indeed, Sherlock Holmes and I are very much alive and well, living quiet lives, he on his Sussex bee farm and I in a small house in the Kensington district, not far from Hyde Park. It would be difficult to explain our longevity, but a hint at the reason for this is given in the very last story of this volume of work.

Only last year I received a telephone call from the Baker Street Associates concerning a long lost edition of Holmes stories that I had written, a copy of which they had discovered in some obscure book shop in New South Wales, Australia.

I had, after the publication of my original fifty-six stories and four novels, decided to produce one more collection of Sherlock Holmes adventures. This book was called THE NEW ADVENTURES OF SHERLOCK HOLMES. Unfortunately the book was released in 1914, on the eve of World War I. The number of copies produced was minimal and, with the war close at hand, there seemed little interest in the exploits of my redoubtable friend. Another unfortunate incident occurred when, during those first months of the war, paper became in short supply, most of it going to the war effort. Because of this, I quickly withdrew the book from circulation and never had occasion to return to it. Very few books were sold during those troubled times and what few copies of my book were printed ended up on the remainder shelves until the book was completely forgotten. Now, all these years later, there is renewed interest in these long lost exploits of my good friend and, thanks to the efforts of the Baker Street Associates and their close work with me, the book will once again be published. Because of the extensive period of time between the original publication of this book and the present edition, I have chosen to change the title to THE LOST ADVENTURES OF SHERLOCK HOLMES.

Times have drastically changed since those quieter days of Victorian England into which I was born and lived my younger years. But I am proud to say that both Holmes and I have had the good fortune to live through the Second Great War, the coming of radio, the cinema, television and the exploration of space. All these things were only dreamt of in my time.

11

Now, with the stark reality of this world knocking on our door, I feel it best to return to an earlier time when all things moved slowly and people took the time to understand the intricate ways of life. With the publication, once again of this long-lost book, I am proud to loosely paraphrase the American author Vincent Starrett: "It shall always be Sherlock Holmes and Victorian England."

Written this day,
25 JULY 88
by Dr. John Watson

# The Lost Adventures of
# SHERLOCK HOLMES

"Do not turn around! I have a revolver pointed at you both! Put your hands up, gentlemen!"

# 1

# THE ADVENTURE OF THE SECOND GENERATION

## I

NOTWITHSTANDING the large success of my medical practice of late, my losses have been great these last few years.

Anna, my second wife, had been killed in a four-wheeler accident only a short time ago. This heavy grief also rekindled that which I had felt at the death of my first wife, Mary. May they rest in peace. In addition, there was the loss of my companionship with Sherlock Holmes, who had long since retired to his Sussex bee farm.

Without realization on my behalf, I had filled the void accorded by these losses by allowing my practice to grow to the point of nearly consuming my own health. Fatigue, indeed near exhaustion, had crept into my daily routine of treating the many patients who relied on me for their cures.

The circumstance of which I laboriously speak occurred through the early part of 1909. Spring had finally come, and it was shortly after a bout of soulful longings for happier times that I received a note from Holmes pleading with me to suspend my practice for a few weeks and come visit him for a time.

Here was my chance to recuperate from the weariness that plagued me, and to indulge in pleasant reminiscences with my old friend.

Without hesitation, I informed my secretary to put all patients on notice that I would be unavailable for a fortnight. I glanced at the note again. Holmes would have a dogcart awaiting me at the railroad station, therefore I must take the 11:05 A.M. eastborn train this very day to the station in Paddlewaite, near the Sussex downs.

I laughed, for Holmes, my dear friend Holmes, still had not lost his very presumptuous nature!

There were times, not a few I might add, that the irony of Holmes' retirement to a bee farm in Sussex struck me with an unrelenting fervor; a fervor that caused me to vacillate between bewilderment at his seeming complete change in character and an uncanny urge for heartfelt laughter at the unlikely nature of that change.

I have, in the past, accurately portrayed Holmes' dislike of country life, even extending to a reluctance to expend time in vacationing for any great length at a seaside resort. The visit to the country or the seaside was acceptable to my friend only if it were in the interest of excitement caused by some rare intrigue. Therefore, the metamorphosis of Holmes into a country gentleman interested in pursuing the complexities of nature, rather than the complexities of his fellow man, continued to leave me questioning just how keen my observations of his mental peculiarities had been. These musings I now put aside in preparation for my stay with Holmes.

I soon found myself disembarking from the train and quickly alighting on the dogcart Holmes' manservant had brought to the station especially for me. It was not long before we moved slowly down a winding road surrounded by lush vegetation, soon to be deposited before the modest home of my dear friend, where, excitedly, I stepped up to the door and knocked. In a moment it opened and there, a smile crossing his countenance, his favorite pipe firmly between his lips, stood my oldest and dearest friend, Sherlock Holmes.

"Watson, my dear man, I'm gratified that you accepted my invitation!"

In a rare gesture, even for Holmes, he placed his arm around my shoulders and ushered me into his home. I took note that he looked older since last I saw him, but as he spoke to me, I realized, from the keenness of his voice and the sparkle in his eyes, that he would never really grow old.

"My home is now your home, Watson, for the duration of your stay. And, of course, for any other time you wish to visit. But you must relax, my friend, and forget your cares. You have been pushing yourself much too hard."

"How do you know that, Holmes?" I exclaimed, always astonished by his keen observations.

"When have you ever stuffed your stethoscope into your coat pocket where I can now see it protruding? You have always placed it inside your derby when in a hurry. And you are one of the tidiest men I know, yet your shirt shows signs of chemical staining and your collar is creased, indicating that you have been working yourself so hard you have forgotten just those things that have always shown you as possessing the habit of cleanliness. No, Watson, you have not been yourself of late. Come, sit down and forget your worries, for you are on vacation and on vacation you shall be!"

Beyond these quick observations, Holmes never asked me what had caused my state of exhaustion for he knew, and rightly so, that time here in the country with my old friend would put things aright. I soon found myself deep in conversation with Holmes, talking of our many past exploits. In a while we lapsed into the comfortable silence that can only exist between friends such as Holmes and myself.

After a while he picked up his beloved violin and began to play some haunting melody, his long thin fingers caressing the instrument.

"Beautiful, quite beautiful, Holmes," I intoned.

"Thank you, Watson," he said, pausing and staring at me for a moment.

"You look uncommonly wistful, dear chap. Are you still thinking of the old days?"

"Yes, Holmes, I am."

"I must admit that I am also. Yes, those were exciting times, Watson, but it is comforting to think that now we will not be disturbed by a jangling doorbell, followed shortly by some poor devil in trouble. Nowadays my greatest excitements are connected with the segregation of the Queen Bee, and the nighttime proclivities of Charles Augustus, my tomcat."

We laughed heartily, the solemn mood of remembrance having been broken.

"I still find it hard to think of you in retirement, Holmes. Do you ever consider returning to active practice?"

"Oh, I consider it occasionally, and then reject the idea. A man should work only up to the peak of his ability. I've passed mine."

"Nonsense," I declared, astonished at his attitude, "you're just as alert as ever you were!"

"Mentally, perhaps, but not physically."

I could see Holmes retreating into himself then, as his thoughts turned elsewhere. I knew these signs, for they were an indication of boredom. The same kind of boredom that had, in the past, inevitably sent him hurrying to his syringe and his comforting seven percent solution. Although Holmes no longer relied on that dreadful substance for relief, I was determined to prevent a sense of boredom from setting in, at least as long as I were here on holiday.

I had not mentioned to Holmes that I had met a strikingly beautiful young lady on the train who had engaged me in casual conversation. It was this conversation, combined with Holmes' approaching withdrawal that prompted me to bring up the young lady in his presence.

"Holmes, would you consider handling a small problem which I am about to tell you?"

"If it's a personal problem that affects you, Watson, you know I'll do anything I can."

"It's not my problem, Holmes, it's the problem of a charming young lady I met on the train. In conversation she revealed that you knew her mother quite well, and—"

Holmes stared at me, a look of bewilderment crossing his face.

"Her mother?"

I was about to reveal everything that was said to me, when suddenly there was a knock on the door.

"Come in," responded Holmes, irritated by the interruption.

When the door opened, there stood a small man in an ill-fitting servant's uniform, his hair dishevelled and pulled back in an attempt at neatness. In his hand he held a piece of paper.

"Yes, Deevers, what is it?"

"I'm sorry to disturb you, Mr. Holmes, but your man said I might come in. My master, Mr. Litton-Stanley, instructed me to deliver this note. He also instructed me to wait for a reply."

Holmes took the note and, reading it, fell into a state of anger.

"What confounded impudence! You tell your master there is no answer to this letter!"

"But he told me I must get a reply, sir."

"You may tell Mr. Litton-Stanley that I will instruct my solicitors to reply to his message in due course!"

"Very good, sir," replied the little man who promptly left, agitated by my friend's angered words.

"What is it, Holmes?" I questioned, filled with curiosity over this small incident that so upset Holmes.

"Read it for yourself," he said, thrusting the note at me. I took it and read aloud.

"*Keep your filthy bees where they belong. One of my guests was stung yesterday. If this happens again, I will have the police run you out of this place!*"

"Good Lord," I exclaimed, "what an offensive letter!"

"The man himself is even more offensive," returned Holmes, "He's a retired manufacturer who thinks that his immense wealth entitles him to domineer the local residents!"

Holmes took the note back, and tossed it on a nearby table. I watched as he paced back and forth for a moment, then he went to his familiar Persian slipper, took some tobacco and stuffed it into his pipe. He had calmed down somewhat as he lit the pipe, then turned and faced me.

"Well, Watson, you can see how that man seems to get at my nature. But let us not spoil a nice sunny afternoon by continued discussion of him. Please go on with the story of the young lady you met on the train."

"The poor woman seemed in dreadful trouble. I do wish you would help her."

I gained his full attention now, the signs of withdrawal Holmes had shown earlier had completely vanished.

"You say that she told you her mother knew me?"

"Yes."

"What's her name?"

"Norton. Irene Norton."

"Norton," he said, quizzically, "I don't seem to recall—but of course! Where is the girl, Watson?"

"She's staying at the Red Lion, in the village."

"Then ring her on the telephone, and ask her to come over here as fast as she can. Of course I'll help her!"

Before my eyes I watched Holmes come to life, his eyes sparkling as of old, his frame tense with expectation. This was the Holmes of the inquisitive mind, of the expert logic that I had known to solve so many a mystery in those pleasant and intriguing days in Baker Street.

"I'm delighted Holmes. But what made you change your mind so suddenly about taking on a case? I thought you were finally and irrevocably retired."

"Is your memory so short, Watson, that you can't remember Irene Adler? Surely you haven't forgotten that, in the case you call A SCANDAL IN BOHEMIA, I was completely fooled by her!"

"By Jove, that's right! You always referred to her as 'THE WOMAN.' But how does this young lady, Irene Norton, fit into the picture?"

"Think, Watson, think! Irene Adler married a barrister named Jeffrey Norton! Ah, I see you are beginning to understand. Tell Miss Norton to come at once. She is the daughter of 'THE WOMAN'!"

It was but a short while later that Irene Norton arrived from the village. Holmes gestured for her to be seated. He stood there a moment staring at this lovely woman, then quietly seated himself across from her, while I sat well enough away that I might take any necessary notes without intruding on their conversation. There was an awkward moment, as I remembered the incomplete glimpse of Irene Adler I'd had through a window some twenty years ago. I was now able to place the familiarity of Miss Norton's features, as I compared them to my memory of those exquisite features of her mother. Both mother and daughter were breathtaking and I observed that Holmes also was taken by this young lady.

"Mr. Holmes," she said, smiling, "I've heard so much about you from mother. She says you are the most clever man in England."

"Your mother flatters me, my dear child. Did she ever tell you of the circumstances under which we met?"

"No, Mr. Holmes, though she did tell me you were a witness when she and my father were married."

"True, though the occasion was rather a little unusual." Holmes leaned forward, pulling his watch chain out and extending it towards Miss Norton.

"This golden sovereign I wear on my watch chain is a small memento of that day. I also have a rather charming photograph of your mother."

"Forgive me for interrupting," I ventured, "but it might be wise to tell Mr. Holmes about your troubles, my dear."

"Quite right, Watson. Reminiscences can wait until we have dealt with your problem, Miss Norton. Just what is troubling you, my dear?"

"Mr. Holmes, I'm being blackmailed! By a neighbor of yours, a Mr. Litton-Stanley. Do you know him?"

Holmes and I looked at each other and I spotted a smile of chagrined amusement on his face.

"Yes, indeed I do know the man," Holmes said, puffing hard on his pipe. "What hold does Mr. Litton-Stanley have over you?"

"He has some letters," she continued, her face blushing somewhat, "some rather indiscreet letters of mine that I wrote to a friend of his last year."

"How did he obtain these letters, Miss Norton?"

"He must have stolen them. I don't know how, but when I was staying at his house a few weeks ago, he told me that he had them and asked 5,000 pounds for their return!"

"This is astonishing," I blurted out, but Holmes gestured for me to remain silent for the moment.

"And why, Miss Norton, should he consider your letters, even indiscreet letters, worth so large a sum?"

"I'm engaged to be married to Lord Weston's son. That awful man, Litton-Stanley, knows that if my fiancée saw the letters, the marriage would never take place."

"Have you told your mother?" Holmes asked.

"Oh no, she'd never understand!"

"Hmm, she might surprise you on that score, I think," Holmes said as he rose and moved to gaze out at the countryside from one of his windows.

"And your father?"

"Daddy's a barrister. He most certainly would not understand."

"And so you come to me. Why?"

"Mother has told me about your abilities and, in any case, I've read Dr. Watson's stories."

"Watson," Holmes chided, "your stories will land me in serious trouble one of these days. Now, Miss Norton, what exactly do you want of me?"

"Please, get the letters back for me."

"But how, my dear child?"

"Steal them, of course."

I sat there, shocked by the words of this beautiful young lady, astonished by the idea that she would place Holmes in the category of a common thief.

"Really, my dear young lady," I ventured, "how could you think that my friend—"

Holmes cut me short.

"No, my dear Watson. Don't be shocked. Miss Norton is a forthright girl like her mother before her. It's most refreshing!"

"Mr. Holmes, you can't say you won't help me."

"No," Holmes spoke up, turning to face the desperate young lady, "I don't think that I can say that. In any case, I have a slight personal score to settle with Mr. Litton-Stanley, myself. He's rude, and has no understanding of bees."

"And how are you going to steal the letters?" I asked, quite dismayed by the entire matter.

"That problem requires a little thought," returned Holmes.

"I could tell you how to do it, Mr. Holmes."

I turned towards Miss Norton, again astonished by her words. Holmes smiled, taking all this in in his inimitable way, then moved to seat himself as before.

"Really now," he said laughingly, "this is delightful, my dear. You explain the problem, and also the way of solving it. How easy a detective's work might be if all clients were equally helpful. Tell me, what is your plan?"

"Tomorrow is the servant's half day off at Mr. Litton-Stanley's. He'll be alone there during the afternoon."

"How do you know that fact?" Holmes asked.

"My maid was 'keeping company,' as they say, with Deevers the butler when I was staying there a few weeks ago. She found out everything from him. My letters are kept in a filigree box in his desk."

"With your enterprise, my dear," Holmes interjected, "I'm surprised you didn't try to open the desk yourself."

"I did," she returned, "but it's very sturdy and has a combination lock. However, I'm sure that you and Dr. Watson can think of some way of getting the letters. Particularly if Mr. Litton-Stanley is alone in the house."

"We shall do our best, Miss Norton," came Holmes' reply as he stood and graciously bowed to this rather astute young lady. He took her hand and led her to the door. I stood and followed. Miss Norton turned to us at the doorway, an anxious look on her face.

"Promise me one thing, both of you."

"What is that?" I returned in curiosity.

"Don't read the letters, will you? I'm . . . I'm really rather ashamed of writing them."

"Of course we won't, my dear child," I added reassuringly.

"You're both so sweet to me. How can I thank you?"

"Thanks would be a little premature at this point," Holmes said. "Do forgive me now as I must take time to give this problem some thought."

I nodded a goodbye as Holmes ushered Miss Norton out. He stood in the doorway a moment, his gaunt frame immovable as he watched the young lady walk lightly up the garden path. When he returned and we were both seated comfortably, he pulled out his pipe and lit it.

"Interesting, Watson. A charming and interesting young lady."

"It seems a difficult problem finding a way to rob Mr. Litton-Stanley."

He laughed, puffing vigorously on his pipe.

"Heavens no, Watson. I should say it's only half a pipe problem. In the meantime, let us relax and enjoy the evening hours to come."

"Hmm," I said, "what unusual circumstances. Tonight, we relax. And tomorrow, a touch of daylight robbery!"

## II

Holmes, a master of disguises, had, at various times fooled me by his ingenious use of makeup. But none of Holmes' past efforts surprised me as much as what he did the following morning. I felt quite the fool as I stood there, made up by his deft hands to look like a country doctor. A Scottish doctor by the name of Hamish, long beard and all.

"Holmes," I said in irritation, "it's quite one thing to disguise yourself, but to put me through such machinations is intolerable!"

"Watson," he replied, ignoring my remarks, "you look wonderful! Quite the appearance of a doctor of the old school!"

"But Holmes," I pleaded. He placed his hands on my shoulders and spoke in the gentlest of tones.

"Watson, you do me the honor to not only be my friend, but to accompany me on this small adventure. Please bear with this annoying contrivance for but a short while. It is essential that you be disguised."

How could I resist my old friend Holmes? He was right, of course, for we both knew we were together again, even for a short while, and truly, the game was afoot!

I accepted with a slight nod and a smile.

"I knew you would understand, Watson. Now, let us commence with our bit of intrigue!"

It was not long that Holmes and I stood in front of Mr. Litton-Stanley's home, an elegant Tudor mansion with long windows that reached almost to the floor, and surrounded by much shrubbery. Without hesitation Holmes pounded on the door.

"Remember Watson, since you are a real doctor, it should be easy to assume the role of a doctor, even a Scottish one. Wait! Here comes someone!"

In a moment the door was opened and there stood a tall, formidable man. A man of great strength with large hands. His face was sharp featured with a high forehead and a great crop of dark hair, specked with gray. In an instant Holmes fell into the role of a rather firm, but frail Nonconformist parson.

"Mr. Litton-Stanley?" he asked.

"That is my name."

"Mine is Appleby and this is my friend, Dr. Hamish."

"Glad to meet you sir," I added, "I've heard a great deal about you."

"What can I do for you?"

"If we could come in a moment," Holmes smiled, "I'll explain our mission."

"Very well," said Litton-Stanley reluctantly, "come into the study."

He strode before us, his huge frame moving clumsily into the study. There he turned and gestured for us to have a seat. Holmes and I seated ourselves comfortably while the huge man leaned against a nearby table.

"We are raising a subscription list," Holmes began in an awful high-pitched voice, "for a charity hospital in Paddlewaite, just across the downs. You are a prominent resident here and we thought you might like to donate a few guineas."

"I'm really not very interested. I've given as much to charity this year as I can afford."

"Ahh, it's a fine cause, sir," I added, "I'm giving my medical services three days a week, and the Reverend Appleby is donating his services, too."

"Who else has contributed to this fund?" asked Litton-Stanley, crossing his arms.

"All your neighbors, sir. We just came from the bee farm over the downs," said Holmes. "The owner gave us a check for five guineas!" Litton-Stanley clenched his fists as a frown crossed his brow.

"Holmes gave you five guineas, did he?"

"Aye. A very nice gentleman, Mr. Holmes," I added. "We're proposing to name a ward in the hospital after him."

"Is this list of subscribers going to be published in the local papers?"

"Oh yes, Mr. Litton-Stanley, yes," Holmes said, smiling his utmost.

"I'll give you TEN guineas!"

"Oh, thank you sir," Holmes remarked in mock amazement.

"I'll get my checkbook."

Litton-Stanley sat at his desk, his back to us. As he unlocked his massive roll-top desk and pulled out his checkbook, Holmes turned to me and whispered in my ear.

"Quick Watson, the chloroform!"

"Now, who do I make this check payable to?" Litton-Stanley said as I moved quietly behind him, my arm poised. Before an answer was forthcoming, I was upon him, having poured some of the chloroform from a small vial into my handkerchief. He struggled for a moment, his huge frame rising from the chair, dragging me effortlessly with him, but Holmes held him steady with his strong hands as the chloroform took effect. Soon he slumped forward as I placed him back in the chair, leaning him gently against the desk.

"Very neat, Watson," said Holmes, a grin crossing his face.

"Is the filigree box in the desk?" I asked.

"Yes, as a matter of fact, here it is, Watson!"

In one gesture, he had pulled it from the drawer he suspected it might be in and showed it to me. Then, almost as quickly, he went to its lid and opened it. I found myself in a rage, prompted by his action and what he had earlier promised Miss Norton.

"Holmes, don't open it! You promised you wouldn't!"

"I just wish to make sure that—"

Holmes never finished his sentence, for a voice somewhere in the room interrupted him.

"To make sure of what was there, Mr. Sherlock Holmes?"

Holmes and I were taken by surprise, but before we could turn around and see who it was, he again spoke.

"Do not turn around! I have a revolver pointed at you both! Now place the box on the table, Mr. Holmes. And put your hands up, gentlemen!"

"I know that voice," Holmes said calmly, as he placed the box on the table, "it's Deevers, the butler."

"Quite right, sir."

"Well Deevers," I said furiously, "you needn't point a revolver at us. Your master isn't injured."

"I'm not in the least interested in my master's health, Dr. Watson. In fact, if he were dead, I should be delighted."

"Then what are you up to, Deevers?" questioned Holmes.

"I'm taking advantage of the situation, sir," he replied quite calmly. "I've been trying to open that desk for weeks. After such kindness on your part, sir, I hate to seem ungracious, but I'm dreadfully afraid I shall have to kill you. Rather, to kill the both of you!"

I stood there, my hands above my head, at a complete loss as to what to do. When I looked at my friend Sherlock Holmes, I saw no trace of emotion on his face, whereas I found myself fighting off the anguish of the moment. I felt sure that Holmes and I would soon be lying dead in Litton-Stanley's house.

"Deevers," Holmes spoke up, "I dislike to interrupt such a melodramatic moment, but why is it necessary to kill us?"

"For months, Mr. Holmes, I have been waiting for an opportunity to steal the Kitmanjar Emerald, and now you have done it for me, sir, and presented me with a perfect alibi."

"The Kitmanjar Emerald?" Holmes questioned, a curious look upon his face.

"Come now, Mr. Holmes, you know the treasure is in this house as well as I do. Apart from the emerald, there is a superb Cellini that would fetch a fine price in the right market!"

"We aren't here after any valuables, my good man," I said, deeply annoyed.

"Please do not call me your good man, Dr. Watson," Deevers said sharply. "It's patronizing and untrue. In any case, whether you were here after the valuables or not makes no difference. Let us say that I've caught you both red-handed! You are completely in my power, gentlemen!"

"I take it that you are going to steal the treasure and pretend that we were responsible."

"Exactly, Mr. Holmes. I shall kill you both, secrete what objects appeal to me and when my master regains consciousness I shall explain that I found three men burgling the house. That I killed two of them, while the third got away with the loot. Who will be able to doubt my word? I shall be regarded as a hero. I might even have my salary raised!"

"Watson, I'm afraid this is the end, old chap."

"What a sordid way to die," I blurted out, "shot in the back like a coward!" I was beside myself in rage. If I had at least half a chance I would have tried to disarm Deevers and thrash him to within an inch of his life! But I was helpless and, in my worry, found myself concerned more with Holmes' safety rather than my own.

"Deevers," Holmes asked, "at least do me the courtesy of allowing us to face the firing squad, will you?"

"Very well, gentlemen, turn around, but don't try any tricks!"

"One last request," went on Holmes.

"What is it?"

"I'm beaten, and I admit it. I am getting old, but in my heyday I crossed swords with some of the greatest criminals in Europe. Attempts on my life have been made many times, but I've always escaped. If this is to be my swan song, at least give me the privilege of shaking the hand of the man who has, at last, bested me."

"Well, sir, I feel that I am stepping a little out of my station, but I suppose the situation is unusual. I hope you don't object to the left hand, sir. I'll keep the revolver in my right."

"Very well, Deevers. There you are."

The two men stood shaking hands while I watched helplessly.

"Goodbye, Mr. Sherlock Holmes."

"Goodbye, Deevers, and my congratulations."

My mind was racing in an attempt to find some way to put an end to this terrible situation, when suddenly Holmes twisted his body, holding onto Deevers' arm. In an instant Holmes applied leverage and Deevers, taken completely by surprise, found himself flat against the floor, his revolver discharging, its bullet imbedding itself harmlessly into the nearby wall.

"My congratulations for being a fool!" Holmes yelled in triumph.

"Well done, Holmes," I said in much-needed relief.

"I may be getting old, but I've not lost my skill at Baritsu. Deveers struck the desk as he fell. Better see to him, Watson."

"He's gashed his head, but it's not serious. He'll be unconscious for a while."

"Good. I think we'll take the precaution of closing this desk drawer. I don't want him to be exposed to further temptation when he comes to."

"Shouldn't we get in touch with the police, Holmes?"

"Police? Great Scott, no, old fellow! After all we're burglars, and we're in disguise. Two facts that would be hard to explain satisfactorily. No, Watson, we must get back to the bee farm as soon as possible, call Miss Norton, and inform her of our success!"

After Holmes and I arrived at his farm, we took off our disguises and, contacting Miss Norton, awaited her arrival. In due time a hansom deposited her at Holmes' doorstep and she was soon sitting before us.

"Mr. Holmes, Dr. Watson, I am so glad to see you back again!" exclaimed Miss Norton excitedly. "Did you get the filigree box?"

"Yes, Miss Norton. And here it is!"

"Holmes, I didn't know you took the box when we—"

"Quiet, Watson. Why not open it, Miss Norton," he said, holding the box out to her.

"Open it, my dear," he continued, "there may not be love letters inside it, but there is a note."

Miss Norton opened the box and pulled out the note, quite puzzled, as was I, by Holmes' actions.

"Please read it to us, my dear," he said, a smile crossing his lips. Miss Norton carefully unfolded the note and read:

"LET THIS BE A WARNING, MISS NORTON. CRIME DOES NOT PAY. IF YOU DON'T BELIEVE ME, ASK YOUR MOTHER. SINCERELY, SHERLOCK HOLMES."

"Mr. Holmes, you knew my secret all the time!"

"Not all the time, but I realized it as soon as I opened the filigree box."

"What on earth are you talking about, Holmes?" I asked in a state of total confusion.

"Miss Norton was under the impression that she could use me as a cat's paw, as a dupe to commit a burglary for her."

"I still don't understand, Holmes," I exclaimed.

"You will remember she asked us to 'promise not to open the box.'"

"Yes, but you did open it just before that fellow held us up with a revolver. What was inside?"

"An impressive green stone which I knew to be the Kitmanjar Emerald!"

"But where is the emerald now?" asked Miss Norton.

"Without Watson realizing it at the time, I slipped it back into Mr. Litton-Stanley's desk and locked it. I brought the box here because I wanted to see your expression, Miss Norton, as you opened it."

"Great Scott! And I thought you were a poor little thing in trouble," I said, dismayed by the realization of Miss Norton's true nature.

Holmes' tall, gaunt figure overshadowed Miss Norton as he gazed directly into her eyes.

"What do you have to say for yourself, young lady?"

"I'm terribly sorry, Mr. Holmes, terribly sorry. It seemed like a wildly exciting idea, but I really didn't mean to steal it."

"Oh, of course not, no, no," Holmes said cynically, "Of course you didn't. You meant *me* to steal it for you! Miss Norton, I'm convinced you know that your mother once outwitted me, and you presumed to think that you could do the same. I should turn you over to the police."

"Please don't, Mr. Holmes, you can't do that!"

"I certainly could!" Holmes exclaimed angrily, "but I'm not going to, for two reasons: First, you are young and impressionable and this may teach you a lesson. And, in the second place, I have a . . . well, a great admiration for your mother. But I warn you, Miss Norton, you have had a narrow escape—a very narrow escape!"

Miss Norton was as white as a sheet. Tensely, she rose from the chair she had occupied, drew a handkerchief from her sleeve, and pressed it against her cheek. She took a deep breath and looked at Holmes with the slightest of tears in her eyes.

"Mr. Holmes, before I go, there is one favor I'd like to ask you."

"Really, What is it?"

"Could I keep this filigree box with your note inside it? It would be a reminder all my life of how we met."

Holmes turned to me, smiling.

"Well, what do you say, Watson?"

"It isn't your box to give, Holmes."

"True, old fellow, quite true. But I fail to see how we can return it now without disclosing our share in the attempted robbery. In any case, I don't like Mr. Litton-Stanley. I think we might indulge in a little petty larceny without feeling too guilty. Very well, Miss Norton, you may keep the box."

"I shall always treasure it. Thank you. Goodbye, Dr Watson. Don't think too badly of me. Good night, Mr. Holmes."

Before I realized it, Miss Norton was gone, leaving Holmes and I to reflect upon the days events. I am sure that Holmes was deeply affected by this young lady, for, as the daughter of "THE WOMAN," Miss Norton had brought back to my dear friend many thoughts and emotions that would remain his, and his alone, in this quiet moment after her departure. Holmes turned slowly, seated himself comfortably in his favorite chair, lit his pipe, then leaned his head back, eyes closed, deep in thought. I sat across from him, myself in thought; but I wanted to ask him some questions about these recent events. I waited for a moment longer, then interrupted his reverie.

"Holmes, forgive me for disturbing your thoughts, but I found you surprisingly lenient with that girl. Do you suppose her mother put her up to the whole thing?"

"That possibility had occurred to me," he said, opening his eyes. "Yet I have a feeling that—"

Holmes was cut short by a knocking on the front door.

"Come in!" he yelled in irritation. "The door is open!"

"Were you expecting anyone, Holmes?"

"No."

There was no mistaking the man in the doorway. It was Litton-Stanley.

"Good evening, sir," Holmes said, "This is an unexpected honor."

"Sherlock Holmes," he blustered, "we haven't been the best of friends, I know, but you've got to help me now. I'm in serious trouble!"

"Oh, indeed? Won't you sit down? This is my friend, Dr. Watson. And now, sir, what is your trouble?"

"I've been robbed, Holmes!"

"Robbed?" Holmes said in mock surprise. "What was stolen?"

"Well, my greatest treasure. The Kitmanjar Emerald was removed from its case, and then mysteriously returned, loose, in my desk afterwards. But there's a priceless Cellini missing."

"Have you any idea who the burglars might be?"

27

"It was a gang, I'm sure of that! A couple disguised as a clergyman and a doctor came into the house on the pretext of raising money for some hospital. They overpowered me with chloroform."

"Dear me, dear me, how very unpleasant for you," said a chagrined Holmes.

"When I came to, I found my butler, Deevers, lying beside me in a pool of blood. The brave fellow must have wrestled with the thieves, but they got away. He's in hospital now. Holmes, you've got to help me."

"The Kitmanjar Emerald was returned, you say, but a Cellini is missing?"

"Yes, it's an exquisite filigree box, in which I kept the emerald."

"A filigree box!" Holmes exclaimed, standing up suddenly in total surprise.

"Yes, it's a genuine Cellini. It's worth several thousand pounds. Holmes, you must help me solve this business!"

Holmes sat down, laughing under his breath.

"I'm sorry, Mr. Litton-Stanley, but I'm afraid I can't help you. I've retired. Yes, and I intend to remain in retirement. Good night, sir."

"But Mr. Holmes, I'll pay you any fee within reason!"

"My decision is final, sir." Holmes insisted, returning to his pipe. "Good night."

"I might have known I wouldn't get any help from you," he said in scoffing tones, then, turning his great hulk away, slammed the door behind him. I looked at Holmes who sat there laughing, his head bent back in glee.

"Holmes, she fooled you again!"

"Yes, the little devil! She knew that box was a Cellini all the time!"

"Confound you, Holmes, you don't seem in the least bit angry at her!"

"I know I should be, but I'm not, Watson. What splendid audacity! What superb nerve the child has."

"Holmes, you MUST get that box back from her!"

"And I shall, Watson. Or rather, I shall persuade Deevers to do it for me, for the price of our silence."

"But," I asked in complete confusion, "how can Deevers get it back for you?"

"Remember that Deevers walks out with Miss Norton's maid. I am certain that when he explains his predicament, he can prevail upon her to steal the box from her mistress so that he can then return it to its rightful owner."

"Ingenious. I would never have thought of that," I added, now relaxing back into my chair. "By George, Holmes, Miss Norton, when you think about it, is a chip off the old block, all right."

"She is, Watson. And it makes me wonder . . . " he said, his voice trailing off into thought.

"What about?"

"I wonder, my dear chap, how long I can remain in retirement. With such a worthy antagonist at large, it's a challenge. I tell you, Watson, it's an irresistible challenge!"

"You're right, Holmes," I said, buoyed by the idea of his returning to practice, "and I have a few words I wish to say to you along those same lines!"

Holmes rose, glancing at his pocket watch.

"Come, Watson. It is time for supper. Let us eat and you can tell me all you've been about and how things are doing in London."

Not only was the dinner served by Holmes' manservant one of the most pleasant I have ever had, but the entire fortnight was of such renewing value to me that I came away with greater peace of mind than I have had in years.

I had, in those two weeks of rest, come to know Holmes in a more complete way, understanding his need to depart from the complex nature of his fellow man to the natural surroundings of the Sussex downs and their calming effect on this most brilliant and moody friend.

In my own case, its salutary effect was such that it has given me new energy, enabled me to confront my grievous losses, and spurred me into renewed excitement over collecting together my many notes and unfinished stories, that I may once again tell of the astonishing adventures of that most famous of consulting detectives, Sherlock Holmes.

Holmes pulled out his magnifying glass and began to look over the safe with great care.

# 2

# THE APRIL FOOL'S ADVENTURE

THE cold and foggy weather seemed endless these last few days and I found, after a hard day at my practice, that I wanted to settle into my most comfortable chair and catch up on some reading I had neglected. I had stoked the fire high to push back the chill in the room and was glancing over a number of books in my library to see which one would catch my attention. It was then I noticed my dispatch box tucked away on the upper shelf of one of my bookcases. It had not been opened for a goodly number of years. I had promised myself that I would again begin to write about the many adventures I was witness to with my dear friend, Sherlock Holmes.

Of course, this is what I had really wanted to do, I suddenly realized. Not to read, but to write. I hurriedly pulled down the box, dusted it off, then seated myself comfortably in my favorite chair and began foraging through the voluminous notes I had taken over the years.

After a while I came across an unfinished story about one of Holmes' earliest cases. I began reading, and the entire case came back vividly to my memory. Hurriedly, I went to my desk, took out paper and pen and began to write. It was an unusual case which actually had started as a prank.

The case of which I speak occurred only a little while after Sherlock Holmes and I had first met and taken up lodgings together at 221 B Baker Street. Holmes was a profound mystery to me then. I had shared our lodgings with him for a month before I was even certain of his profession, the knowledge of which I learnt, to my awe and astonishment, when our first adventure A STUDY IN SCARLET took place. And even after that adventure I wondered at

31

times what I had let myself in for sharing lodgings with such a strange companion. It was in one of those moods of doubt and confusion that my story begins.

Late one March evening I found myself in the neighborhood of Piccadilly Circus. It was cold, and the steady drizzle of rain had dampened my spirits. I felt that a glass of wine and the sound of music would put me in a better mood. And so, I entered the Criterion restaurant. As I sat with a glass of rare vintage port at my elbow, the orchestra playing a dreamy Strauss waltz in the background, I relaxed, feeling my old self again.

Suddenly, I felt a clap on my shoulder; I turned and, to my amazement, young Stamford was standing before me, the young man who first introduced me to Sherlock Holmes.

"Watson, or should I say, Dr. Watson! How are you my dear chap?"

"Well, hello Stamford. Fancy us meeting here again. Come and sit down."

"Thanks. I'm glad to see that you're not holding any grudge against me."

"Why on earth should I do that?" I said in astonishment.

"For introducing you to Sherlock Holmes. I've reproached myself ever since. I think he's as mad as a hatter."

"Not at all," I laughed, "he may be eccentric . . . in fact I'll admit that he *is* eccentric, but he's an extraordinarily interesting fellow. He'll make a great name for himself as a private detective one of these days. You see if I'm not right, Stamford."

"I saw something about him in the paper the other day."

"Yes," I added, "I expect that was the Lauriston Gardens affair. He's a brilliant man, Stamford, quite brilliant, I tell you. Though I must admit he's difficult at times. He works like a fiend, as a rule, but occasionally a reaction sets in and for days at a time, he'll lie on our sofa hardly uttering a word or moving a muscle from morning to night. It's a bit depressing, I must say."

"I think he takes himself too seriously," mused Stamford.

"Perhaps you're right."

A sudden smile came to Stamford's face, as he leaned in close to me.

"How would you like to join in a little plot?"

"A plot? Against Holmes?"

"Well, its just a rag, you know. We thought it would be rather fun!"

"We?" I said with curiosity.

"Murphy and I. We were just talking about it. Here, let me call him over."

Stamford turned and gestured to a young man who was seated at a nearby table.

"I've seen him before somewhere, haven't I?"

"I'm sure you must have, Watson. He's been round at Hospital, and any time you go into the British Museum, you'll find him there. Nice fellow, but dull, definitely dull."

"Yes, Stamford?" said the young man as he came forward.

"This is a friend of mine, Dr. John H. Watson. This is James Murphy."

"How do you do. I think I have seen you at Hospital."

"And I know I've seen you, Dr. Watson."

Stamford gestured for Murphy to be seated. Once we all made ourselves comfortable, I served them some wine, and a conversation was soon struck up.

"I was just telling Watson about our little plot," Stamford said gleefully.

"Now look here," I chimed in a little annoyed, "I'd like you fellows to realize that Holmes is a very good friend of mine!"

"Don't worry, Watson," said Murphy, "It's all in good fun. Don't you realize what the date is tomorrow?"

"The first of April, isn't it?"

"Yes, April Fool's day!"

"Oh, now I see," I said, greatly relieved, "you're going to play an April Fool's day joke on Holmes!"

"Yes, that's our plan!"

"Well, it's hardly our plan, Stamford. It's really Lady Ann Partington's idea. You see, Dr. Watson, Holmes was very rude to her when she was at Hospital recently, and she wants to . . . well, you know, take him down a peg or two."

"Sounds innocent enough. I must say he is inclined to be rather arrogant at times," I mused. "What exactly is your plan?"

"We'll need your help, Watson. You must be careful not to give the joke away," said Murphy.

"I bet you a fiver that Holmes falls for the whole story," Stamford laughed, "hook, line and sinker."

Murphy, in a conspiratorial air, gathered us closer together. He described a most amusing plan to trick Holmes by his own over self confidence. It was a fascinating idea and I readily agreed to do my part in fooling my friend.

The following morning, Lady Ann Partington called on my friend Sherlock Holmes. Mrs. Hudson ushered her in and Holmes quickly stood to greet her.

"Lady Ann, I am flattered that you have called to see me in my professional capacity."

"Surely, my good man, you didn't think this was a social call. You were much too rude to me in Hospital the other day for that!"

"That was the point I was trying to make," Holmes said with a forced smile. "Please sit down, won't you?"

"Here," I added, "take this chair, won't you, Lady Ann. It's by far the most comfortable one in the room."

"Thank you, Dr. Watson," she returned, seating herself.

"And now, what can I do to help you?" questioned Holmes.

"You've heard of the Elfenstone Emerald?"

"Oh yes, yes indeed," Holmes said, "a magnificent stone of very considerable value. An heirloom in your family, I believe?"

"That is correct, Mr. Holmes. I keep the stone in a wall safe in my bedroom. However, this morning, when I had occasion to go to the safe, I discovered that the emerald had been stolen!"

"Stolen? Great Scott, what a shocking business. Of course, you want Mr. Holmes to recover it for you?"

"A remarkable deduction, my dear doctor." Holmes said impatiently. "Now, Lady Ann, when you opened the safe did you observe any signs of it having been tampered with?"

"Mr. Holmes, I think it rather stupid to sit and answer questions here in Baker Street. Why don't you come over to my house in Cavendish Square and examine the safe for yourself? You are a detective, aren't you?"

"Lady Ann," Holmes said with great annoyance, "just now you accused me of rudeness. I assure you that at least mine was unintentional."

"Oh, come, come, Holmes. Don't be so touchy," I quickly added in an attempt to prevent the flaring of tempers.

"I can promise you a substantial fee, Mr. Holmes."

Holmes' face turned hard for a brief moment as he looked at Lady Ann.

"I'm a struggling practitioner in a new profession, aye? My poverty, but not my will, consents."

"I pay thy poverty," Lady Ann retorted, "and not thy will. You see, Mr. Holmes, I too can quote my Shakespeare. My carriage is waiting, gentlemen. Let us drive over to Cavendish Square at once, shall we?"

Holmes bowed politely to Lady Ann, then gestured for me to get our hats and coats. Within a short while we were traveling through the streets of London in a four wheeler, to shortly be deposited at Lady Ann's door.

She ushered us into a most glamourous living room, filled with heavy drapes, the finest china and one of the most ornate pianos I have ever seen. Lady Ann went to one wall, pushed a large portrait to one side, revealing a safe.

"This is the wall safe, Mr. Holmes."

"Ummm," my friend said as he took a close look, "not too difficult a safe to crack for an expert. You placed the emerald in it last night, you say?"

"Yes, when I went to bed. And this morning, it had gone."

"Surely Holmes," I spoke out, "this is a good occasion to use that magnifying glass that you're always flitting about with."

"An excellent occasion, my dear doctor. That's why I brought it with me."

Holmes pulled out his magnifying glass and began to look over the safe with great care. I had to stifle a small laugh as Lady Ann smiled at me. We both knew what my friend Sherlock had no knowledge of; the clues he would find were part and parcel of our April Fool's hoax on him.

"Well, that's very interesting."

"What is it, Mr. Holmes?"

"This safe was opened by an expert. There's no sign of its having been forced open. Hello, what's this? Watson, look here, there's a peculiar tarnish on the steel knob. It was obviously handled by someone whose fingers are habitually stained with chemicals."

"Are you sure, Holmes?"

"It's quite elementary, Watson. Lady Ann, please tell me where those doors lead to," he said, gesturing to the large double doors at the end of the room.

"My boudoir."

"I should like to examine it if I may."

"But, of course."

He stepped to the door, never once missing a chance to observe everything he could see. It was amazing to watch him as he would pause, glance at something through his magnifying glass, or touch something then rub his fingers against it to get its texture or feel. Shortly he was in the other room and a good distance from Lady Ann and myself. Whereupon she turned to me in excitement.

"Dr. Watson," she whispered in delight, "this is the most beautiful April Fool's day fraud I've ever played."

"I say, Murphy was right. He has fallen for it, hook, line and sinker. Just the same, Lady Ann, I'm beginning to feel guilty about all this. I can't help feeling a bit disloyal."

"Nonsense, doctor, it's all in fun."

"Are Stamford and Mr. Murphy listening?"

"Yes, they're next door, in my drawing room. I'm sure their ears are positively glued to the keyhole."

"I do hope Holmes won't be angry with me," I said, my feelings of guilt rising to an uncomfortable state.

In a short moment Holmes had retraced his steps and stood before us.

"There is nothing of any interest in there. The windows haven't been tampered with. We may presume, therefore, the thief did not enter by an upstairs window. Lady Ann, this room has not been touched since you've discovered your loss?"

"No, Mr. Holmes. I told the servants to leave the room exactly as it was while I came to fetch you."

"Splendid!" he said, looking around, "a deep pile carpet, aye? Couldn't be better! I can tell you this, Lady Ann: The thief was a tall man with a long stride."

"Come now, Holmes," I contradicted, "I know your methods. There aren't any footprints on this carpet that you can identify, even with your magnifying glass."

"My dear doctor, I've studied many crimes and I've never seen one yet that was committed by a flying creature. As long as a criminal remains upon his two legs, there must be some trifling displacement which can be detected by a keen observer. I assure you that the marks on this carpet indicate the thief was a tall man with a long stride!"

I was about to speak again, but Holmes turned away and pulled forth his magnifying glass to look at some minute item.

35

"Traces of tobacco ash, Watson. Pipe tobacco. Shag tobacco that sells at four pence an ounce."

"Now really Mr. Holmes," Lady Ann questioned, "how can you possibly identify an individual tobacco?"

"It's a hobby of mine. In fact, I've even written a monograph on the subject. Now, one more look at the safe itself. If you'll excuse me again, Lady Ann."

As Holmes continued his investigation, I observed that Lady Ann was coming to see Holmes in a far more respectful manner.

For that matter, I was also, for Holmes, in his inimitable manner, was picking up each and every clue we had so carefully left for him!

"Hello," he said aloud, "what is this bit of dust? It's rosin! A distinct trace of rosin! Lady Ann, I suggest that you get in touch with Scotland Yard, at once!"

"You mean that you've solved it, Holmes?"

"I mean, doctor, that I can give you a reasonably complete picture of the thief, and that picture is so individual that I'd be surprised if it would fit more than one man in London!"

"This is pure magic, Mr. Holmes. Please describe him to me," Lady Ann said, seating herself on the couch.

"Well, he's a tall man. The width of his stride indicates that, and he's thin."

"What enables you to tell that, Holmes?" I said with genuine curiosity.

"His footprints have made a remarkably light indentation on the nap of the carpet. Our thief dabbles extensively in chemicals, as indicated by the tarnishing of the knob on the safe. And the traces of rosin would suggest that he plays the violin, also. He smokes shag tobacco. He has a great practical knowledge of how to defeat combination safe locks, and he's obviously in close contact with the criminal classes."

"Just how do you know that, Mr. Holmes?"

"I doubt he would steal a famous stone unless he knew how to dispose of it; through some trustworthy fence no doubt."

"Yes, it's a very comprehensive picture, Holmes. I almost feel as if I knew the chap."

"Thank you, doctor," said Holmes.

Lady Ann could go on no longer. Her laughter filled the room with its bright and cheery sound.

"I agree entirely, Mr. Holmes," she finally said. "Dr. Watson, I think the joke has gone far enough."

Holmes first gave me, then Lady Ann, a complete look of bewildered astonishment.

"Joke?" he questioned, "what do you mean?"

"You're quite right, Holmes," I said laughing. "You're positively uncanny with that magnifying glass. You say there's only one such man in London. What you've done, my dear chap, is given a perfect description of YOURSELF!"

"April Fool, Mr. Holmes!" Lady Ann said with glee, then turned towards the drawing room door. "Dr. Stamford, Mr. Murphy, you can come in now!"

Stamford and Murphy came into the living room yelling "APRIL FOOL." We laughed and joked with Holmes, who, himself, accepted the hoax in good stride. Our laughter subsided shortly and we began to fall into delightful discussion, before Lady Ann interrupted us.

"Gentlemen, come along into the drawing room. Let us drink a glass of wine to Mr. Holmes, who has so graciously forgiven us for the little trick we played on him. And also to Dr. Stamford who thought of the whole idea!"

"I hope there are no hard feelings, Holmes," I said, still feeling guilty for pulling the wool over my friend's eyes.

"No, no, doctor," Holmes said laughingly, "though it was a rather embarrassing experience."

"When Murphy told me about the plan, I just couldn't resist joining them."

Stamford had poured the drinks and gave them to us as we continued to talk.

"You know Murphy, don't you, Mr. Holmes?" said Stamford.

"No, I don't think we've met. How do you do, sir."

"How do you do, Holmes. How did you like the little game we played on you?"

"It was rather a salutary experience. I suppose you gave them all the details to build up the picture of me, Watson?"

"Yes I did, Holmes. Knowing some of your methods, we tried to plant every clue which, I must say, you found."

"A very neat job, gentlemen. And incidentally, this is a perfect example of the dangers of deductions based on purely circumstantial evidence. I shall profit from this little lesson."

"I must say," Stamford added, "it was worth a fortune in emeralds to see your face, Holmes, when you realized what you'd done."

"By the way," I said, looking around, "Where is Lady Ann?"

"I believe she said she was going to fetch the Elfenstone Emerald. She thought you might be interested in seeing it," proffered Murphy.

"She probably feels the sight of it will salve my wounded vanity," Holmes said, a laugh in his voice.

In a moment, Lady Ann returned, pale as a sheet. Holmes and I quickly helped her to a chair. She looked up and grabbed Holmes by the arm.

"Mr. Holmes, the emerald, it's . . . it's not where I hid it! This time it's really stolen!"

All of us stood before Lady Ann, quite stunned by this revelation. Our April Fool's joke had turned completely around, so as to make fools of us all. I was looking at Holmes to see his reaction to this latest news on the emerald, and it gladdened my heart to see a sudden change in him. I must confess that I felt rather ashamed of my part in the prank, for I could see that Holmes' pride had been hurt. But now, only a few scant minutes after we had our laugh, and with a definite crime before him, the difference in Holmes was amazing. He suddenly became a dynamo, quickly galvanized into action as he stood before us, firing questions at all the members of the so-called conspiracy.

"Lady Ann, who beside yourself knew of this fresh hiding place?"

"Both Murphy and I did, Mr. Holmes," said Stamford.

"Yes, after we left our deliberate clues on the safe," Murphy added, "we went with Lady Ann and saw her secrete the emerald in the top drawer of her dressing table."

"We thought it would be all right there," Lady Ann said, "After all, as soon as the joke was over, I was going to put it back in the safe."

"I think our wisest plan, before we question the servants, would be for each one of you in this April Fool's day prank to submit to being searched."

"Holmes," objected Stamford most firmly, "Surely you don't suggest that anyone of us took the emerald?"

"No, Stamford, I don't. But if any one of you four are not guilty, this will be a splendid way of proving your innocence!"

"Steady Holmes," I said, astounded by the implied accusation, "you're not suggesting that Lady Ann stole her own emerald, are you?"

"I'm suggesting nothing. But let me point out that the recent vogue for . . . what shall we say . . . you know, the insurance companies, has provided another interesting motive for these 'so called' thefts."

"I resent your insinuation! It's outrageous!"

"Lady Ann," Holmes insisted, "if I am to recover your emerald, I must at least consider every possibility. A search is the most immediate practical action, therefore I would suggest that perhaps you could retire into the next room while I persuade these gentleman to submit to being searched. Then, with all due respect, I shall have to call someone in, of your own gender of course, to have you searched."

"Very well," retorted Lady Ann in frustration, "but I think you're in danger of making a fool of yourself once again!"

As Lady Ann prepared to leave, Murphy stepped forward and raised his hand, drawing all attention onto himself.

"Wait," he said, "don't . . . don't go, Lady Ann. A search won't be necessary."

What do you mean, Murphy?" I questioned.

"I must throw myself on your mercy, Lady Ann. I confess that I stole the emerald! After you put it in the drawer, Lady Ann, I slipped back into the room and took it out."

Everyone was staring at Murphy.

"That's a criminal action!" I exclaimed.

"I know it," he returned. "But I'm poor. I need money desperately for my mathematical research. I knew the emerald was priceless and I couldn't resist the temptation to take advantage of a joke. Here Lady Ann, here's the stone. Please, I beg you, do not prosecute. Please don't. It'll be my ruin."

It was then I noticed Holmes. While all attention was on Murphy and what he was saying, Holmes had slowly circled round the group and placed himself conveniently next to the man.

"May I examine the emerald?" he said quietly. Without waiting for permission, he took the stone and began to slowly turn it over and over in his hand.

"Well, Mr. Murphy," said an astonished and annoyed Lady Ann, "I won't pretend that I'm not deeply shocked. I must ask you to leave my house!"

"But you won't prosecute me, will you? It was only a moment's temptation."

"No, Mr. Murphy, I won't prosecute you."

I had been watching Holmes closely, and saw a slight smile cross his lips. He reached into his vest pocket and pulled out a very small vial with a clear liquid in it.

"Holmes," I asked, "what are you doing with the emerald?"

"An appropriate question, doctor. Well, knowing something of the deceptive ways of thieves, I came on this case fully prepared to test the emerald when I found it. Now, a drop of this acid from this vial, so, and we shall see."

Lady Ann rose from her chair and came towards Holmes.

"Mr. Holmes, what are you doing? You'll injure the stone."

"No, not if it's a true emerald."

We all gazed at the emerald. Within seconds, the answer came.

"Good Lord, the acid's eating through the stone as if it were sugar!" I exclaimed.

"Then that means . . . " said Lady Ann.

Holmes turned and faced Murphy, staring squarely into his eyes.

"It means, Lady Ann, that Mr. Murphy has just imperiled his honor and his freedom, to steal a singularly beautiful FAKE!"

I cannot tell you how disparaging this incident made us feel. Holmes threw the fake emerald on the table, seated himself before us and quite calmly smiled at Murphy. Lady Ann, in what appeared to be a state of near panic, sat down beside Holmes and looked at him with pleading eyes.

"Lady Ann, I must question your servants without hesitation. Please send them to me, one at a time. In due course, we shall all gather here in this room again. In the meantime, I wish Dr. Watson to restrain all of you in the dining room until my questioning of the servants is over. Watson, please to do me the honors."

I took everyone into the dining room where they seated themselves. While they talked, I quietly fetched each servant and in turn sent them into the living room to be confronted by Holmes. In due course Holmes opened the door and beckoned Stamford and Murphy into the living room. A short while later the door was again opened and Holmes asked Lady Ann to enter her bedroom, there to be searched by a private matron. It was not long we once again were gathered in the living room facing Holmes. He stood by the fireplace, his hands folded behind his back as he glanced from one to the other of us. Lady Ann stepped forward, a look of near panic in her eyes.

"Mr. Holmes, this 'joke' has turned into a nightmare! Is there no way of recovering my emerald?"

"I hope so, Lady Ann. I've been taking steps in their logical order: The servants have all been questioned, and we've searched Mr. Stamford and Mr. Murphy."

"Yes, a most humiliating experience. Made me feel like a criminal!" Stamford said in disgust.

"Well, personally I was only too thankful to submit to a search this time; I knew I had nothing to worry about," added Murphy.

"You, yourself Lady Ann," I said, "you consented to being searched by the private matron that Holmes sent for."

"Only because he threatened to send for the police if I didn't. But, distasteful though it was, I'd rather endure that than have this story on the front pages of the newspapers."

"And in spite of all these rather unfriendly proceedings, we've gotten exactly nowhere as regards finding the emerald!" said a disgruntled Stamford.

"But we have at least eliminated the possibility that the thief is secreting the jewel on his person."

"So you still think it is somewhere in these two rooms, Holmes?" I asked.

"I think so, though there is one remaining possibility."

"And that is?" questioned Murphy.

"That the fake stone was substituted for the real emerald sometime before all of you engineered your April Fool's day joke."

"Oh no, Mr. Holmes, that's not possible. I know it was the genuine emerald I took out of the safe this morning."

"How can you be sure? The substitute was an excellent imitation. Without a chemical test, such as I performed, it would be hard to be certain!"

"I can tell you why I'm certain," Lady Ann continued, "last night my father came to dinner and brought a Mr. Vanderlighter of Amsterdam. He examined the stone. And you'll agree that a jewel expert like that couldn't be fooled."

"That's true, Lady Ann," Holmes said, "and what did you do with the emerald after Mr. Vanderlighter left?"

"I locked it in my safe and went to bed. I didn't unlock the safe again until Dr. Stamford and Mr. Murphy came here this morning."

"That settles it then," I said in excitement. "The real emerald is still hidden somewhere in these two rooms!"

"But where, that's the question," added Stamford.

"I must say," puzzled Murphy, "it's completely mystifying."

"Let's go back to what we were all doing at the exact moment you came into the room, Lady Ann, and informed us of the loss of your stone."

"Why, we were drinking a toast, Holmes," I said.

"Good man, Watson, that's it! Lady Ann, hard thinking is, well, it's thirsty work."

"I'm so sorry Mr. Holmes, let me get you something. A glass of port, perhaps?"

"No thank you, but I do observe that you have a remarkably comprehensive assortment of liquors. I wonder if I might have a glass of Creme de Menthe?"

"Of course, I'll get it for you."

"Creme de Menthe in the middle of the day, Holmes?" I asked, quite puzzled.

"I knew you were eccentric Holmes," Stamford added, "But this is more than I expected."

"Mr. Holmes, this bottle . . . it clinked as I picked it up!" exclaimed Lady Ann.

"I thought it might. Please allow me, madam. Thank you."

We watched as Holmes began pouring out the contents of the bottle.

"I'm sure you won't mind if I waste this liquor on the Aspidistra. Just so . . . . ."

In a moment, there was a clinking sound and something dropped into Holmes' hand. He held it up so that we could see.

"Lady Ann, allow me to restore to you the Elfenstone Emerald."

"Great Scott!" I exclaimed.

Soon we were all talking at once in the wake of our astonishment.

"Ingenious," Holmes said, interrupting our excitement, "the one safe hiding place in the room. Where could a green gem be more effectively hidden than in a bottle of green liquor!"

"Who stole it, who substituted the fake stone?" I asked, my curiosity taking hold. Lady Ann stepped forward and faced all of us.

"Frankly, I don't care. The gem is restored. That's all that matters. I prefer not to take this matter to court. Neither you or I, Mr. Sherlock Holmes, would show up in the best of light. And my father would disapprove of this whole affair, I'm afraid!"

"Just as you wish, Lady Ann," Holmes concurred, bowing to her wishes. "In either case I shall expect your check for my services, in due course!"

Although Lady Ann was somewhat stunned by Holmes' remark, she took it in her stride. Everyone bowed to her and slowly, amidst idle talk about what had happened, we left her lodgings. I hailed a four-wheeler, and Holmes, Stamford, Murphy, and I soon found ourselves in Piccadilly Circus.

"Cabby, pull up over there. We'll get out. Here we are at the Criterion again, Stamford. Won't you come in and join us for lunch?"

"Thanks, Watson, but I'll keep the cab and go on. I actually have a patient this afternoon. A rare and delightful experience for a young and newly established doctor, as you probably know."

"As rare and delightful as a client is for a young detective, Stamford?" Holmes laughed. "I quite understand, and I'm correspondingly grateful to you for your profitable hopes."

"I'm glad it was profitable for you, Mr. Holmes. Personally I feel pretty stupid about the whole thing. Well, goodbye!"

Standing there in the cold drizzle, we waved our goodbyes as Stamford left. Murphy seemed pensive and very quiet. I turned to him as he stood waving goodbye to his friend.

"You're remarkably quiet, Murphy."

"Well, I'm afraid my conscience won't let me do much talking, Doctor. I'm heartily ashamed of myself. Thanks for the lift. I'll leave you chaps here."

"Nonsense," Holmes insisted, "You must join us for lunch, and no buts about it! I insist, come on."

"That's awfully nice of you."

"Come, come Murphy, anyone of us could make a foolish mistake," I said. "It's just lucky you didn't have to pay for yours."

In a moment we were inside the Criterion and seated to the strains of a lovely Viennese waltz. The waiter poured us some select wine and we perused the menu.

"By George," I exclaimed, "I'm as hungry as a hunter. How about you, Murphy?"

"No, I'm afraid I have very little appetite. This whole case has upset me dreadfully."

"You mustn't take it so much to heart, Murphy. By the way, doctor, I'd like to have your opinion on the case. Who do you think staged the theft of the emerald today?"

"It's perfectly obvious to me, Holmes. Lady Ann Partington did it herself to collect the insurance money. If she hadn't, she'd have insisted on your finding the thief. But you needn't worry, Holmes, you'll get your fee all right, I'm sure of that."

Holmes laughed and shook his head.

"I'm not worrying about the fee, but I can assure you that Lady Ann did not engineer that fraud today."

"You mean that it was Stamford?" I said, puzzled.

Holmes turned to face Murphy.

"Tell him who was responsible, Murphy."

"But, how should I know?"

"Oh come now, Murphy," Holmes said in all seriousness as he leaned in towards the man, "let's not fence any longer. You did an excellent job. A superlative job. I was almost sorry to spoil it for you."

"I don't think I understand you, Mr. Holmes."

"Oh yes you do, Murphy!" There was a touch of anger in Holmes' voice now. "You're a splendid actor, too. I was so 'deeply touched' when you had apparently stolen a fake jewel, while all the time you knew that the real one was safely hidden in the bottle of Creme de Menthe! To be abstracted later, at your leisure! Ha, ha! You scoundrel!"

"Holmes," I said, "do you mind telling me what's going on here? I'm completely and absolutely in the dark!"

"Surely it's obvious, my dear doctor. The imitation emerald was a brilliant copy."

"What makes you so sure of that, my dear Holmes?" said Murphy.

"Because this April Fool's day hoax was only conceived yesterday. At least that is what you wished the others to believe. Such a superb paste gem could not have been made on such short notice. Therefore, it must have been prepared by someone who knew about the hoax before it was arranged. Now, Watson, when Stamford told you about the plan last night, whose idea did he say it was?"

"He told me it was Lady Ann Partington's plan."

"Precisely. And yet Lady Ann referred to it today as Stamford's idea. Obviously you, my dear Murphy, presented the plan to each as the notion of the other! And so, only you could have arranged the real theft behind the hoax. I repeat. A splendid job!"

"Thank you, Mr. Holmes," Murphy said, no longer seeming the shamed young man of before. "May I also compliment you on your cleverness in frustrating my plot?"

"Look here," I said in bewilderment, "what is all this? One of you is a criminal, the other is a detective. Yet you're throwing each other compliments as if you were in the same profession!"

"The dividing line between the criminal and the criminal investigator is thinner than you might imagine, Watson."

"How very true, Holmes," Murphy added, staring directly at my friend, "would you consider coming over to my side of the line? Together we would make an unbeatable team."

Holmes laughed heartily.

"You flatter me. Nevertheless, I must decline your offer, Mr. Murphy."

"What a pity. On your side of the line, you'll never be a rich man. By the way, for your edification, my name is not Murphy, though Stamford insists on thinking it is."

"Then what is your name, you scoundrel!" I exclaimed in anger.

"Your friend Holmes says the word 'scoundrel' so much better than you, doctor. Uh, my name? My name is M-o-r-r-i-a-t-y."

"Oh, indeed?" said Holmes, "spelled M-O-R-R-I-E-T-Y?"

"No. Dear me, I have so much trouble with my name. People will either misspell it or mispronounce it. I'm afraid I will have to begin calling it the way it looks. M-O-R-I-A-R-T-Y."

"Moriarty," Holmes observed, "I shall remember that name. I have a feeling we shall meet again."

"I trust that we shall. You've won the first round, Sherlock Holmes, I admit that. But I believe a return match is indicated."

"I look forward to it, Moriarty. And now, Watson, I can't stand your baleful glare any longer. Let's order lunch, shall we?"

And that is how it came to pass that the strange and terrifying conflicts between Holmes and Moriarty began. Little did we realize then what this first meeting would portend in the future. It was a time of beginnings for both men, and, if I may humbly add, for myself, in practice as a newly established doctor and friend to Holmes and his many adventures.

"By the time the police get here, you and your friend Holmes will be blown to kingdom come!"

# 3

# THE CASE OF THE AMATEUR MENDICANTS

MY friend Sherlock Holmes, whatever he may be with his moody and driven nature, always placed human justice and the natural flow of life before all other things. He abhorred fools and despised the cunning who took advantage of others. He especially hated the murderer, for that kind was the worst, taking life from a human being and bringing grief and pain to everyone.

And yet, if it were not for the murderers and thieves, there would be no Sherlock Holmes. How strange that his intense hatred for the criminal is the one thing that continues to make my good friend so productive. It was thoughts such as these that reminded me of one of the most unusual cases I and Holmes found ourselves involved with. It began on a rather stormy November night in 1887. The rain had been pouring for days, and the only consolation was the clean and breathable air it had provided.

On this night in question, I was nodding in front of the fire, a good book of stories in my hands. I'd had a very tiring day, I remember. It was about the hour that a man gives his first yawn and glances at the clock, when suddenly, the front doorbell jangled discordantly.

Mrs. Hudson had long since retired to bed, and Holmes, after a long and arduous day's work, was also asleep, so it was I who crossed to the window and opened it. The rain and cold came rushing in as I tried to prevent as much water as possible from soaking the rug. It was extremely dark, but I could just see the outline of a figure standing on my doorstep. It looked like a woman. Suddenly a cultivated voice called up to me.

"Is the doctor in?"

"Yes, madam," I yelled through the wind and rain, "I'm the doctor!"

"Then please come at once! It's a matter of life and death! I have a carriage waiting!"

I could sense the pain in her voice and I reassured her that I would be down immediately. I closed the window, scribbled a note to Holmes, grabbed my coat, hat, and my bag, then went downstairs and into the rain.

A carriage was standing at the curb, but I could not see any trace of the lady who called me. The only person in sight was an old and repulsive looking beggar woman, dressed in rags and tatters. After a moment of bewilderment, I approached her.

"My good woman, did you see a lady leave here a moment ago?"

"No doctor, she didn't leave, she's still waiting for you."

I was astonished, for the voice coming from this sad woman in tatters was that of the cultured voice that had called up to me in my rooms.

"Forgive me, madam, but those clothes of yours . . . I thought you were a beggar woman."

"There isn't any time to discuss that now!" she said frantically. "Please get into this carriage!"

"But, my good woman, where's the driver?"

"I'm going to drive. Please get in!"

I entered the carriage, then turned and stuck my head out as she pulled herself up into the driver's seat.

"Are you sure that you can handle those horses, Madam?"

"Of course I can!" she yelled, then snapped the whip in her hand and we were off! I could not help thinking how absolutely extraordinary this all seemed to me.

As the carriage rushed through the rain-soaked streets I tried to find out where we were going, but the woman insisted I not ask her any further questions. I sat back, the cobble stone streets whirling by under our feet and the rain running down in rivers against the glass of the carriage windows. I pulled my coat tight up around me for it was bitterly cold. And as I was bumped and jostled throughout this mad, racing drive, my thoughts turned back to my home where, only moments before, I was in the warm comfort of my favorite chair. A particularly bad bump shook me back to reality. I saw that we were in the warehouse district not far from the waterfront, for I could hear the fog horns and boats sounding a short distance away. I knew there were no dwellings here, for this was strictly a business district and a place of often dealt shady crime. Suddenly the carriage pulled up in front of one of the warehouses.

"Why are we stopping here, madam?" I asked, not without some trepidation on my part.

"Because this is where we are going. Please hurry! Follow me down these steps!"

I stepped from the carriage and rushed forward into the safety of a doorway through which she had entered. She gestured to me and I followed her down a long and deep staircase to the basement of the warehouse. It was quite dark, but there was a crack of light coming from a small opening in the middle of the door. She was about to knock on the door, when I stayed her hand.

"Madam, do be so kind as to tell me where you are taking me."

"We have a . . . a club here in the basement," she said in hesitant tones. "Come, you'll see for yourself in a moment."

She knocked in a pattern. One, a break, then three. She did this only one more time. One, a break, then three. We waited a moment and the small flap covering the opening in the middle of the door was pushed aside. The silhouette of a man blended with the streaks of bright light that burst from the opening.

"Who knocks?" said the man.

"Number seven," said the lady in rags.

"Give the password."

"To the lanterns."

"You may enter."

As the small flap closed I turned to the lady in wonderment.

"This must be a very secret club of yours, madam."

"It is, doctor."

The door was opened and a small man eyed us both as we passed him and walked down a short corridor. I seemed to hear piano music from a distance.

"Madam," I insisted of her, "I do wish you'd tell me where you are taking me. This looks like the entrance to an opium den or a thieves' kitchen."

"Don't worry, doctor, you are in no danger."

She swung open a second door and the piano music filled my ears. There before me was a luxuriously furnished large room, filled with talking people, some of them in full evening dress and others in beggars clothing!

"There, doctor, does that look like a thieves' kitchen?"

"I can't believe my eyes, madam. What a strange collection of people! Absolutely amazing!"

Suddenly, looming up before me was a large man, deeply scared, with fiery eyes and a head of hair that was pulled back and tied, like that of a gypsy. He was in beggar's clothes, with a dagger stuck through his belt.

"Number seven," he said, "who is this man?"

"He's a doctor. I went to fetch him."

"I thought I said there were to be no strangers inside here!"

"Now look here, my good man," I said angrily, "I've been extremely patient so far, but my temper is beginning to wear a little thin. Either let me see your patient at once, or show me out! My time is valuable and I don't propose to waste it!"

"I'm sorry, doctor," said the lady, who then turned to the tall and steely man. "Where is Julian?"

"He's in the back room," he said with a gesture, pointing to a large door to one side. "And if you know what's good for you Dr. what-ever-you-call-yourself, you'll forget everything you see in here!"

"Stop threatening me, sir! I'm not in the least interested in your blasted club! Just take me to the patient!"

Without a word, the tall man walked to the room, I following with the lady beside me. This second room was smaller, but it too was exquisitely furnished.

"This is the man we want you to examine, doctor," said the tall one, pointing to a well dressed gentleman who was lying on a velvet couch.

"Well, someone had better tell me what happened to him," I said.

"He fell down the stairs leading into the club room," said the young lady.

"Why did you move him?"

"We wanted him to be comfortable."

"That's the worst thing in the world you could have done," I said in dismay, "never move a person with an injured skull!"

"Is he going to be all right, doctor?" said the young lady.

I examined the gentleman as she spoke, then, heaving a great sigh, I turned to the lady.

"No, madam, I'm afraid he isn't. His neck is broken. He's dead."

"Julian, dead!" the lady exclaimed, her hand against her trembling mouth.

"You are sure of that, doctor?" the tall man asked, eyeing me suspiciously.

"Of course I'm sure of that, my good man. I'm afraid you need an undertaker now, not a doctor."

The tall, gruff looking man leaned over the body a moment, shook his head, then turned towards the door.

"I must tell the others," he said. He entered the main room and raised his arms.

"Quiet, everybody, quiet! Julian is dead."

A murmuring was set up as the various beggars and well dressed people began to talk among themselves. A few of the club members stepped forward and went into the room to observe the now dead Julian.

"This is terrible," said one small man dressed in impeccable clothing. "Who is this man?"

"He's a doctor."

"For Heavens sake, we must get him out of here at once. We don't want any strangers nosing about!"

Some of the members began protesting my presence with anger.

"Just a minute," I said loudly to assuage their nervousness, "I assure you, ladies and gentlemen, I haven't the slightest desire to stay here one moment longer. If you'd direct me to the door again, madam, I'll try to find a cab myself, in this God forsaken district, and go home!"

"Show him out and give him his money!"

"Follow me, please," said the young lady who had called upon me for my services. She directed me to the door, and accompanied me outside.

"Do you mind, if I don't drive you home, doctor?" she said apologetically.

"Frankly, young lady, I should much prefer it. After this experience I feel my nerves are not in the best of shape."

"You mustn't be angry with me, Doctor, please."

"To whom shall I send in my bill, madam?"

"Here is a five pound note. That should cover your time and trouble, shouldn't it?"

"No, no. It's far too much, madam," I said in surprise at the large amount she was willing to pay me.

"It's late at night, doctor, and it hasn't been a very pleasant case for you. Please take it."

"Very kind of you. Very generous, indeed. I was wondering, however, how you happened to come to me in the first place?"

"I was driving about looking for a doctor, and a policeman directed me to your house. May I come around in the morning for a death certificate?"

"Of course, madam. Do you remember my address?"

"Yes, but I don't know your name."

"Watson. Dr. John H. Watson."

"Dr. Watson?" she said, "not the Dr. Watson who is associated with Sherlock Holmes?"

"Well, madam," I said, quite pleased, "I'm flattered that you know of me."

She backed away, a look of fright on her face.

"Good night, doctor. And please, forget about everything you've seen here tonight!"

With that, she turned and ran back into the warehouse, the rain obliterating her in a swirl of darkness. I stood perplexed for a moment, unable to fathom not only her fright, but the entire reason behind such an unusual band of people assuming such enterprise as this club they were a party to. As luck would have it, I spotted a Hansom a short distance away, turned up my coat collar to protect me from the biting rain and ran to catch it. It was not long I was once again on my way across town, this time to return to the comfort of my warm lodgings. As I sat in the Hansom, I pondered on this amazing late-night rendezvous and decided that it would be best to tell my good friend Holmes about the entire incident.

The following morning found me seated opposite Holmes as we enjoyed an early breakfast. I told him the entire story, leaving out no single detail that I could remember. He sat, listening attentively as he finished the last of the meal.

"And that's the way it was, Holmes. One of the most curious adventures I've ever had without you."

"Very interesting, Watson. You say this underground cellar was luxuriously furnished?"

"Yes, and as I've told you, I was surprised by the amazing mixture of people there. Some in rags and some in evening dress."

"Just like the nursery rhyme. 'Some in rags and some in tags and some in velvet gowns.'"

"Exactly, Holmes. Even the feeling that I was taking part in a story out of the Arabian Nights. I must say though I was pretty angry at the time. However, after a good nights rest, I feel quite differently this morning."

"It would be interesting to see if any repercussions of your strange adventure reach us."

"I doubt it. The woman seemed frightened to death when I mentioned your name."

"We shall see. Meanwhile, I'm expecting a client. If you're not too busy with your practice, I would greatly appreciate your taking some notes and observations on the matter."

"I'd like to very much, Holmes. Do you know who it is?"

"This telegram will tell you much more than I can," he said, handing me the paper that lay on the table near him, "It arrived an hour ago."

He stood and walked to the window. The rain was still coming down, washing the street clean not only of the usual grim and soot, but of all people and vehicles, save for a few passing Hansoms and carriages. I read the telegram aloud.

"'Be at your lodgings this morning to discuss our problem. Stop.' It's signed A.M.S. Pretty high handed message. Be at your lodgings! No 'please.' What do you suppose A.M.S. stands for?"

"I was just toying with that problem," he said returning to his seat.

"Could it be the American Medical School?"

"No, Watson, there's no such body. You are referring to the American Medical Association. The curious tone of the message inclines me to believe that the A stands for Amateur."

"Very possibly. Amateur Maskers Society."

"Or, Watson, the Amateur Murderers Society," said Holmes, laughing. "That would be a nice thought, wouldn't it?"

The doorbell rang and Holmes stood, expectation on his face.

"That is their representative, no doubt, to save us further guesswork."

I went to the window and looked out, hoping to gain at least a glimpse of who it was that was coming to see Holmes.

"Holmes," I said, "it looks like the same carriage that I was driven in last night! But the girl standing on your doorstep is dressed in the height of fashion."

"Splendid, Watson. Unless my guess is incorrect, we have not heard the end of your adventure. Go and meet the lady at the top of the stairs, old chap, and save Mrs. Hudson's legs."

I did as Holmes suggested and opened the door just as a most charming young lady reached the top of the stairs. I ushered the lady in as she acknowledged me with a smile.

"Mr. Sherlock Holmes?" she said, turning to my friend.

"At your service, madam. Won't you sit down?"

"I am Lady Dorothy Broxton."

"But your voice," I said perplexed, "you're the lady who fetched me last night, dressed up as a beggar woman!"

"Yes I am, Dr. Watson. Forgive me for being so mysterious at the time."

"Doubtless you've come to consult me regarding last nights unfortunate accident at the Amateur Mendicant Society."

"How did you know what the initials stood for, Mr. Holmes?"

"It's not too difficult. After hearing Dr. Watson's story of last night's happenings, the connotation seemed obvious, am I right?"

"Perfectly. Last night when Dr. Watson told us Julian was dead, we thought it was an accident."

"And now," Holmes interrupted, "you think it is murder? Lady Broxton, if you expect my help, there must be no more mystery. Just what is this Amateur Mendicant Society?"

"I'm afraid it might be a little hard for you to understand our motives. We're a group of people, rather wealthy people I suppose, who find pleasure in deliberately leading a seamy life disguised as beggars. We use the basement that you were in last night, doctor, as our headquarters. We keep our beggar's clothes there, and change out of them before we go home."

"What a fantastic idea," I said, disgruntled by the whole thing.

"What a futile and worthless way of spending your leisure time, Lady Broxton."

"I suppose it must seem so, Mr. Holmes. But we are curious to learn how the other half lives. Of course, there's a certain thrill in rubbing shoulders with the police. At least we do some good."

"Indeed?" Holmes said with curiosity, "I should be interested to learn how."

"The money we make as beggars we give to charity."

"Oh, do you really? And you feel that this gesture on your part absolves you from any responsibility to the real beggars whose livelihood you are impairing!" Holmes said in disgust.

"I hadn't thought of it just like that," admitted Lady Broxton, "Then, I suppose you won't want to help us, Mr. Holmes?"

"That's quite another matter, madam. As a professional detective I cannot afford to be a moralist. Yes, I will investigate this case for you, though I warn you my fee will be an extremely high one!"

"Money doesn't matter, Mr. Holmes, as long as we can solve Julian's death without bringing the police into the case."

"Lady Broxton," Holmes snapped, "Who is the dead man? The man you refer to as Julian?"

"Julian Trevor, the poet. He was the one who started our society."

"Julian Trevor, yes, I've read some of his work. Decadent. Distinctly decadent."

"What makes you think that he was murdered, Lady Broxton?" I asked.

"After you left last night, Dr. Watson, there was a terrible scene. Do you remember Sidney Holt?"

"Was he the tall fellow who was so unpleasant to me?"

"Yes, that's the one. He said that he saw Lord Cecil deliberately trip Julian as he came to the head of the staircase."

"Lord Cecil being whom?" asked Holmes.

"Lord Cecil Dearingforth, son of the Earl of Meerschaum. There was a bitter argument. Cecil accused Sidney of doing the same thing to Julian. They had a dreadful fight, ending up with Cecil threatening to go to the police. That's when we decided to send a telegram to you, Mr. Holmes."

"So, the proof of murder depends on such flimsy evidence as to whether the dead man fell or was pushed."

"Mr. Holmes," Lady Broxton begged, "even though you don't approve, please help us, won't you?"

Holmes, in his own dramatic way, moved to the window, staring out at the endless rain, deep in thought. He turned suddenly towards us.

"Yes, Lady Broxton, I will."

"Then you'll come back with me now to our headquarters?"

"I shall join you within the hour. In the meantime, my old friend Dr. Watson can go with you."

"But Holmes," I protested, "what can I do without you?"

"You know my methods, Watson. Act accordingly."

"Very well, Mr. Holmes, I shall take Dr. Watson with me. But you promise you'll be there?"

"I promise you that I will be there, madam."

I looked at Holmes in puzzlement, but he averted his eyes. Lady Broxton stood and went to the door; I following reluctantly.

"Lady Broxton, I'll meet you at your carriage. I want to get my hat and coat," I said as an excuse to stay a moment.

As Lady Broxton continued down stairs I turned to Holmes in agitation.

"Holmes, what are you up to?"

"Go with her and ask me no more questions," he whispered, "I shall join you within the hour."

"Holmes, there's a glint in your eye," I returned, "I don't think you believe her story."

"Of course I don't, Watson. Now go with her, old fellow, and keep your wits about you. The game's afoot!"

To return to such a dismal and deploring place of death and intrigue did not sit well with me, but Holmes had asked me to return and return I did.

As I awaited his arrival, I took the time to question a few of the members of the Mendicant Society, but gained no further clues as to the reason or the cause of Julian Trevor's death.

I was just finishing my questioning of Sidney Holt, the tall gentleman who was so rude to me only hours before. He was still being rude.

"I'm afraid that I don't find your story very convincing, Mr. Holt," I said to him as he stood over me.

"Oh don't you now? Then suppose you stop asking questions until Sherlock Holmes gets here. He's the man we've engaged to settle this business, not you! We're paying for his services, not those of his assistant!"

"Mr. Holmes asked ME to conduct this preliminary investigation," I said coldly, restraining my anger. "I am perfectly familiar with his methods, so keep a civil tongue in your head if you want Holmes to continue with this case!"

"I'm not answering any more questions until he gets here!"

"Insufferable fellow," I said under my breath as I turned away from him. "Lord Cecil, you say that you saw Holt deliberately trip the dead man as he came down the stairs last night?"

"Yes I did, doctor."

"Now where were you standing, sir?"

"At the head of the staircase. Holt was beside me and as Julian came by he deliberately—"

Lord Cecil was interrupted by a small, aged man who spoke nervously.

"Excuse me, please, excuse me, number 11, but there is a strange man just come in. He is dressed as you when you work, but I do not remember having seen him here before. He speaks very rough."

"Did he give the correct signal?" asked Lord Cecil.

"Yes, and the password, sir."

"He must be a new member," said Lady Broxton who had been standing beside me during the entire time of my preliminary investigation.

"I suppose we'd better see him. Bring him in," said Lord Cecil with great agitation, "A bad time for him to come here, confound it!"

Almost immediately a large man, dressed in tattered clothes and sporting a great beard came forward.

"Quite a nice place you got here!" he said. "Certainly do yourselves proud, don't you?"

"Who are you and how did you get in here?" asked Lord Cecil rather suspiciously.

"I gave the signal and the password, just like Julian told me to. I'm a friend of Julian's and he told me to meet him here."

"Who are you, really?"

"Are we all friends here?" said the bearded man, glancing about.

"Yes," Lord Cecil reassured, "you can talk freely."

Suddenly this strutting, ill-dressed ragamuffin of a man bowed deeply. Now, when he spoke, it was with a slight Spanish accent.

"Then permit me to introduce myself. I am Don Louis Jose Fernando de La Storez, at your service."

"Why do you want to join us?" asked Sidney Holt.

"When Julian tell me about this . . . well, it tickle my . . . how you say . . . my funny bone? It is so charming an idea. Aficionados of Mendicancy."

"Well, I suppose he's all right," Sidney Holt said, eyeing the new member.

"Of course, I am all right. Now where is Julian, please. He will vouch for me."

"He's in the other room," Holt went on, "he's had an accident."

"An accident? Not a bad one, I hope."

"A very bad one. Dr. Watson, you'd better take him in there and break the news to him," said the cynical Holt.

I gestured for the man to follow me. We entered the room and a look of shock crossed the man's face.

"Your friend is dead, I'm sorry to say. His neck was broken last night in some brawl."

"Yes, but I do believe it was an accident, Watson," came the now familiar voice of my friend and companion.

"Holmes!" I exclaimed, completely taken by surprise.

"Quiet, old chap, quiet," whispered Holmes.

"But not quietly enough, Mr. Sherlock Holmes!" Sidney Holt exclaimed, his tall frame blocking the doorway. "Come on now, come back to the others and let's all take a look at you! Come on, get moving, both of you! This isn't a popgun I've got in my hand!"

Holt forced us by gunpoint to join the others.

"Sorry Holmes, I've given the whole thing away."

"That's all right, old chap," he returned.

"Cecil, Dorothy, come here! I want you to take a look at the great Sherlock Holmes! Walked into our trap just like any stupid policeman! I don't know why you had to dress up for it, Mr. Holmes. We were waiting for you here anyway, you know."

"I was well aware of that, Mr. Holt. You see, I knew I was walking into a trap."

"How did you know that, Mr. Holmes?" Lady Broxton said, quite surprised.

"Lady Broxton, the story that you brought to us today was so obviously a false one. Just as there is no Amateur Mendicant Society!"

"Then who are they, Holmes?" I asked.

"Go ahead, Mr. Holmes," Holt laughed, "tell him. Let's see how much you really do know!"

"Why should I tell you what you already know?" Holmes offered, a cynical edge to his voice.

"Go on, talk, if you know what's good for you," Holt said, brandishing the gun at Holmes.

"Oh, you are so persuasive, aren't you, Mr. Holt. Very well. Undoubtedly Julian Trevor's death last night was an accident. You fetched a doctor, Lady Broxton; a very natural move, and later discovered that the doctor in question was the old friend of Sherlock Holmes. You were all afraid that I'd become interested in your unusual society, so you invented that very thin story about the accident being a murder. You wanted to lure ME here, so that I could be disposed of. Then you could all continue your nefarious works without hindrance."

"Well, now, aren't we clever. And what is our nefarious work, may I ask?" Holt questioned.

"Your password gave me a clue. 'TO THE LANTERNS.' The cry of the French Revolutionists. They strung aristocrats up on lampposts; or shall I say lanterns? Then again, the combination of curious costumes in a luxurious establishment in a low class area posed another question: What political belief provides a common meeting ground for misbranded aristocrats and dangerous commoners?"

"And how did you answer that question?" asked Lord Cecil.

"Very simple, my dear sir, in one word: NIHILISM. Its doctrine of assassination and overthrow of government could find every chance of being put into practice by all of you at the forthcoming jubilee celebrations to be held here in London! This would account for your beggar's clothes. A beggar would have greater freedom of movement in a crowd than an ordinary person."

"You're a clever man, Mr. Holmes," Lord Cecil said coldly. "Too bad you'll have to die. I'll get the rope."

"What are you going to do with him?" Lady Broxton asked in shock and bewilderment.

"Do?" Holt said, "give him a first hand taste of Nihilism, of course. They can't live. They know too much."

"You can't possibly do this," I protested. "You know the police will track us here!"

"By the time the police get here, you and your friend Holmes will be blown to kingdom come!"

Lord Cecil returned with the rope. Holt tied Holmes wrists together.

"Ah, mind that bandaged wrist of mine, will you? It's confoundedly sore."

"Now isn't that a shame," Holt laughed, pulling the rope even tighter. "Is this any better? Tie up the doctor, Cecil, while I bind up Holmes' legs."

"I can't go through with this!" Lady Broxton yelled, "I just can't stand by and see two innocent men murdered! Nothing was said to me of this. It isn't right! If you go on with this, I'm going to the police!"

Holt slapped Lady Broxton across the face. I wanted to thrash the man, but could do nothing as Lord Cecil finished tying my wrists and legs together.

"Tie her up as well, Cecil. We don't need any soft people in our midst. Now, Mr. Holmes, I'm going to fetch a little invention. A little invention I'm sure you'll be interested in."

Lord Cecil stood over us, admiring his handiwork. Holmes, Lady Broxton and I were tied most securely, our three chairs facing each other in a small circle.

"It's a pity both of you didn't learn to mind your own business. Quite comfortable, all of you?"

"You're a filthy traitor to your country," I said bitterly, trying to release myself, but to no avail. Lord Cecil merely laughed.

"There we are," Holt said, returning. "An example of Michail Petrov's mechanical genius. This bomb will blow the entire building sky high, and the three of you with it. I'll just set the clock mechanism for five minutes, which will give us plenty of time to get out of here."

Holt placed the bomb on the floor in the center of our small circle so that we could all face it and hear its deadly ticking.

"A charming picture. The three of you bound hand and foot sitting together, watching a bomb. Well, tah, Dorothy. Think of our cause during the five minutes. As for you, Mr. Holmes, and your friend, good riddance to bad rubbish!"

With that, Sidney Holt joined the others as they hurriedly left their secret hideout. A deathly silence fell upon us. Holmes, confound him, sat quite serenely while I continued to struggle with the ropes. Lady Broxton broke out into a terrified fit of crying. I turned to Holmes, realizing it was no use to try and break free. The ropes had been tied with an expert hand.

"Holmes," I said quietly, "I blame myself for this. If I hadn't been so infernally noisy when I recognized you, we wouldn't be in this mess."

"It wasn't your fault, old fellow; I'm sure they suspected me, anyway."

"I must say, it seemed to me that you told them a great deal more than was necessary about your suspicions. Surely you could have pretended ignorance."

"I suppose I could have prevented their capturing me if I had planned more carefully, but I was concerned for your safety as well as—"

Holmes was interrupted by Lady Broxton's hysterical screaming.

"I can't die yet, I'm not ready to die!" she screamed.

"Courage, Lady Broxton, courage. Tell me, was I right in assuming that your associates are Nihilists?"

Lady Broxton calmed herself as best she could, even though we were all deathly aware of the ticking bomb.

"Of course, they are," she said, "they are planning to assassinate the Prime Minister during the Jubilee celebration."

"The Prime Minister!" I yelled. "Great Heavens, Holmes, we've got to get free!"

"Assuming that some miracle happened," Holmes went on, still addressing Lady Broxton, "and we did get free, and your former associates were arraigned in court, would you testify against them?"

"Of course, I would. But what chance is there of that? That clock, that devilish clock, why doesn't it stop ticking!"

Lady Broxton was beside herself with anguish.

"If it bothers you that much, Lady Broxton, I'll stop it for you."

With that, Holmes gently removed his hands from where they had been tied and reached for the bomb.

"Holmes, your hands are free!"

"Of course they are, my dear fellow. The bandaged wrist I mentioned to Holt concealed a razor edged blade. I cut through the ropes almost before our friends had left the room."

Both Lady Broxton and I looked at Holmes in total disbelief.

"Then why did you keep us in this suspense, Mr. Holmes?" asked Lady Broxton who, for the first time, began to return to her old self.

"I wanted to be quite sure that you testify in the forthcoming trial, Madam. There we are, that renders the bomb harmless. An interesting device, but of simple construction."

Before Holmes had even finished his words, we could hear police whistles outside.

"Ah ha," he said smiling, "those whistles mean the police have sprung the trap that I have set for your associates, Lady Broxton. It's lucky for you that you've had a change of heart, otherwise I suspect that, once free, you would try to escape, and there would be one more to receive a full sentence."

Lady Broxton lowered her head in shame as I turned in joy to my friend.

"Holmes, you had the place surrounded with police when you came in here."

"Of course I did, Watson. Here, let me undo your ropes."

"No wonder you were so calm. No wonder you told them so much. You wanted them to show their hand!"

"Precisely, old fellow, and they obliged me most satisfactorily. They attempted our triple murder, and are self confessed anarchists. With the evidence of Lady Broxton, I'm sure that we can put them where they all belong. Considering it's barely noon, I think you'll agree, Watson, that this is a very comprehensive morning's work!"

With Lady Broxton turned over to the police to await her testimony at the trial, Holmes and I caught a Hansom and went home. It was still pouring outside, but as we gained the entrance to our lodgings at 221 B Baker Street, the warmth of a fire, I for a cup of hot tea and a pipe for Holmes, all seemed well. And well they were.

I fell dizzily to the ground as Holmes leapt forward to struggle with the mysterious figure behind the lantern.

# 4

# THE ADVENTURE OF THE OUT-OF-DATE MURDER

## I

"FOR goodness sakes, Holmes, I insist that you stop your constant fiddling with those chemicals and potions and come with me now!"

"Later, Watson, later," he returned as he poured a brackish substance from one test tube to another.

"Just look at the weather," I persisted, pointing to the window. "It is beautiful out. This the first year of the new century, and one of the finest September's we have ever had, with fresh air and blooming flowers, and all you wish to do is sit here with your smelly bottles and experiment. Outrageous!"

He said nothing, but went right on with his work. I stood there a moment demeaned by his total indifference towards me.

"Holmes," I said, restraining my rage, "just look at you. You haven't stopped this for weeks. You've stayed up for days on end working with all this and spent even more time on that new invention Scotland Yard calls 'FINGERPRINTS.' You've got bags under your eyes, you've lost weight and you've hardly touched any food Mrs. Hudson and I have offered you!"

He looked up from his work and faintly smiled.

"And I've enjoyed every minute of it, Watson. Or would you rather I turn to my seven percent solution out of boredom than tackle some project that may save a life sometime in the very near future?"

"That tears it, Holmes! As your friend, as well as a doctor who can see an attack of nerves

59

and total breakdown approaching, I must insist you come with me!"

With that I took the test tube out of Holmes' hand, put it back in the rack and grabbed his hat and coat.

"Here, take these; we're leaving this afternoon. I've already booked a train for Eastbourne. As your doctor I must demand immediate rest for you."

"My dear Watson, what ever shall I do without you to look after me? Still, I have so much work to do and—"

"As I thought," I interrupted. "Well my fine friend, I've put out all necessary clothing on your bed with a suitcase beside them. Arrangements have been made and we are off for a fortnight's vacation. It's that or Hospital for you, Holmes!"

That was how I forcibly persuaded my good friend Sherlock Holmes to accompany me on a well-deserved rest. The first few days of our vacation were spent in soothing idleness. Once persuaded to take this vacation, Holmes began to enjoy himself. Both of us were regaining the energy that only rest can provide.

On the morning of the third day Holmes, a dash of color back in his cheeks, and a hint of the old sparkle in his eyes, suggested that we should call on his good friend Evan Whitnell, curator of a nearby museum. And so, just after lunch on that September day, we hired a carriage and soon found ourselves in Professor Whitnell's private office at the museum.

"My dear friend, Evan," said Holmes, "your recent discoveries in this part of England have made you world famous instead of just nationally famous. My congratulations."

"Why thank you, Holmes. Thank you very much," Whitnell said, beaming at us.

"Professor, I do wish you'd tell me about your discoveries."

"With pleasure, Dr. Watson. Less than two months ago I was excavating on the downlands in this neighborhood, when I was fortunate enough to discover a number of underground caves. Caves saturated with a heavy deposit of lime that gave clear evidence of having the property of rapidly mummifying any flesh, human or animal, deposited in them."

"Extremely interesting," I said, "and what treasures have you unearthed, Professor?"

"A number of mummified specimens of animals clearly belonging to bygone eras. My prize specimen is the body of a large wolfhound. The inscription on its collar identified the animal as having belonged to some local squire in the year 1748!"

"Amazing! I didn't know limestone had such qualities of preservation."

There was a knock on the door and Professor Whitnell's assistant came in.

"It's Lady Clavering, Professor. She asked me to tell you that she was in the museum."

"Oh, yes, I almost forgot. Show her up here," said the Professor, who then turned to us, a great smile on his face. "I'm most anxious for you both to meet her, and she, in turn, is even more anxious to meet you. I dined with her last night, and when I told her that you were coming here today, Holmes, she insisted on meeting you."

"Whitnell, you scoundrel," Holmes said laughing, "there's a twinkle in your eye. I suspect that Lady Clavering is here to consult me in my professional capacity, and that you engineered the meeting."

"Well, Holmes, perhaps I might have dropped a hint," said the Professor with genuine amusement.

"I warn you, Professor," I said sternly. "Holmes can not become involved with another case. He's completely run down and needs the rest."

"Don't worry, doctor, all that Lady Clavering requires is a little advice. I knew you wouldn't mind, my dear Holmes."

"Of course not, Whitnell."

Another knock on the door and a most beautiful young lady came in, dressed in quite fashionable clothes.

"Ah, there you are, Helena, my dear." said the Professor, who then introduced us to her.

"Please sit down here," he went on, "I may as well tell you, Helena, that our little plot has already been discovered."

"Oh dear, and I was just getting ready to exert all my feminine wiles in an attempt to persuade you to help me, Mr. Holmes."

"The Professor tells me that you are in need of a little advice, Lady Clavering."

"Yes, Mr. Holmes. I put my problem simply: Five years ago my husband, Sir George Clavering, left me. I haven't seen or heard tell of him since. I now wish to remarry, but of course I cannot do that without having my husband declared legally dead."

"My dear Lady Clavering, I can't help feeling a solicitor is the proper man to consult, not a detective such as I."

"Perhaps," I added, "you are suggesting there might have been foul play in connection with your husband's disappearance?"

"No, Doctor Watson. The Claverings are a strange family; self-willed and head-strong. George and I were not happy together and I believe he disappeared deliberately."

"You've reported his disappearance to the police, of course?"

"Yes, Mr. Holmes, but they have never been able to trace him."

"This kind of thing has happened in the family before, Holmes," said the Professor. "Tell them about Sir Nigel, Helena."

"He was one of my husband's ancestors. He walked off one day in 1777 and was never seen again. George knew of the legend, and he often threatened to do the same thing himself."

"But your problem, Lady Clavering, is not that of your husband's fate, but rather of your own freedom."

"Yes, Mr. Holmes."

Holmes stood, a wry grin upon his countenance, as he pulled forth his pipe.

"Well, I'm afraid my advice can be of little consolation to you. The law has specified the number of years that must elapse before anyone disappearing can be declared legally dead. I would suggest that you possess your soul in patience until that period has passed."

"Oh dear," Lady Clavering said in great disappointment, "and I was hoping you would be able to think of some terribly clever way of getting round the law, Mr. Holmes."

"Lady Clavering," Holmes said in consternation, "sometimes, perhaps, my methods may be unorthodox, but I assure you that 'getting round the law,' as you put it, is a procedure I do not indulge in."

"Now I've offended you, Mr. Holmes, and it is the last thing on earth I meant to do, I assure you."

"My friend's a little touchy about matters concerning his professional honor, you know." Holmes laughed loudly and joyfully.

"Nonsense, my dear Watson. I'm not touchy, and I'm not offended. Now may I suggest we all examine the Professor's latest treasures? And after that, perhaps, he'll take us for a stroll on the downs. I'm most anxious to examine those lime pits of his."

With the relaxed atmosphere that Holmes now evoked, we spent some time with the Professor in looking over the vast treasures housed so carefully in his museum. In a short while, the Professor took us on a stroll of the downs, where a gentle breeze and the bright and warm day mixed with the delightful songs of various birds lifted us into a most pleasant and relaxing mood.

"The lime pits are about a mile from here," said the Professor, pointing up ahead. "It's a nice walk across the cliff tops."

Holmes had lit his pipe and seemed intensely interested in the surrounding landscape.

"I'm sorry Lady Clavering didn't want to come with us. A charming woman, even though she did rub you up the wrong way, Holmes."

"A beautiful woman, Watson, but I must confess her charm eludes me. Her lack of concern about her husband's fate seemed completely unnatural."

"Not if you'd known her husband," the Professor chimed in, "He was a tyrant and a bully, both in his home life and in the village!"

Nothing more was said as we continued our walk through the beautiful downs. Shortly, some distance ahead, we saw a figure approaching. It was a young man, in simple clothes, who whistled as we walked.

"Hello," I said, "who's this coming towards us?"

"It's Timmy. Daft Timmy they call him in these parts. He isn't quite right in the head, poor fellow, but he's perfectly harmless. Has two passions in life: Birds, and bonfires. Hello, Timmy."

Timmy approached the Professor, clutching his cap in his hands.

"I've got something beautiful to show you. Oh, it's so beautiful."

"Well, what is it, Timmy?" asked the Professor.

"Look. It's in my cap. See. Oh, isn't it lovely!"

There, nestled gently in Timmy's cap, was a small bird's egg.

"It's a robin's egg," Holmes said, quite delighted.

"I found it when I was bird nesting. Did you ever see such a blue egg?"

"It's a beauty, Timmy," I said. "Where did you find it, my boy?"

"Down by the lime pits. Oh, I'm going to build a lovely fire on the downs tonight. I'll let you come and watch it if you give me a shilling."

"Now you be careful, Timmy," the Professor said sternly, "or you'll be in trouble again."

"Timmy doesn't get in trouble anymore, now. Not since he had Sir George carried away."

"Sir George Clavering used to whip Timmy when he found him on the downs," the Professor whispered in an aside to Holmes.

"Timmy," said Holmes with great curiosity, "tell me, how did you have Sir George, as you put it, 'carried away'?"

"I told my birds about him. I told them how he used to beat poor Timmy, and they said they would carry him off and drop him over the cliffs! And that's what they did, because he never came back again."

The sound of hoof beats reached our ears, and we turned to see a great hulk of a man come riding up. With a massive head of red hair flowing in the wind, I could just make out the deep set, burning eyes and the angry face as he moved towards us.

"Oh Lord," said the Professor in dismay, "here comes Harry, Sir George's brother. Now there will be trouble. Timmy, you had best run."

"No," said Timmy in fear, "Timmy can't run. He'll break his pretty blue egg."

In a flourish of flying dirt, Harry Clavering pulled his horse up to an abrupt halt before us. He stood up in the saddle, now looking even more menacing, as he scowled at Timmy.

"Timmy! Get off my land! If I catch you here again, I'll take my riding crop to you!"

"But he hasn't done anything!" objected the Professor.

"Go on, be off with you, do you hear!"

"I'll tell my birds about you, that's what I'll do," said Timmy backing away. Then he turned to us with a smile.

"Don't forget my bonfire!" he yelled, and off he went across the downs, clutching the robin's egg close to his breast.

"Infernal scoundrel! Hello, Whitnell."

"Hello, Harry. Have you met Sherlock Holmes and Dr. Watson?"

Harry Clavering looked down at us from his horse, utter disgust on his face. I wanted to thrash the man for his insolence to poor Timmy.

"Oh, Sherlock Holmes, the professional nosey parker, aye? Yes, Helena was just telling me about you. I'm very angry with her for talking to you about my brother. It's a private affair, and I intend it shall remain one, you understand, Holmes?"

"The devil with your brother, sir, and with you! And I'd advise you to remember that you are not addressing a half-witted villager who can't defend himself!" Holmes burst forth angrily.

"If you know what's good for you, you'll do what I say!"

And with that, he turned his horse around and rode off, whipping at the poor beast with his riding crop.

"Impertinent jackal," I said, quite inflamed, "he spoke to you as if you were a stable boy, Holmes!"

"Really?" Holmes laughed, "he was quite refreshing. I'm reminded of an apt quotation of my young friend James Elroy Flecker: 'Thine impudence have a monstrous beauty, likened to the hind quarters of an elephant'!"

"He's almost as much disliked as his brother before him."

"Tell me, Professor, does he succeed to the title when his brother is declared legally dead?" asked Holmes.

"Yes. And what's more, he's Helena's unofficial fiancée, the worst luck!"

"I see. Personally I'm beginning to get a trifle bored with the affairs of the Clavering family. Let's go on to the lime caves, shall we?"

Whitnell led the way and soon we came upon a great cavernous opening that led down. Here and there about the cave entrance were picks, shovels and wheelbarrels, indications of Professor Whitnell's work. The sun was at the proper angle and its light penetrated the cave opening, giving us a chance to see its gigantic size and a portion of its depth. We continued walking, ever downward, watching ourselves carefully, lest we stumble on the broken limestone on the floor of the cave.

"These caves are amazing," I spoke, "we must be fifty feet below the level of the ground now, aren't we, Whitnell?"

"More than that, I should say."

"The rock formation is most unusual. I see now it is a series of caves connected by a veritable honeycomb of tunneling."

"Quite right, Holmes. I think I'll light my lantern now. It's getting darker, and I haven't explored this particular cave before. I've had a wall cave in on me a couple of times, so you had best watch where you are walking. Let's go deeper, shall we, but do watch your step."

Professor Whitnell led the way, but Holmes, in his always deep rooted curiosity had strayed away towards one wall, carefully glancing over the rock formations.

"Hello," he finally said, "what's this in the crevice here? Looks like a mummified bird of some kind."

The Professor raised the lantern higher to better observe Holmes' discovery.

"It is," said the Professor in excitement, "A beautiful specimen!"

"Judging by its markings, a black streak here, and bars of white in the tail, I'd say it was a peregrine."

"That's exactly what it is, Holmes, a falcon. Dating back a couple of hundred years, I should say. And in a perfect state of preservation. This is a treasure."

While Holmes and Professor Whitnell were examining the bird, I had wandered further on to what appeared to be a large pile of broken stone wedged against one wall.

"Seems to be another cave over here," I said, "I'll try to remove some of this—"
Suddenly the stone crumbled away, coming down full force to the floor of the cave.
"Good Lord, the whole wall has collapsed!"

"Watson, you're not hurt, are you?"

"No, no, Holmes, I'm all right."

"Why, you've unearthed another cave, Dr. Watson," the Professor remarked, "Let's go in.
I think we can just manage to crawl through."

Holding his lantern aloft, Whitnell crawled through the opening, followed by Holmes and
myself. Our clothes were now caked with limestone dust.

"Great Scott," I commented, "I don't believe my eyes!"

"Magnificent!" Holmes exclaimed, "Whitnell, this is a treasure, indeed. Look here. A
perfectly preserved body dressed in 18th century costume, powdered wig and all!"

"Yes, and there's no mistaking who it is. Look at that typical beak profile. It's a Clavering!
And it isn't hard to identify which one."

"You mean the one that Lady Clavering told us about this afternoon?" I asked.

"Exactly," returned the Professor, "without doubt, this is the body of Sir Nigel Clavering,
who disappeared in 1777! Let's search his pockets, but be careful, as this material is quite old
and can tear and crumble most easily. We might find some identification. Ah, here's a snuff
box of the period. And some coins."

"Yes," I said, "and the inscription of George the Third is still visible on them. Hello, here's
his diary. This is unbelievable. I say, what are you up to, Holmes?"

"I'm examining the body, Watson. This man was murdered! Look at this wound just above
the heart, obviously inflicted with a sharp instrument, probably a dagger. This is interesting!
An entirely new experience for me. The opportunity of solving an unsuspected murder
committed well over a hundred years ago. Pass me that diary, Watson old chap, and let's see if
the poor devil was aware of his fate."

"Rather hard to read," I said, observing the diary with Holmes, "all the S's look like F's."

"A peculiarity of the 18th century writing, Watson."

" 'They are faying,' " I read aloud, "I suppose that means 'saying' . . . 'They are faying in
the coffee houfef that my brother Harry haf been coveting my wife.' "

"This is amazing, Holmes," said the Professor in wonderment, "see how history repeats
itself. It's an exact parallel of the situation existing today. Harry is coveting his brother's wife,
Helena, and Sir George has not been seen for five years!"

"What an extraordinary coincidence."

"If it were one, Watson," said Holmes. "As it is, it's one of the most ingenious frauds I've
ever seen. The clothing appears authentic, so do the coins and the faded ink, also the paper of
the diary. And due to the peculiar mummification of the body, it would be almost impossible
to say how long it has been here. Nevertheless, I am convinced that this is a recent corpse, and
undoubtedly, that of Sir George Clavering!"

"What makes you so sure, Holmes?" I said, quite puzzled.

"The writing in the diary. The 18th century used an S that looked like an F, it is true, but never at the end of a word. You will recall, Watson, that you were reading h-a-F, haf, for h-a-S, has."

"That's perfectly true, I was."

"That would be incorrect in genuine 18th century writing. No, obviously this is an extremely clever attempt to disguise the comparatively recent murder of Sir George Clavering."

"But this is terrible, Holmes," said the Professor, "and yet I believe you are right!"

"I'm sure of it!"

"What are you going to do about it?" I said.

"Do? You and I will mount guard over the body, Watson. You, my dear Whitnell, if you don't mind, will be good enough to go and fetch the police."

And so it was that Holmes' old friend Evan Whitnell went for the police, leaving us in the limestone cave. It was cold and dreary and, without the lantern to give us light, totally dark. No matter how hard I tried, I could not see Holmes through the pitch black of the cave. Only our voices told us where we were as we sat upon the limestone floor.

"Holmes," I finally said in fatigue, "what do you suppose is keeping the police? Whitnell must have gone over an hour ago, and the lantern with him. Here we are sitting in this dreadful darkness in a smelly cave fifty feet under the cliffs, with a mummified corpse."

"Quite true, Watson, but I don't . . . ah ha, here comes the lantern."

I stood up, turning to the bright light that approached us.

"Whitnell, over here!" I yelled.

"That you, Whitnell?" said Holmes.

We could here footsteps on the cracked and broken limestone as the lantern hung in the air as if by magic, getting closer and closer to us.

"That lantern's blinding me, Holmes. Is that you, Whitnell? Answer, can't you?"

I could barely make out a form behind the blinding light of the lantern. I turned to Holmes who quickly stood up, a look of trepidation on his face.

"Look out, Watson!"

Suddenly I was hit across my shoulder and head. I fell dizzily to the ground as Holmes leapt forward to struggle with the mysterious figure behind the lantern. In a brief second Holmes collapsed lifeless to the ground, and just before I fell into unconsciousness I could hear the peeling of demonic laughter coming from the figure that stood over us, the sound echoing and echoing through the giant caverns!

## II

"Watson, old fellow, wake up. Come on, that's it!" I heard Holmes' distant voice become clearer as I regained my senses. I felt, rather than saw my old friend crouching over me.

"What the devil happened, Holmes?" I said as I unsteadily got to my feet.

"Whoever that was with the lantern knocked you down with a spade. I fought with him, but my feet slipped on the crumbling limestone and our adversary got the better of me. I'm afraid he was able to knock both of us unconscious."

"Good gracious, my head feels like I'd been hit with a sledgehammer," I said, feeling the damage.

"Anything serious, Watson?"

"No. Just a bad cut on the back of my neck; the blood has already coagulated. I think I'll be all right."

"Well, our assailant had the advantage. With that blinding lantern it was impossible for either of us to see what was going on until it was too late. I only came round minutes before you, Watson."

"Where the devil are we?" I said, again trying to see in the darkness.

"I took the liberty of checking that out. It seems we are in the bottom of a deep, and narrow pit. Our assailant must have dragged us here when we were unconscious."

"Can we get out, Holmes?"

"Possibly," he said, "get your coat off, and your shirt. I've already done with mine, and tied them together. Come on, Watson, off with them!"

"Whatever for?" I said feebly, still dazed by the blow I'd received.

"Dear me, that blow on your head must have been severe. I'm trying to make a kind of rope, Watson, a rope to get us out of here!"

"What's the good of a rope unless there's someone on the ledge above us to pull us out?"

Without answering me, Holmes began whistling as loudly as he could.

"What are you whistling for, at a time like this?"

"I'm whistling for help!" he said impatiently.

"Then why not shout?"

"A whistle carries farther."

I sat down to gather my strength and continued to rub my head in an attempt to increase circulation and dull the pain I was feeling. Holmes must have continued his whistling for some ten or twenty minutes before it finally grated on my nerves.

"Who could possibly hear that, Holmes?"

"Daft Timmy, I hope. Remember he was having a bonfire on the cliff tops tonight. My whistle is that of a nightingale, a song unheard in Sussex at this time of the year. If he does hear it, I'm sure it will bring him down here."

"I hope you're right. Seems to me that Whitnell and the police will never find us here. We shall mummify just as the filthy murderer intended us to!"

"Courage, Watson, I—"

Holmes and I heard whistling from a short distance above us. It grew louder until a figure stood at the edge of the pit.

"It's worked, Watson! It's Timmy, carrying a burning log!"

"Nightingale," said Timmy peering down into the pit, "pretty birdie, what are you doing down there?"

"Timmy!" yelled Holmes, "I've tied these clothes together to make a rope. I'm going to throw them up. You ready? Catch!"

Holmes bundled the clothes together and threw them with all his might. Timmy caught the clothes and stood looking down, puzzlement on his face.

"Now, Timmy, lower it to us!"

"Oh, I shouldn't do this. They'll whip me."

"No, no one will whip you, Timmy. And we both want to give you a shilling to come up and see your bonfire."

"That's different," Timmy said in excitement, "two shiny shillings. I'll lower the rope."

In a moment I was at the top of the pit, lowering the rope to Holmes, who then climbed out to join us. Exhausted, we rested for a moment. Timmy, poor boy, had to be told there was no nightingale. His disappointment soon vanished when we gave him two shillings to take us to his bonfire. Cold and weak, we stood before the fire, our hands outstretched, gathering in the warmth of the flames.

"Did you ever see a finer bonfire?" said young Timmy, the flames dancing in front of his happy face.

"Never, Timmy. It's lovely."

"It's the most comfortable sight I've seen for the last couple of hours," I said, as the damp and cold slowly ebbed from our bodies.

"Just one thing's bad, though. Somebody tried to burn a book in my lovely fire. It must have been when I was off getting more wood. I found it when I came back, and I pulled it out of the fire, and stamped on it I did. See, here it is."

Timmy showed us the book. There was no mistaking it.

"It's the diary that we found on the body in the limepits."

"Precisely, Watson. Now I begin to see daylight."

"People shouldn't burn books," Timmy said angrily, "books are nice, like birds and bonfires. They are nice to be near. Oh, you must still be cold. I'll get more twigs to burn, I will."

Timmy quickly ran to fetch more wood, leaving Holmes and I to contemplate the day's events.

"Now, that we're alone, Holmes, I can see why we were attacked tonight. The murderer knew that we were going to the caves and was afraid that his devilish plot wouldn't stand up under your scrutiny, so he watched us. When we discovered the body and sent Whitnell off to fetch the police, he knew he had to get rid of us."

"And who do you think that somebody is, old fellow?"

"That's easy. There's only one person strong enough to knock us both unconscious and shift out bodies. The dead Sir George's brother, Harry Clavering."

"I think not, Watson. Didn't you observe as we entered the caves that pickaxes and wheelbarrows were much in evidence?"

"Yes, they were, of course."

"Strength was not required, under the circumstances. Placing us in a wheelbarrow would be an easy method to transport us to the pit. We were extremely vulnerable in the darkness. Any man with a modicum of cunning could have disposed of us, or, any woman, for that matter."

"Holmes," I said in surprise, "you're not suggesting that Lady Clavering is the guilty party?"

"Holmes! Watson!" came Professor Whitnell's voice from a distance as he and two policeman came running up, "thank heavens, you're safe. I've had the police with me for the last hour, but we couldn't find you. You weren't where I left you."

"True. Whitnell," Holmes said, "I want you and the police to take me to Lady Clavering's house at once. After that, I wish to lodge information and make a charge of assault, and possibly a charge of murder!"

Holmes and I were taken straight away to Lady Clavering's where we were first given hot tea and some blankets to warm us. Harry Clavering stood before us, his arm around Lady Clavering. Professor Whitnell sat before us, deep concern showing on his face over the condition we were in. Holmes sat Lady Clavering down and told her the entire story of the discovery of the body in the limepits, trying to break the news of Sir George's death as gently as possible.

"That, unfortunately, is the story of how we found your husband's body."

"This is horrible, Mr. Holmes, horrible."

"But who in thunder could have planned such a devilish plot!" said Harry Clavering.

"Why did the murderer attack you and Watson?"

"There, my dear Whitnell, you have the key to the murderer's identity. The man who so cunningly conceived and executed the murder of Sir George could never have bungled the job of disposing of Watson and myself, unless he had meant to bungle it!"

"You mean he didn't mean to kill us?"

"Exactly, Watson! He merely wished us out of the way while the incriminating evidence was removed."

"You mean the diary," I added.

"Of course I do. You will recall we found it partially burned in Timmy's bonfire."

"Then it was Timmy who—"

"No, no, my dear Watson," Holmes said, cutting me short. "Surely it's obvious one person, and only one, knew that the diary was the key to the murderer's identity. The man who was present when we discovered it and detected the fraud!"

"Great Scott, you mean Professor Whitnell!" I said in total disbelief. Everyone in the room stood in rigid shock as Holmes looked at Evan Whitnell with steely eyes.

"Whitnell, you? You murdered my brother?" Harry Clavering yelled in shaking anger.

"Evan," Lady Clavering gasped, tears in her eyes, "no, it isn't true."

Professor Whitnell sank back in his chair, pain written across his face. It was over, and he understood. There was no fight in him, just a beaten man. He looked at each one in turn, then heaved a great sigh; almost a sigh of relief that his play acting was over.

"I did it," he said quietly, "because I love you, Helena. All these years there has been nothing in my life that meant anything, but you. I thought that if George were out of the way I could make you care for me. Then, when I realized you loved Harry, I was mad with jealousy. And so I planned to conceal George's body forever. It was a clever plan. You said so yourself, Holmes. If it hadn't been for you, it would have worked."

"Yes, it was diabolically clever, Evan, but I'm afraid that no amount of cleverness now can prevent you from paying for your crime. I am truly sorry, old friend. Constable, you have your man. Our work is done."

A terrible stillness seemed to engulf the room. No one spoke, for no one had need to say anything more. The police took their man, and I watched, saddened at heart by this turn of events, as Holmes stood by the window watching his old friend being taken away. It was almost night and, with the kind invitation of Lady Clavering to stay till morning to recuperate from our experiences, we retired in silence.

The next morning found us once again walking along the cliffs in fine fettle.

"Some rest I'd gotten you into, aye, Holmes?"

"Dear Watson, you should know by now that it doesn't take much to invigorate me and return me to my old self," he said quietly.

As he spoke, my eyes scanned the horizon, observing the birds, the land, and enjoying the fresh and breezy air.

"Holmes, look there on the point. Timmy's bonfire is still burning away."

"Yes," Holmes said contemplatively, "Timmy's a simple fellow, with simple tastes."

"Why are you so gloomy this fine morning? You solved the case brilliantly."

"My dear fellow, my faith in human nature has been sadly shaken. Evan Whitnell was a good friend, and an old one. It's hard to be instrumental in sending him to the gallows."

"I understand, Holmes," I said, "but you must admit he richly deserved it."

"Yes, yes, I know he did, that's quite true, but it's depressing just the same."

Holmes and I walked on in silence. He took his pipe from his inverness and was about to light it, but he stopped, slowly placing it back in his pocket. It was a time for quiet, for Holmes had to face his pain alone, even though I was there at his side. We stopped and Holmes looked out over the cliffs in a mood of intense contemplation. I walked some distance away, leaving him to his thoughts. In a few moments, he turned to me.

"Come on, Watson, let's continue our walk home across the downs."

"I heard Sir Harry offering you a fee this morning. Did you take it?"

"No I didn't, but I did accept his offer of an acre of land on the downs over there near the abbey ruins. You can see them silhouetted against the sky."

"An acre of land? What on earth would you do with that?"

"Well, Watson, when I retire, and I shall retire some day, I've often thought of bee farming. This would be a heavenly spot for such a venture."

"I can't imagine you as a bee keeper."

"Why not? After a life spent unraveling the tangled affairs of human beings, it would be soothing in the twilight of one's days to study the exact and predictable behavior of bees. Singing masons, building roofs of gold. Ah well, my dear Watson, one day perhaps. Perhaps."

"Watson! Gregson! Grab his arm! Look out for that razor!"

# 5

# THE CASE OF THE DEMON BARBER

I have mentioned, in my various stories about my good friend Sherlock Holmes, that he was most proficient at makeup and has, at various times, done some acting in solving a case, such as in A SCANDAL IN BOHEMIA. Holmes makes little reference to those times when he has donned makeup and assumed a role in order to gain access to someplace or someone he would otherwise be unable to contact. One such case, where his actual acting on stage played an important part in solving a mystery, began on a winter's night in 1896. Holmes and I had gone to a theatre in the east end of London to see a performance of the famous old English melodrama called *"Sweeney Todd, the Demon Barber of Fleet Street."* Todd was a murderer of voracious appetite who placed his victims in a specially constructed barber's chair, cut their throats and then pressed a lever that would swing the chair over and decamp the unfortunate victim into a horrible cellar beneath his shop. We had taken a private box and were watching one of the closing scenes with Holmes leaning forward in his chair following the action on the stage with obvious delight, I beside him equally engrossed. An actor by the name of Mark Humphries was playing the part of Sweeney Todd, and it was evident to me he was playing the role up to the hilt and enjoying it immensely. With long strides he would cross the stage, brandishing his arms about as he talked, making every move and gesture a bold action. I felt it highly overdone, but amusingly interesting.

As the curtain lowered, the audience rose as one and cheered. I turned to Holmes, laughing as I did so, and saw a deep smile of amusement on his face.

"Upon my soul, Holmes, that fellow Mark Humphries is the most florid actor I've ever seen on a stage."

"I find him enchanting, Watson. It seems to me he's really caught the flavor of this 'murderous monsterpiece.' After all, a restrained performance of the barber Sweeney Todd would be unthinkable."

"Perhaps you're right," I said, "but I must say his makeup seems rather overdone. No barber would wear such an enormous beard. It would be impractical. Most likely to get in the customer's faces. By the way, Holmes, I noticed from the program that Mark Humphries as well as being the principal actor is also the owner of the company."

"Yes," Holmes said as he leaned back and lit his pipe, "the current trend towards the actor/manager is a very healthy sign, I think."

We said no more, but relaxed, looking down at the audience as they slowly moved towards the exits. We would soon be joining them when the crowd had thinned out a bit. There was a knock at the door leading to our box, and Holmes and I turned just as a gentleman entered.

"Excuse me, but is one of you gentlemen Mr. Sherlock Holmes?"

"Yes, I am."

"I was asked to give you this note."

"Now who on earth knows that you're at the theatre, Holmes?"

"We'll soon find out," he replied, opening the small envelope that contained the note, "well, this note is from Mark Humphries, our actor/manager. It says 'Dear Mr. Holmes, I recognize you in your box. Please come to my dressing room as soon as you can. My sanity, and even the safety of London perhaps, depends on your compliance!' "

Holmes and I looked at each other with curiosity.

"'My sanity and the safety of London?' I wonder what on earth he means, Holmes?"

"That, my dear fellow, we can only discover by going backstage to meet him." Holmes rose, gathering together his walking stick, gloves and top hat. I did likewise as we casually made our way through the few remaining members of the audience until we had stepped onto the stage, crossed behind the curtain, and down the side of the theatre to the backstage entrance. Standing at the stage door was a man almost as tall as Holmes, dressed not in workman's clothes, but that of a well to do gentlemen. It was he that approached us as we reached the stage door.

"Mr. Sherlock Holmes?" he said.

"Yes?" my friend returned.

"My name is Lindsay. Derrick Lindsay. I'm the business manager of this theatre. Mr. Humphries asked me to meet you at the stage door and take you to his dressing room."

"Very kind of you. This is my colleague, Dr. Watson."

Mr. Lindsay acknowledged my presence and gestured for us to follow him. As we walked down a long corridor, actors and actresses in various appearances of disarray came running back and forth as they went about their chores of changing into street clothes and removing their makeup. I was deeply fascinated by all this while Holmes simply took it in his stride.

"Excuse me asking, Mr. Lindsay," Holmes said, "but surely you must be related to that distinguished actor of some years back, Litton Lindsay."

"He was my father, Mr. Holmes."

"Ah, indeed. The resemblance is extraordinary," Holmes mused.

"With such a heritage, Mr. Lindsay, you must love the theatre," I added.

"It'll probably sound like heresy," laughed Mr. Lindsay, "But I hate it. However, it is the only thing I was trained for, and there's good money to be made in it, sometimes. And money's the thing I both like and want. Mr. Holmes, I do hope you will be able to help Mark Humphries. He certainly needs it. Now Mark's wife and I think . . . There's Mrs. Humphries now. Maria!"

A most beautiful woman turned and approached us. She walked with great dignity and it was quite easy to see she was very cultured in her ways. I remembered seeing her in the play tonight. Mr. Lindsay introduced us to Maria who immediately approached Holmes with a look of deep concern on her face.

""Mr. Holmes, I'm so grateful that you're going to see Mark. He's in such a dreadful state. There have been times lately when Mr. Lindsay and I have been afraid he's going out of his mind. Haven't we, Derrick?"

"Indeed we have. We're both deeply worried about him."

"In that case, I hope I can be of service. Which is his dressing room?"

"Number One, next door to mine," said an anxious Mrs. Humphries. "Derrick, I think it would be better if Mr. Holmes and Dr. Watson go in alone. I'm sure Mark will speak more freely if we are not in the room."

"A very good idea, Mrs. Humphries," Holmes said, "we'll see you later on." We turned and went to the end of the corridor, where Holmes knocked, and a voice yelled through for us to come in. We did so and I was quite shocked, for the man seated before us at the dressing table was in total turmoil. Half his makeup was off, giving him a twisted look with the grease paint smeared diagonally across his face. I looked closely at the one eye he had cleaned and could see it was not only twitching, but seemed bloodshot, which is usually caused by lack of sleep. Add to that his bulk and nervous nature and the man looked like a beaten creature whose eyes darted strangely from his dressing table to Holmes.

"Sherlock Holmes, thank Heaven you're here. Please close the door," he said as he continued to remove the evening's makeup.

"Mr. Humphries, this is Dr. Watson, my colleague, and a man I trust implicitly."

"Watson. Yes, I know of you, also. Sit down, won't you? You're wondering why I asked you to come back and see me, of course."

"Naturally, sir," Holmes said, seating himself across from Mr. Humphries while I sat to one side.

"Well, I won't beat about the bush and waste your time. I'll come straight to the point. I'm going mad! I know it sounds fantastic, but it's true. I've often heard of actors beginning to live their parts off the stage. The same parts they play on the stage. Well, it's happening to me. I'm turning into another Sweeney Todd!"

"Are you suggesting, sir, that you are a potential murderer?" Holmes asked pointedly.

"Yes, I am!"

"What reason do you have for holding that belief?" Holmes continued.

"Reason! Listen to this," Mark Humphries said visibly shaking, "three times in the past week I've wakened in the morning to find my boots covered with mud, and my razor stained with blood!"

"Great Scott!" I exclaimed under my breath. Holmes leaned forward, pressing on with his questions.

"You've had no recollection of any untoward events during the night?"

"None."

"Have you ever been addicted to the unfortunate habit of sleep walking?" I asked.

"Not to my knowledge, doctor. And if I had been, surely my wife would have told me about it."

"Your wife . . . yes," Holmes said contemplatively. "Where do you live, Mr. Humphries?"

"We have a flat here above the theatre."

"Mr. Humphries, you say that on three separate occasions on waking in the morning, you have found a bloodstained razor and mud covered boots. Can you show us this proof?"

"No, no I can't. I was always so frightened my wife would see them, that I cleaned them before she had the opportunity of finding them."

"That's a great pity, sir," I said. "They would have been very valuable clues in a case like this."

"I couldn't risk my wife seeing evidence like that, doctor," Humphries said frantically. "She'd know the truth; that at nighttime, while she's asleep, some devilish, hidden urge has overcome me. An urge that causes me to prowl the streets of London, razor in hand, looking for a victim. Mr. Holmes, you've got to help me. I'm certain that, without knowing it, I've been committing murder. And if you don't help me, I'll go on and on!"

The man was beside himself, trembling in a totally distraught state, his nerves on edge, his very being shattered.

"Mr. Humphries, please," Holmes snapped, "try to calm yourself. I'll undertake the case. It's a very unique assignment. In effect, Watson, I'm being engaged by a possible murderer to prove him guilty! Now, Mr. Humphries, compose yourself enough that your wife will suspect nothing of what you and I have spoken. In the meantime, I have some preliminary work to do on your case before I fling myself full force into your problem. I will contact you shortly."

Holmes and I excused ourselves and left the room. Outside we saw no sign of Mrs. Humphries nor Derrick Lindsay.

"All the better for us, Watson," was Holmes' comment. "I don't want them to know a thing yet. Come on old chap, we're off to Scotland Yard."

"Scotland Yard? Whatever for?"

"You'll see when we get there."

Outside the theatre we caught a cab and made our way to Scotland Yard, Holmes seated comfortably across from me, his lit pipe smoking away like some chimney on fire. I could see he was in deep concentration, no doubt on the case at hand. Between the theatre and Scotland Yard, I mused to myself, Holmes would probably have called it a "one pipeful" time of concentration.

And I was correct, for Holmes had just finished his pipe as we stood waiting for Inspector Gregson to finish checking on what Holmes had asked of him.

"Well, Mr. Holmes," Inspector Gregson said, returning from his careful look through Scotland Yard's files, "I've finished going through all the records."

"What have you found?" Holmes asked.

"In the last two months we haven't had one case of an unsolved killing with a razor, sir."

"Any mysterious disappearances, Inspector?" I asked.

"Bless your heart, doctor," chuckled Gregson, "there's never a day passes without one or two of them. Here's a list of them, Mr. Holmes, if it's any use to you."

"Thank you. Come on, Watson, in the morning we can go back to the theatre and set our friend's mind at rest. I'm much obliged to you, Gregson."

"Glad to be of service, Mr. Holmes."

We returned to Baker Street where Mrs. Hudson, rather annoyed and disgruntled, set up a hasty late dinner for us before we called it a day. As I expected, Holmes was glancing over various newspaper clippings from the past months looking for some evidence to contradict Inspector Gregson's findings while I prepared for bed.

The next day brought us once again before Mark Humphries in his dressing room. Holmes begged the man to relax as he seated himself.

"We examined the homicide records at Scotland Yard after leaving you last night, Mr. Humphries. There have been no unsolved razor murders in London during the past fortnight."

"And therefore," I added, "you may rest easy on that score, sir."

"But it proves nothing. Remember that in the play Sweeney Todd's victims are never found either."

"Yes, thanks to a singularly horrible ingenuity in disposing of them. But this is *real* life, Mr. Humphries."

"Then how do you account for the bloodied razors and the mud soaked boots?" Humphries said disdainfully.

"Are you sure they aren't just in your imagination, sir? You admit that your wife's never seen them. The whole thing could be, shall we say, an overdose of Sweeney Todds?" I said.

"I do admit that I'm suffering from a surfeit of that."

"Then why not drop the play from your repertory?" Holmes asked.

"Our manager, Derrick Lindsay, won't let me. It's our best money maker and he's always got a keen eye to business. Mr. Holmes, I can see that you still don't believe my story. So I've saved some evidence for you, evidence that I found this morning!"

From a bottom drawer in his dressing table, Humphries pulled a pair of muddied boots and a blood stained razor.

"Look at these. Now what do you say? Do you still think it's my imagination?"

"Splendid!" Holmes exclaimed. "At last some real clues to work on!"

"How can you be so overjoyed at this evidence, Holmes? It happened to me again, last night! Do you realize that I am a murderer? I'm a menace to society! For Heavens sake, lock me up before I do some more deathly damage!"

"Mr. Humphries, I'd like to take these objects back to Baker Street where I can perform some chemical tests. You have no objections, I hope?"

"Objections? Good Heavens, no," he replied, almost whimpering.

"Excellent. You've told no one of this fresh discovery of yours?" Holmes asked.

"No one, not even Derrick Lindsay."

"Derrick Lindsay," I asked, "that's your manager, isn't it?"

"Yes. The best friend I've ever had. Except for his father before him. It was Derrick who helped me back on my feet two years ago when I put on that disastrous production of MACBETH. I don't know where I'd be today if it weren't for him."

"You lost a great deal of money on that production, sir?" Holmes asked.

"Nearly every penny I had."

"Indeed. By the way, where is your wife, Mr. Humphries?"

"She's in her dressing room next door. We have a matinee today and we're preparing for it."

"I'd like a word with her, if I may. Watson, wait here for me. I won't be a moment."

While Holmes left to talk to Humphries' wife, I opened my bag and pulled a sedative out, dissolving it in a glass of water on the dressing table.

"Mr. Humphries, take this. In your nervous state it will not be long before you end up with complete exhaustion, such as to be unable to perform on the stage. This sedative will help. There's just enough here for you to refresh your nerves before your matinee. I suggest you lie down on your couch and in no time you'll be ready for today's performance."

Shortly after Mr. Humphries lay on the couch, Holmes returned. I gestured for him to be quiet. Humphries looked up as Holmes bent over the man.

"We'll take your leave now, sir. Don't worry, I shall get to the bottom of this quite soon."

We left the poor soul to rest and hailed a cab. On our way back to Baker Street, Holmes told me all that had transpired with Mrs. Humphries, which I shall endeavor to detail here as closely as I can to the actual event. When Holmes left the dressing room he immediately knocked on Mrs. Humphries door.

"Who is it?"

"Sherlock Holmes."

The door was only slightly opened, revealing Mrs. Humphries in makeup as she was just finished her preparations for the matinee.

"You want to talk to me, Mr. Holmes?" she asked questioningly.

"For a moment. May I come in, Mrs. Humphries?"

"Couldn't we talk on the stage? It's empty."

"I should prefer to come into your dressing room, if you don't mind. What I have to say is confidential."

"Very well then, come in," she said coldly.

As soon as Holmes was ushered in his eyes widened, for there he saw a man sitting on a chair by the dressing table.

"Mr. Holmes, may I introduce Señor Vennelli, our musical director."

"How do you do, sir."

"It is a great pleasure to meet the so great Señor Holmes; I have so admired you," Vennelli said, bowing deeply.

"Señor Vennelli, if you don't mind," Holmes said curtly, "I wish to speak to Mrs. Humphries alone."

"I quite understand," he returned, then, bowing once again, left the room quietly, closing the door behind him.

"Mr. Holmes, I'm really awfully glad of this opportunity to talk to you. Tell me truthfully please, what is your opinion of my husband?"

"I haven't formed a definite opinion, yet. Except that it is possible he's the victim of a fraud. But for the moment, I want to ask you a few questions, if you don't mind."

"Of course not, Mr. Holmes."

"Has your husband ever shown evidence of being a sleep walker?"

"A sleep walker? Oh no, never."

"Are you a light sleeper?" Holmes continued.

"Yes, I am. Exceptionally so. Why?"

"I was just curious."

"You're being very mysterious, Mr. Holmes. Can't you tell even me what is going on?"

"I promised your husband the answer to that question before tonight's performance. I'm afraid I can't tell you any more until then."

"I see. And now, may I ask a question?" she returned.

"Certainly, though I won't promise to answer it."

"You said just now that my husband might be the victim of a fraud. What did you mean?"

"Again I am afraid that you must wait for the specific answer to that question. However, there's another fraud being practiced on him that I can speak of now."

"What fraud?"

"The fraud that *you* are indulging in, Mrs. Humphries," Holmes said in restrained anger.

"What do you mean?"

"Of course this particular fraud is none of my business but, when I almost force my way into your dressing room and find your musical director with a quantity of rice powder on one shoulder and suggestions of rouge on his cheek, it doesn't take a great deal of intelligence to deduce that your husband is being deceived!"

"How dare you! Get out of here, at once!"

"That's exactly what I propose doing. No doubt I shall see you later on. Good day to you, madam."

And with that, Holmes left to return to Mr. Humphries' dressing room.

"That's insufferable, Holmes. It's bad enough Humphries has to live with this Sweeney Todd thing he is going through," I said when Holmes had finished his tale.

"Yes, such are the machinations of life, my dear Watson. Ah, here we are at Baker Street."

Once in the comfort of our lodgings, Holmes went to work with his microscope and chemicals running several tests while I, the latest newspaper in hand, casually read through numerous articles. After some time I looked up to see Holmes still at his work.

"Well Holmes, what does the microscope tell you about the mud on the boots and the bloodstains on the razor?" I asked.

"I've drawn a blank on the mud, old chap. It's an extremely common type to be found in most parts of London."

"And the blood?"

"I'm examining that now."

"This is as strange an occasion as ever I remember, Holmes. Here you are trying to prove a man innocent when he insists that he's guilty."

"By George, Watson, here's the answer! This blood is definitely not human blood. I suspect it's canine. Now a Sweeney Todd madness would hardly drive its victim to kill dogs, therefore it's obvious Mark Humphries is the victim of a devilish plot!"

"Then he's not a murderer." I exclaimed.

"No. Come on, Watson, we must go to the theatre at once and give him the good news."

Once again, and with what I thought was for the last time, we drove by cab to the theatre. The stage door guard had by now come to recognize us and immediately let us in. We stood before Mark Humphries' dressing room as Holmes knocked.

"Why doesn't he answer, Holmes? It's only three quarters of an hour before curtain time."

"He must be in his dressing room. I'll knock again."

Holmes pounded on the door, then, annoyed with waiting, tried the handle and opened the door.

"Holmes, look, he's slumped over his dressing table."

"I hope we're not too late. Here, give me a hand with him."

We carefully pulled him upright. It was then we saw the blood covering the dressing table, the same blood that had so deeply stained his clothes.

"We are too late," I said. "His throat's been cut."

"Poor devil," Holmes murmured, a bitter, self-accusing tone in his voice, "I promised him a solution to his troubles before the night was over. Little did I think the solution would be death."

"It looks to me as if his worry over his supposed madness has caused him to commit suicide," I sighed.

Holmes looked at me abruptly, sudden anger in his eyes.

"Suicide? Rubbish, Watson, it's murder."

"But the razor clutched in his hand."

"Placed there by the murderer before rigor mortis had a chance to set in. In any case, scrutinize the wound. Does that look as if it has been done by a suicide?"

"I don't see why not," I insisted.

"Look closer, old chap. The depth of the wound is even, whereas a suicide's cut always wavers towards the end. No, this is murder, Watson, and I think I know who did it. But I have little evidence and therefore must lay a trap."

"What kind of a trap, Holmes?"

"I haven't time to tell you now. Every moment counts. Off with you to Scotland Yard and get Inspector Gregson. Bring him back here as fast as you can."

"Right you are, Holmes," I said, then turned to leave, but my friend stayed my movement.

"Watson, tell absolutely no one except Gregson of Mark Humphries' death. If anyone here asks you about Humphries, tell them he is well and that his problems are solved."

"But the performance of the play?" I questioned.

"Don't worry about that. Now off with you to Scotland Yard! And hurry!"

I was off immediately for Inspector Gregson, but I had no idea that finding him would take so long a time. The duty officer informed me that Gregson was out on another case and was expected back quite soon. I paced the floor of the front office, constantly glancing at my watch as an endless period of time seemed to pass by with my patience about to snap. Finally, after waiting for almost an hour, Gregson appeared.

"Gregson, you must come with me. There's been a murder at the theatre. We mustn't waste a moment!"

"Murder? What murder? What's this all about?" he asked as I pulled him into the cab which I had waiting outside the Yard.

"'I'll explain everything on the way to the theatre. Cabby, a shilling if you can get us back in 10 minutes!"

And in a little over the allotted time, the cab pulled up to the stage door.

"The performance, if there is one, must be nearly over by now. Come on."

We entered the theatre and moved quietly towards the wings.

"I wonder who the devil is playing Sweeney Todd?" I said in surprise.

Gregson and I stood in the wings almost close enough to touch the actors. I gazed at Sweeney Todd in bewilderment.

"This is impossible, Gregson," I whispered, "there's Mark Humphries on the stage. But I saw him with his throat cut!"

"Well, I don't believe in ghosts, doctor," he returned, scratching his head.

"Great Heavens, it's Holmes!"

I stood there transfixed. Holmes was perfection, not only in the role of Sweeney Todd, but in his exact duplication of Mark Humphries' every gesture and movement. Even his voice sounded the same. Yet through the padding and the makeup there was the unmistakable Holmes. The Holmes that only I could know so well. The Holmes who still delightfully amazed me with his deeds and cunning and his observations, all of which gave him the gift to do what he now did on stage with stunning adroitness. I have seen Holmes don various disguises and act several roles, but these were in the real world. Now, I was watching Holmes on the stage, in the theatrical world of make believe, and I saw all his magnificent acting ability come to the fore, revealing another aspect of this brilliant man I had not really understood before. Suddenly the play was over and I saw Holmes rush towards me as the last curtain call finished.

"Thank Heavens you are both here!" he said.

"Holmes, what are you up to?"

"Surely that's apparent, Watson. I've disguised myself as the dead man hoping to force the murderer's hand."

"You're running a terrible risk, Mr. Holmes."

"Part of my profession, Gregson. But it didn't work. It didn't work, confound it."

"What didn't work?" I asked.

"The murderer still hasn't tipped his hand. I wonder if I've underestimated him."

"It looks as if you have, sir. And if you don't mind my saying so I think you'd have been a lot wiser to let me handle the case as soon as you found Mr. Humphries' body, instead of going in for all this dressing up stuff."

Holmes stood there as if he hadn't heard a word Inspector Gregson had said. It was that look of intense concentration I was so familiar with.

"But of course!" Holmes suddenly shouted, "Now I see it. Only one person could have killed Mark Humphries."

"Who, Holmes?" I asked.

"Do as I say and I'll show you. I'm going to Humphries' dressing room now, alone. Give me a few moment's start, and then follow me. Out of sight, but within earshot."

Holmes quickly left and we watched as, again assuming the movements and gestures of Mark Humphries, he entered the now dead man's dressing room.

Gregson and I secreted ourselves in a stairwell not far from the dressing room.

"You know, doctor," Gregson said, "I'm very fond of Mr. Holmes, and yet there are times when I get so angry with him. He shouldn't risk his life like that."

"You know Holmes, Gregson, he'll never change," I said, somewhat bemused.

"Well if he doesn't, one of these days he's going to wake up and find himself dead," Gregson said. I laughed at the Inspector's serious but unintentionally humorous comment. Abruptly we both became aware of shouting coming from the dressing room.

"You devil!" shouted the voice, "how many times do I have to kill you?"

"Gregson, quickly, Holmes is in danger!"

I rushed to the dressing room door, Gregson at my side. I flung open the door and there, before us, a razor in his hand, stood Derrick Lindsay. Holmes was struggling with the man, desperately trying to keep the razor from his throat.

"Watson! Gregson! Grab his arm! Look out for that razor!"

Thank Heavens Holmes maneuvered Lindsay so his back was towards us, allowing us to come up from behind and disarm the man. Gregson pulled the razor away from Lindsay, then hit him hard across the jaw, stunning him. Lindsay fell to the floor, at first moaning in pain, then weeping in distress, bits of the beard Holmes wore on stage clenched in his hand.

"Very neat, Gregson," Holmes said, quickly regaining his composure.

"Are you all right, Holmes?"

"Perfectly. Thanks, old chap, though I'm a little tired. Gregson, my dear fellow, will you take over from here? I think I've had enough melodrama for one day."

Gregson took charge of the killer as Holmes sat down at the dressing table and removed the remainder of the makeup until he was once again in his regular clothes, pipe between his teeth and a smile of complete satisfaction on his face.

In a short while we hailed a cab and returned to Baker Street, where we settled in for the night.

"Ah," Holmes said, easing himself into a chair, "how pleasant, Watson, to be back in Baker Street again. A crackling fire, my dressing gown and your company combine to make a soothing end to a somewhat violent day."

"Yes, it's been a most unusual case, Holmes. I still don't entirely understand it. The original idea, of course, was to try and drive Mark Humphries mad by making him think that he was a murderer. That accounted for the boots and the bloodstained razor."

"Precisely, my dear fellow, and the killer, having conditioned his victim by this trickery, then murdered him, trying to make it appear a suicide. Now who had a motive?"

"Three people, I believe, Holmes. Mrs. Humphries, her lover, Señor Vennelli, and Derrick Lindsay. I must say that I suspected the wife."

"So did I for a while. And yet it was illogical. She knew, and we may therefore presume her lover knew, that I was suspicious of her."

"Then she must have known that you promised her husband a solution to his troubles before the night was out. It seems highly improbable that she, or Señor Vennelli, would have faked his suicide at that point."

"Quite right, Watson," Holmes said as he lit a cigar, "so I investigated Derrick Lindsay's affairs and found that what Humphries had referred to as the 'kindly act of a friend' in helping him back onto his feet, was in reality the mortgaging of his entire theatrical effects. Lindsay stood to inherit the theatre on Humphries' death, therefore, I was convinced he was the killer."

"And then after he murdered him he saw what he thought to be Mark Humphries on the stage."

"Ah, that's where I was slow and stupid, old chap," Holmes said smiling. "I couldn't imagine what motive gave Lindsay the cold clear nerve to suppress all reactions when he saw his supposed victim revived on the stage. Only later did I realize."

"Well, Holmes, what was the motive that made him hold his hand?"

"The characteristic that ruled his life, Watson. Avarice! A morbid love of money. You see, if he'd attacked me during the performance, he would have had to refund the money to the audience. His greed conquered all other passions. It made him wait until the performance was finished before he attempted my life."

"You know, Holmes, now that the case is solved, I'll tell you something in confidence. At the end of the play tonight, when you were waiting for Lindsay to tip his hand, I was afraid that you'd made a mistake, that you'd slipped up on the case."

"And I, Watson, will tell you something in confidence," he said leaning towards me, "there were two of us that felt the same way."

"Now you're being modest, Holmes."

"I assure you I'm not, my dear chap. In fact, in the future, if it should strike you that I'm . . . well, getting a little overconfident of my powers, or perhaps taking a little less pain over a case than it deserves, kindly whisper 'Sweeney Todd' in my ear, will you. I shall be infinitely obliged to you!"

Holmes sat back, blowing large puffs of smoke into the air as I chuckled quietly. Yes, Holmes never ceased to amaze me.

As Holmes clung desperately to the side of the mountain, the tents, the guides, and all their equipment were buried beneath hundreds of feet of thundering snow.

# 6

# MURDER BEYOND THE MOUNTAINS

## I

"HOLMES!" I said in anger, "the least you could do is tell me what transpired during those months you spent in Tibet!"

"What?" he replied his eyes still at the microscope, "and have you write it all up as another one of your highly exaggerated stories about my so-called exploits?"

I said nothing. I merely sat there, pencil in hand, ready to write, as I stared at Holmes. The deathly quiet at last penetrated his thoughts and he looked up to see me sitting there, anger across my face.

"I must apologize, old friend; it was a thoughtless thing to say. Can you forgive me?"

"I don't know, Holmes. It's been two years now that you have refused to even utter a word on what happened during that period you were presumed dead. You've sorely tried my patience each and every time I have asked you for information!"

Holmes put his microscope aside and came to sit before me. His face was filled with a look that I could only assume was that of anxiety. He seemed hesitant to speak. Finally, leaning forward, he looked at me with a sense of friendship and compassion that I had seen only rarely before.

"My dear Watson, do try to understand that, for me, those three years I spent wandering throughout the world are of the most personal nature. It is not easy for me to speak of them, even to you. Much transpired then that has affected and changed the inner core of my being, and it is for that reason I have found it difficult to reveal any of what I have gone through."

"Holmes," I said, letting go of my anger, "why didn't you reveal at least this much to me before? I would have understood."

"Call it a stubbornness on my behalf. Or a reluctance to talk about my experiences during that period. I merely resisted your curiosity with as much patience as I could muster."

"Holmes, I am truly sorry. I shall not bring it up again."

"No, Watson," he returned, surprising me by his change of mind, "I believe you are right. I should have gotten some of this off my mind long ago. There is one experience I had that almost shattered me as a man. I shall reveal it to you if you will bear with me."

"Of course."

Holmes had, in the few years since he had returned to Baker Street, referred to his having wandered about the world to such places as Persia, Egypt, and the south of France. But that was all. He never revealed to me, until now, any of his actual exploits. As I sat listening and taking notes, Holmes graphically depicted to me one of the most interesting adventures he had ever had. I shall try to do justice to this amazing story by putting into my own words exactly what Holmes revealed to me.

For two years, Holmes spent his time in Tibet, where he disguised himself as a Norwegian explorer by the name of Sigerson. His object being to visit the forbidden city of Lhasa.

Holmes, accompanied by native guides, had spent weeks climbing upwards through the Tibetan mountains in an effort to reach his objective. Finally, he found himself standing on the outskirts of his tiny encampment, high in the Tibetan snows. Surrounding him were the excited group of native guides, their fur-capped faces and shaggy sheepskin coats making them appear like strange animals, as they stood there gesticulating wildly.

The freezing wind whirled great clouds of snow away from the mountain top that loomed above them. Holmes felt a premonition of impending disaster as the leader of the guides approached him.

"Sire, my men will go no further. They say the Goddess of the Mountain is angry! If we climb further, she will swallow us up! She will bury us!"

"But we cannot go back now!" Holmes yelled through the ever increasing wind. "We have come so far. Over a thousand feet! Eight hundred feet higher and we shall reach the pass where we shall be safe!"

"I will not go!" yelled one of the men. "We can stay back there in the tent, until the Goddess of the Mountain tells us we can go further!"

"He is right," added the leader, "we can't go!"

The men moved to stand together in defiance of Holmes, as he looked about and saw the danger as the snow and wind increased, swirling around them like snakes ready to pounce and kill.

"Fools! Fools! If you stay here in the wilderness, there might be an avalanche and you will all be buried! You will be swept away! The only road to safety lies upward!"

The men stood their ground, protesting wildly that they would go no further. Their fear of the Goddess of the Mountain was greater than their concern for themselves. Holmes saw it was useless to argue with them.

"Then I shall go on, alone!"

He turned away and slowly, painfully, began the long climb up the side of the mountain some eight hundred feet to the safety of the pass above. Holmes was the only one who survived. As he struggled through the pass that led to safety, the icy gale lashed at him in a frenzy of numbing cold and stinging snow.

A few moments after he reached the top, the avalanche occurred. The tents, the guides, and all their equipment were buried beneath hundreds of feet of hurdling, thundering snow. The way behind him was now closed. It was impossible to go back and attempt to rescue any of the guides. Holmes turned his sight to the freezing rock and snow that lay ahead. Alone, unaided, he descended the path that led to the plateau beyond, for the Goddess of the Mountain was still angry. Through the knifing wind and snow he battled on, without food and without much hope.

Even Holmes was helpless in that battle of man against the elements. What happened in that next thirty-six hours, he never really knew, except that the wind howled and the driving snow slashed at him without mercy. Finally, unable to endure the ever increasing cold and pain, his mind began to wander. He became delirious, tracking about in the snow, gesturing and mumbling to himself in a dreamlike state that bordered on death.

"Watson, dear boy, hand me my violin, will you?—Moriarty, I want to introduce you to the Goddess of the Mountain; I think you have a lot in common—221 B Baker Street, Cabby, and for heavens sake, get me there as fast as you can, I think I've caught a chill!"

Though his mind was wandering, his great strength, combined with his instinctive urge for self-preservation, kept him on his feet. When finally he returned to normal consciousness, he found himself in a primitive cart drawn by two oxen as it jogged along a rough road. Although it was cold, the sun was shining on him, giving him some relief from the intense freezing he had lived through. Next to him was a woman who slowly fed him warm broth from a cup. For a moment the woman looked at him with a comforting smile, then put the cup aside.

"No wonder you look puzzled, poor man, you can't make up your mind whether you are in this world or the next."

Holmes, through swollen and bleary eyes could see that this was no native woman who was comforting him.

"Who are you?" he asked weakly, still assuming the role of Sigerson, the Norwegian explorer. "And how did I get here, please?"

"My name is Ilene Farley. I'm a medical missionary. I found you wandering out of your mind two days ago, just beyond the mountains, at the foot of the village. And, well, I've taken you under my wing, so to speak. We're going to the monastery of Pancha-Pushpah."

"I am most grateful to you, Miss Farley. You have saved my life. Permit me to introduce myself. My name is Sigerson. Olaf Sigerson, a Norwegian explorer."

The young woman laughed.

"Oh no. No, your name is Sherlock Holmes, and you're a famous English detective. Mr. Holmes, you have been delirious for the last two days. In your ravings I was delighted to learn that the great Sherlock Holmes did not die two years ago at the Reichenbach Falls."

"I can see that further simulation at a disguise is useless, my dear young lady. However, I must implore you to keep my secret. It is essential that for a while longer the world continues to think me dead."

"You need not worry, Mr. Holmes. I'm a great admirer of yours, and I promise that no one will ever learn your secret from my lips. Now, try to drink a little more broth. You are dreadfully weak."

"Thank you so much," Holmes smiled.

With great effort Holmes lifted himself up on one elbow and drank again from the cup. Suddenly, from the roadside, a voice began to yell.

"Help me, please! Please to give me help!"

Miss Farley looked around and saw a man beside the road.

"Another white man travels the road to Pancha-Pushpah. Stop the cart! Do you need help?"

"Ah, thank you, lady. My own cart has broken a wheel. You are going perhaps to the monastery of Pancha-Pushpah?"

"We are."

"Good. Feodor Dimitrivich Borodin, Imperial Russian envoy will travel with you. Please to make room. Ah, spasiba!"

The Russian was large, muscular and had a blazing red beard. He smiled as he pulled himself onto the cart. Holmes leaned close to Miss Farley.

"Remember my secret," he whispered to her.

"The cart may proceed," the Russian said with authority, then turned to Miss Farley. "Your name please, young lady."

"Ilene Farley. I'm an American medical missionary."

"I do not approve of missionaries," he frowned, "but . . . you are very beautiful. So Borodin will forgive you. Who is this lying on the floor? He looks half dead."

"I am half dead," said Holmes, attempting a smile. "My name is Sigerson, I am Norwegian."

"What is a Norwegian doing in Tibet?"

"I have been exploring the mountains. And what, may I ask, is a Russian doing in Tibet?"

"What is a Russian doing? Ha! You shall see, my friend. To Holy Mother Russia shall belong Tibet! But now, let us relax. We have some hours ahead of us before we reach the monastery. You like vodka, Miss Farley?"

"I'm afraid I don't drink."

The Russian bellowed with laughter. Holmes watched every move he made, fascinated by this gruff man's authoritative air.

"Borodin will teach you to drink. Then he will sing you songs of his native Russia. We shall be happy!"

He placed a small flask to his lips and gulped greedily of the vodka. He wiped his lips with his sleeve, then burst into song. Every note jarred Holmes' already aching and weary head. It seemed like an eternity to my poor friend, but finally, the cart, with its strange, assorted trio, arrived at the gates of the monastery. It was an edifice, Holmes told me, of great antiquity and of breath-taking beauty, built in the shadow of a giant mountain.

Before long, Holmes was fed and bathed and made comfortable in his own quarters. Weakly he walked about, trying to regain his strength. At one point, he requested a chance to speak to the abbot of the monastery, and spent a few moments with him. It was not long before he and his two companions were summoned into the presence of the head abbot himself; a man of great age and infinite wisdom. The faint chanting of religious music could be heard coming from another part of the monastery, as the old abbot stood before Holmes and the others, keenly observing them before he spoke.

"My dear Miss Farley, my dear gentlemen. I have welcomed you to this monastery, and yet, each one of you has come to me separately, and asked that he be given permission to go to the sacred city of Lhasa. I cannot give that permission, my children."

"Borodin has traveled a long way," the Russian said in restrained anger. "Russia will be most unhappy if he does not get the permission!"

"I am an explorer, reverend sir," Holmes said. "Will not that fact entitle me to some consideration?"

"I too have traveled a great way, sir," added Miss Farley.

"My children, I realize your claims, but the permission is not in my power to grant. Tibet is ruled by our Chinese overlords. In any case, I will ask you to turn your heads. The gentleman approaching us has preceded you in residence here. He also wishes to tread the road to Lhasa."

"You have new visitors, I see," said the tall man who now approached Holmes and the others.

"Yes, my son. Permit me to introduce you. This is Sir Harvey Forrester from Great Britain, and this is Miss Ilene Farley from America, Feodor Borodin from Russia, and Mr. Olaf Sigerson from Norway. Please be seated, everyone. My children, the Chinese ruler in this province has heard of your presence here. He has announced his intention of visiting you. Before he arrives, I should like to ask you each a question. Four of you, all from different countries, have traveled here to the mountains of Tibet. At this monastery, I can offer you refreshments, the opportunity of acquiring wisdom, and peace. What more do you seek that you must go to Lhasa? I shall ask you each that question in turn. You, Miss Farley, what do you seek?"

"I seek the opportunity to bring both God and health to your Tibetan people."

"And you, Mr. Sigerson?"

"I seek to chart the true course of your mountains; and so to bring knowledge to the world."

"And you, Feodor Borodin?"

"I seek to bring about complete understanding between the great peoples of Tibet and Russia. If I succeed, the Tsar and his family may consider turning to Buddhism."

"Indeed?" smiled the abbot incredulously, then turned to the last of the group, "and you, Sir Harvey, as representative of the British government, what do you seek?"

"I shall not join in this contest of wishful thinking," he said mockingly. "I merely remind you, sir, that your government has signed a treaty with mine!"

"And was not that treaty forced upon us by our Chinese overlords? No my children, you have advanced brave reasons, but I cannot help remembering that the streams of Tibet bear gold nuggets the size of hazelnuts. You foreigners in your pitiful ignorance esteem gold . . . ."

Suddenly, a large gong interrupted the abbot as its sound filled the vast halls of the monastery.

"That signals the arrival of Wah-tzun, the Chinese emissary. Your problems will soon be settled, my children. I will acquaint him with your requests."

The abbot bowed deeply and hurriedly left to meet up with Wah-tzun. As the rest of the companions mumbled to each other in frustration, Holmes laughed gently under his breath, a large smile crossing his face.

"Why are you smiling, Mr. Holmes?" said Miss Farley.

"I'm smiling, young lady, at the name of the Chinese overlord, Wah-tzun. I must avoid falling into old habits and saying 'Elementary, my dear Wah-tzun.'"

In a moment the Chinese overlord entered the room, robed in elegant clothes, bedecked with gold and jewels.

"Silence! Silence! The abbot has told me your wishes. I have made my decision. American lady and Norwegian will not be allowed. Only Great Britain and Russia have treaties with my country."

"I insist that I have prior right over the Russian representative," demanded Sir Harvey. The Russian stepped forward, his great bulk pushing Sir Harvey aside.

"How dare you! I represent the Tsar! And Russia is your neighbor. I demand my diplomatic privilege!"

The overlord looked at the two men standing before him, their fists clenched, ready to do battle.

"Follow me. I will decide these things, not you!"

The overlord turned and walked away, the two men following as they ranted at each other, demanding their rights brought about by their respective treaties with China. Holmes and Miss Farley watched until the great oak doors at the end of the room closed tightly, leaving the two standing alone.

"Well, Mr. Holmes, it looks as if you and I, at any rate, don't get to Lhasa."

"No," said Holmes, deep in thought.

"You look worried. Does the journey to Lhasa mean so much to you?"

"It isn't that. I'm worried about the potential danger that hangs over this monastery. Violent forces are at work."

"What do you mean, Mr. Holmes?"

"As you know, Miss Farley, I've some specialized acquaintance with these matters, and I tell you that I rarely see more clearly exemplified that emotional tension which leads to one thing: Murder! That is what I am afraid of, young lady, murder!"

Holmes, of course, was almost always right in his assumptions. He had an uncanny knack of being able to quickly decipher the elements that lay beneath the surface of various actions and deeds and piece them together with newfound conclusions of the most accurate kind. So it was in this case. Later that day, as the sun was setting over the mountaintop, sending its golden rays through the open windows of the monastery, the old abbot walked slowly in the inner gardens, talking to the man whom he thought was an Norwegian explorer.

"My dear Mr. Sigerson, what can I do to help you? Our conversation has pleased me, and I can see that you are a man of rare perception and knowledge, and one worthy to enter Lhasa, but I can offer no hope. Mr. Wah has already rejected the applications of both the Englishman and the Russian."

"He did that?" Holmes said in surprise.

"He did, my son. He told me they were both very angry and they threatened him."

"If anything were to happen to the Chinese emissary, would you have the right to grant permission for a journey to Lhasa?"

"Yes. Until the new envoy arrives from Peking. But what are you suggesting, my son? This monastery is a haven of peace, a backwater far from the troubled stream of life. No violence has ever occurred here."

"I hope it never will, and yet . . . The Chinese envoy was frightened, you say, reverend sir?"

The old abbot seated himself upon a stone bench in the last rays of the day's sun. Holmes sat beside him.

"Yes, he was frightened, my son."

"He has left the monastery, of course?"

"No," he returned, shaking his head, "those who come here even for a short visit must break bread with us, and sleep at least one night. Mr. Wah is quartered in the cell you see before us."

"Would you mind if we call on him, reverend sir?"

"Of course not, my son, though you will but waste your breath in talking to him. He will not give you permission to take the road to Lhasa."

Holmes helped the old abbot to stand and they quietly walked over to the emissary's room. Holmes knocked on the door.

"He sleeps, my son. Let us not disturb him."

"If you don't mind, reverend sir, I must waken him. If he can be wakened." Holmes knocked again, and then again, louder each time.

"What can be wrong?" said the abbot, the first signs of doubt crossing his face.

"I think I know," said Holmes, "I'm going in."

Holmes pushed the door in and the two men stepped inside. The emissary lay on his bed, his eyes open, staring blankly at the ceiling above.

"There is your answer, reverend sir."

"He is dead?" said the old man in disbelief.

"Yes sir. Strangled with his own queue."

"No," said the abbot, "the poor misguided man has taken his own life."

"No sir, look at those marks on his shoulder. He has been murdered."

"Murdered? But what are we to do?"

"As it happens, reverend sir, I have had a certain amount of experience in my own country with this kind of violence. If I were to produce the murderer for you, with absolute proof of his guilt, would you authorize my going to Lhasa?"

"Yes. Since, for a few days, that permission is now mine to give, I will grant it. You fill me with a strange confidence, but how will you find this taker of life?"

"I cannot tell you now, sir, but I shall find him! All that I require is a little assistance from you, sir."

"Of course, what is it?"

"Let us both leave the cell. Post a guard here and give him strict orders that no one is to enter unless accompanied by me."

"Very well. But, my son, where are YOU going?"

"Before very long, sir, I hope to be on my way to Lhasa."

# II

Holmes paused a moment, deep in thought. Slowly, he lit his pipe and went to the window to gaze down upon Baker Street and its busy people and passing hansoms. He turned to me, a sad and forlorn look upon his face.

"All this," he said with a sweeping gesture, "and all that outside, Watson, is often quite meaningless to me. When I crossed the Tibetan mountains, struggling to save my life, I came to realize how insignificant we are in the scheme of things. Nature does not care if we live or die, it goes on, regardless. When I awoke on that cart, understanding that I had come close to death, I began to see things differently. In the monastery, surrounded once again by people, I had meaning again. And therein lies the power of nature, my dear friend, that in its complete neutrality towards us, it allows us to see life as a gift or as a hindrance. I see it as a gift. When I suspected the Chinese overlord was dead, I knew I had to find the murderer, not just because it was a challenge to me, or a way of stimulating my mind as other cases so often have done, but because this tragedy would forever affect the monastery and the very essence of peace and tranquility that resided there."

As Holmes spoke I continued to take notes, listening carefully to his every word.

Realizing that I was not there to help him, Holmes decided to enlist the aid of Miss Farley, the American girl. Immediately after he left the cell of the murdered man, he'd gone to Miss Farley and told her of the tragedy. They quickly returned to the scene of the crime, where Holmes saw that his instructions had been carried out, and a guard was barring the entrance to the dead man's cell.

"The abbot gave you your orders?" Holmes said to the guard.

"Yes. You may go in."

They entered the cell, Holmes gesturing for Miss Farley to close the door behind them.

"You're sure your nerves are up to this, Miss Farley? It's not a pretty sight."

"I've seen sudden death before, Mr. Holmes. In any case, I wouldn't dare feel frightened, I'm so flattered that you asked me to help you."

"You were the only one who knew my true identity, that is why I suggested you take my old friend's place. You see, I need . . . what shall I say? . . . I need a sounding board for my deductions. Wait, here, I'll light a match."

Holmes took a candle from a table and lit it. The room was filled with light, revealing the body of the overlord to Miss Farley. She gasped in horror and stepped back. Holmes touched her shoulder to calm her.

"I warned you it wasn't a pretty sight. Hold the candle, will you please, Miss Farley."

Holmes inspected everything in sight in his usual manner.

"This isn't hard to re-construct. The killer stood behind his victim, holding him by the left shoulder, so. Wound his queue around his neck and pulled back. Yes, the marks are self evident. Hello, what's this on the floor at his feet?"

"A cigarette," said Miss Farley, "dropped as it was burning, I should think. And now it's nothing but ash."

"Exactly. Ash. Now which of the visitors at the monastery smoke cigarettes?"

"Yourself, Mr. Holmes, the Russian, and Sir Harvey, the Englishman."

"I think we may justifiably omit myself from the list of suspects," added Holmes with a look of chagrin, "so that narrows it down to two. Look here, Miss Farley, there are clear traces to the naked eye not only of tobacco ash and paper, but of cardboard!"

"Cardboard? But what does that signify, Mr. Holmes?"

"That the case is nearly solved! Come on, young lady, we must pay a visit to Borodin's cell at once!"

Holmes, accompanied by Miss Farley, hurried to the quarters of Feodor Borodin, where they found both Borodin and Sir Harvey Forrester arguing. Both men turned as Holmes entered.

"Ha! Mr. Sigerson, can you believe that Sir Harvey can do nothing but argue with me all the time. It is disgraceful. Come in, both of you. We will drink vodka and I will sing songs from our Mother Russia for you. Anything will be better than arguing with Sir Harvey!"

"We have not come here to listen to songs, Feodor Borodin," said Miss Farley in disgust. "The Chinese envoy was murdered tonight!"

"Yes, yes, so we have been told, my dear. Sir Harvey and I are very happy because of his death, are we not?"

"Well, I won't pretend I'm not," said Sir Harvey, raising a glass of vodka to his lips.

"Feodor Borodin," Holmes said, "you were in the cell at the time of the murder!"

Borodin turned towards Holmes, his face suddenly becoming a mask of rage.

"That is a lie, Norwegian!"

"I can prove it. In that cell I have just found ashes, totally burned cigarette ashes that included fragments of cardboard. Only a Russian cigarette has a cardboard mouthpiece."

"He's very obstinate tonight, Sigerson. We've just been having a political argument. Couldn't agree on a single point, except on the dangers of the common man. He was telling me of the most extraordinary revolution on his estates. Do you know they chopped off one of his hands?"

Holmes was surprised, looking quickly at Borodin's hands.

"Your hand, Borodin, quickly, which one is missing?"

"As God is merciful, it was my left hand."

"Then what is that hand beneath your glove?" asked Holmes.

"Is made of wax, my good Norwegian, is made of wax. Come, see for yourself."

Borodin carefully removed his glove, revealing a hand made of bees wax that was tightly bound to his wrist.

"Extraordinary!" exclaimed Sir Harvey.

"It is more than that. It is conclusive proof!"

"What do you mean, Mr. Sigerson?" Miss Farley asked in confusion.

"I cannot tell you now. I must leave for the moment. Let me warn you: The three of you would be well advised to keep an eye on each other! Meanwhile, I must see the abbot."

"But why?" implored Miss Farley.

"Because now I know who murdered Wah-tzun!"

Before the full impact of what he had implied could be comprehended by the three suspects, Holmes was gone, leaving them to their own devices. Through the open door a thin mist was edging its way into the room, slowly encompassing the three people who stood there. Feodor Borodin was again taking long drinks of vodka as he eyed the other two. Sir Harvey Forrester sat back in a chair, resigned and waiting for the final verdict. Miss Farley stood, her hands at her chest, shivering, frightened and unable to move.

It was done. As Holmes sat at the foot of the abbot, the sounds of chanting could be heard not so far away in the sacred temple. The abbot looked toward the mountain as the mist began to slowly dissolve with the coming of the sun. He turned to Holmes and, smiling, placed his ancient hand upon my friend's shoulder.

"The pink fingers of dawn are stealing across the mountain top, my son. Soon, you will be on your way to Lhasa."

"Yes, reverend sir, you have kept your promise," Holmes said in a voice so soft and gentle it was almost a whisper.

"And you have kept your promise, Mr. Sigerson. The Chinese soldiers have arrived, and the taker of life has been given into their custody. Before you leave, my son, I want you to do something for me."

"Anything, reverend sir, what is it?"

"The hooded figure in the corner is that of the monastery scribe. He keeps our annuls. I want you to explain, for our records, how you knew which one of the three was the taker of life."

"It was not difficult, sir," offered Holmes, "the killer had gripped Wah-tzun's shoulder with the left hand while his right was used to strangle him. Therefore the Russian Borodin could not be the killer since his left hand was artificial."

"Quite so, it was as you told me made of wax. Then—"

"But the clue, reverend sir, of the cigarette pointed directly to the Russian. It had been planted there to deliberately incriminate him. Now, there is no plain police force in Tibet, am I correct?"

"We need no police for there is no crime here, my son. But do continue."

"Why should the cigarette be planted to incriminate the Russian? Who could arrest him? Who could bring the Russian to justice? Unless the murderer knew there was someone capable of making the deduction that the Russian was guilty, all from a handful of cigarette ash. Therefore, the murderer had to be the one person who knew my true identity. Miss Ilene Farley, the supposed missionary."

"Ah," smiled the abbot, "she was no missionary, as it transpired when she confessed. And no American."

"No. A secret service agent of German origin, seeking to reach Lhasa before the Russians, and infuriated by Wah-tzun's denial of passage. Any secret service is better off without such employees."

"She will pay for her mortal sin, my son. May she redeem herself in her next place on the wheel."

The distant gong from Lhasa sounded. The abbot looked down upon Holmes, a look of deep sadness crossing his face.

"My son, you are about to leave me, and I shall never see you again. Though evil and death came to Pancha-pushpah, and to my monastery in the caravan that brought you here, I shall miss you. I shall miss you, greatly."

"And I you, reverend sir," said Holmes with the heaviest of hearts.

"Would you consider staying here? I can only offer you peace, a shelter from the outside world, and quiet companionship."

"Ah, three great gifts, sir. But I cannot take them. My work is not done. I must go on."

"Of course, my son. It was an old man's dream. One last question."

"What is it, sir?"

"You spoke of your true identity, just now. Who are you, my son?"

Holmes gazed into the old abbot's eyes and was deeply shaken by their calm and beauty.

"Reverend, sir, I cannot tell even you the answer to that question. One day, if I pass this way again, but not now. Let us just say that I have wandered through a world of trouble, just as you have remained tranquil in a world of peace. I hope, sir, that we shall meet again."

"I hope so, too. Goodbye, my son."

"Goodbye, reverend sir, good bye."

Holmes rose, and with great reluctance, bowed deeply to the abbot, who gave him his blessing. He walked to the entrance of the monastery, the abbot watching him with eyes of wisdom.

Holmes turned at the entrance for one last look, managed a sad and weak smile, then turned back towards Lhasa. He walked slowly up the rough trail towards Lhasa, knowing in his heart that he had to move on in his quest for the inner knowledge he yearned. In Lhasa he would find some of the answers that had plagued him throughout the years of his life.

And, although he would not reveal his deepest most inner feelings to me, I knew, as he sat before me finishing this strange story, that my dear friend had, indeed, found something of the inner peace we all seek. A better understanding of that precious soul within all of us. The answers he came upon helped him make up his mind to once again return to England and his life here in Baker Street. For which, I must admit, I am most thankful.

"Yes," said Holmes, "I can see now the trickle of blood oozing from the base of his skull."

# 7

# THE CASE OF THE
# UNEASY EASY CHAIR

THIS strange tale began on a cold winter morning in 1897 as Holmes and I had just concluded our breakfast. We were seated on either side of a cheery fire in our Baker Street lodgings. A thick fog had rolled down between the line of houses, and the windows opposite loomed like dark shapeless eyes that stared at us through the swirling yellow mist. It was what most people called a London pea soup fog. Our gas was lit and threw its flickering light on the white table-cloth and china, for the breakfast table had not been cleared. Holmes was busy cross-indexing his records on crime while I was engrossed in one of Clark Russell's fine sea stories.

Our morning was not destined, however, to be a quiet one, for shortly after 11 o'clock Mrs. Hudson ushered a young lady into our rooms. A young lady who seemed to be in serious trouble as she shakily seated herself opposite us, constantly pulling at her handkerchief. I presented her with the usual courtesies on first meeting.

"I'm Dr. Watson, and this is Mr. Sherlock Holmes."

"How do you do, gentlemen. I must apologize for not giving my name to your housekeeper, but I have to be most careful. Of course, you're wondering who I am, and what's brought me here."

"My own theory," Holmes said, smiling kindly, "would be that you are Miss Harriet Irvin, and that you have come to me to elicit my aid in proving that Mr. Binyon did NOT murder your father."

"Holmes," I said in astonishment, "what on earth are you talking about?"

"You are absolutely correct, Mr. Holmes," returned the young lady, "but, how did you know?"

As usual I sat listening to Holmes again explain how, through deductive logic, he arrived at his conclusions.

"You are wearing very new and extremely expensive mourning clothes, presumably for the first time, since a few basting threads are still in evidence. You wear no wedding ring, so evidently you are not in mourning for a husband. The only man who's death the papers announced in the past few days, and who left a young daughter wealthy enough to purchase such garments, is Sir Edward Irvin. And since the police have already made an arrest, obviously you wish me to disprove the police theory, and intercede for young Binyon."

"Mr. Holmes, you're wonderful! That's just what I want you to do. You will, won't you?"

"Miss Irvin, I've studied the newspaper reports very carefully. It would seem to me that Scotland Yard has arrested the right man."

"Well, I'm very sorry," I chimed in, "but I didn't read the newspaper reports. I haven't the faintest idea of what you're both talking about!"

"Then let me bring you up to date, my dear Watson. And please correct me, Miss Irvin, if I make any mistakes. Three days ago Sir Edward Irvin, the father of this young lady, was found stabbed to death in his study. The only entrance to the study is through an anteroom, where his secretary had been sitting ever since Sir Edward was last seen alive. And the secretary swore that no one had entered or left the study."

"The secretary's name being Binyon, I suppose," I added.

"Correct. Under the circumstances, it's hard to see that any other arrest was possible."

"And yet I know he's innocent, Mr. Holmes."

"How do you know that, Miss Irvin?" I asked.

"We were in love. We were going to be married. I don't care what the police say; a woman knows these things. Robert Binyon did not kill my father."

"Did your father approve of the engagement?" I continued.

"Well, no, not exactly."

"If one were to be exact, Miss Irvin," said Holmes, "wouldn't one say that your father absolutely forbade the marriage?"

"Yes, he did."

"And Inspector Lestrade, who took on the case, assumed that was the motive for the murder."

Miss Irvin sat nervously, pulling upon the handkerchief more fiercely than ever. Holmes smiled and pointed to it.

"My dear Miss Irvin, if you continue to pull at that poor thing much longer, you may tear it to shreds. Please, do relax and allow me to continue my questioning."

She took a deep breath and sat back in the chair, trying to calm herself. Holmes went on.

"Does your father have any other living relatives, Miss Irvin?"

"His brother, my uncle Peregren. He lives a hermit's life in the country. We've seen very little of him in the last few years."

THE CASE OF THE UNEASY EASY CHAIR

"Was he left anything under your father's will?"

"No. I was the sole beneficiary. Please help me, Mr. Holmes. If you'll just talk to Robert, you'll know he's not guilty."

I turned to Holmes, who seemed to be pondering the evidence so far presented.

"There's no harm in talking to him, Holmes. After all, our old friend Lestrade handled the case, and he's made a good many mistakes in the past, you know."

"Haven't we all, old chap?" Holmes laughed. "Well, Miss Irvin, I'll do what I can, but I promise nothing."

"Bless you, Mr. Holmes."

"Where is your fiancee being held?"

"At Scotland Yard. I talked to him there, just before I came to see you."

"Scotland Yard, eh?" said Holmes rising from his chair, "Splendid! We can talk to Lestrade at the same time. Watson, your—"

"Hat and coat, Holmes?" I said, interrupting my illustrious friend.

"Precisely, old fellow. Your hat and coat."

Holmes and I ushered the lady downstairs while he again reassured her everything possible would be done to help in this case. Once she was off in a Hansom, I hailed another, which took us to Scotland Yard and the redoubtable Inspector Lestrade.

"So, Mr. Sherlock Holmes and Doctor Watson," said Lestrade as we sat before him, "think they know more than the Yard, eh? Come over here to teach us our business, I suppose?"

"Nothing of the sort, Lestrade," I said in irritation, "we came over here to make a few inquiries."

"I tell you, gentlemen, that you're wasting your time. Young Binyon is guilty, whatever his young lady may say!"

Holmes lit a cigar, as a look of mild irritation crossed his face.

"Lestrade, what did the autopsy prove?"

"Just a moment, I got a report of it here on my desk. It won't tell you nothing you don't know."

He handed the report to Holmes who carefully scanned its contents.

"It says here death was instantaneous," Holmes commented. "Caused by some weapon like a long needle, a fine stiletto, or an ice pick, penetrating the brain at the base of the skull."

"And no such weapon was found in the room," added a cynical Lestrade.

"Or on Mr. Binyon?"

"True, sir, but then he had the chance of disposing of it!"

"Just the same, Lestrade," I added, "the murder weapon hadn't been found, has it?"

"No, doctor, but we'll find it. Don't you worry about that!"

"I should like to talk to the prisoner, if you don't mind."

"Why, of course I don't mind, Mr. Holmes. He's in the detention cell just down the corridor from here. Follow me, gentlemen."

Lestrade took us down a dismal corridor towards a barred room at the end.

"Place could do with a bit of paint," I commented.

"What's that, doctor?"

"Nothing. Has Binyon given you any trouble, Lestrade?"

"Trouble? Ha! If all our prisoners were as quiet as him, we wouldn't need no guards, doctor. Nice, quiet young fella. Hard to realize he's a murderer."

"A fact that still has to be proven in court, Lestrade."

"A fact that is going to be proved in court, Mr. Holmes."

Lestrade took out some keys and unlocked the cell door. Seated on a stool at the far end of the room was a young man, thin and pale and slight of build.

"You've got visitors, Mr. Binyon, very distinguished visitors. Mr. Sherlock Holmes and Dr. John H. Watson."

"I'm sorry to see you in this plight, Mr. Binyon," I said.

"Mr. Sherlock Holmes!" he said, rising from the stool, "then Harriet did go to see you when she left here. I'm so glad. You'll get me out of this mess, I know you will."

"Even Mr. Sherlock Holmes can't get you out of this one, young fellow me lad."

"Mr. Binyon," said Holmes, ignoring Lestrade's remark, "I promised your fiancee that I'd try and help you. My obvious course is to go to Sir Edward's house and examine the room in which the tragedy occurred, but before I do that, I'd like to ask you a question or two."

"Ask me any question you want to, sir."

"It was you who discovered the body, I understand. Please describe the circumstances."

Holmes and I seated ourselves on the not so comfortable bunk opposite young Binyon, while Lestrade stood by the barred door.

"Sir Edward was in his study, while I had been working in the anteroom adjoining," young Binyon revealed. "At five o'clock I went in to say goodnight to him, and I found him slumped in his chair with blood streaming down the back of his head. Of course I sent the butler for the police at once."

"Could anyone have entered that room without your knowledge?"

"No, Mr. Holmes, I never left my desk. And there was no other entrance to the room save through my office."

"How about the windows in Sir Edward's room?" I asked.

"They were locked from the inside, doctor."

"You don't need to worry. We examined the window ledges. Not a mark. No one came in that way!" added Lestrade.

"What is your theory of the murder, Mr. Binyon?"

"I haven't one, Mr. Holmes. I'm completely baffled. I'm certain no one entered that room, yet I swear to you that I didn't stab him, though I can understand the police believing I did."

Holmes took a deep puff on his newly lit cigar, then stood up, gesturing for me to follow suit.

"Lestrade, I should like to examine the room in which Sir Edward was murdered."

"Easiest thing in the world, Mr. Holmes. I'll accompany you, if you like. His house is in Knightsbridge. I'd like very much to come with you."

"Why, Lestrade?" said Holmes, a sly smile on his face. "You're convinced that Mr. Binyon is guilty, aren't you? Won't you be wasting your time?"

"Not me," Lestrade said in triumph. "For once I know you're on the wrong side of the case, Mr. Holmes. And I want to be there and see your face when you find it out!"

"I thought as much," said Holmes in low tones.

"What's that?"

"Nothing, Lestrade. Shall we go?"

We bid farewell to young Binyon and caught a four-wheeler which dropped us off in front of the Irvin residence. It was an imposing structure, that of a wealthy man who had spent much money and great pride on his dwelling.

"I imagine, Lestrade, that you still have a police guard inside?"

"Oh yes, doctor," he replied, knocking on the door, "there's been a sergeant guarding the dead man's room day and night. However, we still haven't found the missing weapon, you know."

The door opened to reveal a rather imposing and tall butler. He looked at the three of us rather coldly.

"Yes, gentlemen?"

"I'm Inspector Lestrade of Scotland Yard. We wish to examine the house."

"I must see your identification, sir."

"What are you talking about? I been in and out of this house half a dozen times!"

"I have my orders, sir."

I could see that Holmes was chuckling to himself. I found myself doing the same.

Reluctantly Lestrade showed his identification.

"Is Miss Irvin at home?" asked Holmes.

"Miss Irvin is NOT receiving, sir."

"Great Scott, man," I said in frustration, "can't you give us any information?"

"There's been tragedy in this house, sir, and the truth of it's not known yet. I'm not answering any questions that I don't have to!"

"Stout fellow!" said Holmes with a smile. "Now, may we come in?"

The butler let us in rather reluctantly.

"May I direct you, gentlemen?"

"No thank you. I know this house nearly as well as you do!"

"I think not, inspector. I've served here for 27 years! Now, gentlemen, if you are not needing me, I'll return to my quarters!"

As Lestrade led the way to the dead man's room, I turned to Holmes.

" Bless my soul, that's a sinister looking chap if I ever saw one!"

"Yes, Watson, and he knows something. You see, Lestrade, there is a possibility that Binyon is innocent."

"Yes, I began to see that, sir, when you were talking to the butler."

"You're being rather cryptic, Holmes. What possibility are you talking about?"

"The possibility that Binyon is shielding the real murderer. And whom would he be most certain to shield?"

"You mean his fiancee," I said in surprise, "Miss Irvin?"

"That's right, old fellow."

"Ah, here we are," said Lestrade as we arrived at our destination. "This is the anteroom where young Binyon worked. And that door there leads into the study where Sir Edward was found."

"Nothing's been touched since the discovery of the crime?"

"Oh no, Mr. Holmes. That's why we've had a constable on duty in there night and day. Before the trial we're bringing experts in to test the room for secret panels or anything of that kind."

"Let's examine the dead man's room, shall we?"

We went into Sir Edward's room. It was sumptuously arranged with a large desk and oak paneling everywhere. Seated before us in a chair was a constable.

"Webster!" Lestrade yelled, "get out of that chair and stand up, can't you? You're on duty!"

There was no answer. I moved to the constable's side and examined him. He didn't move as I shook him.

"Great Scott, he's dead!"

"Yes," said Holmes, "I can see now the trickle of blood oozing from the base of his skull."

"Well strike me pink, he's been killed the same way as Sir Edward was!" said a shaken Lestrade.

"I presume you'll agree that Mr. Binyon didn't commit this murder, Lestrade."

"Course not, Mr. Holmes, he couldn't have done it. He's locked up at the yard!"

"Ask the butler to come here, will you?" said Holmes. I could see Holmes was in his element, at last beginning to take over the case from the confused Lestrade. I again bent over the body, examining it carefully.

"Yes, there's a fine puncture here at the base of the skull. By Jove, Holmes, the report mentioned a stiletto or ice pick. A wound like this might be caused by one of those long steel hat pins that women wear!"

"Yes. It's a possibility, Watson, a distinct possibility. And Miss Irvin was wearing a long hat pin this morning, if you remember."

Holmes was quickly about the room, examining every corner and crevice, his eyes darting this way and that as his hands touched the various seams of the oak paneling.

"No, Watson, I cannot discern anything but the finest craftsmanship to this room. There's little chance of secret panels here, I should say."

"And the windows are locked from the inside, eh?"

"Yes. Ah, Lestrade, you've found him. What's your name?" Holmes said to the butler.

106

"Travers, sir."

"You see what's happened, Travers?"

"Yes sir, I see. The constable's been killed just like my master."

"Tell me, Travers, is this room exactly as it was in Sir Edward's lifetime?"

"Yes sir, except that my master was not in the habit of keeping the corpses of policemen in here!"

"Don't try to be funny, Travers," said an angry Lestrade. "Don't you realize that you're mixed up in a murder case!"

"The point of my question, Travers," Holmes went on, "was to find out if any of the furniture in here had been moved lately."

"Not moved, sir, but there has been a piece of furniture added. That armchair the dead man's lying in."

"The same chair in which Sir Edward's body was found! Of course, that's the answer! Travers, when was that chair delivered? And who delivered it?"

"It was delivered the day before Sir Edward died. It came from Silverschwantz's antique shop in Bond Street."

"Ah ha! The game's afoot, Lestrade! See to the removal of this poor man's body, seal the room, and for Heavens sake keep this latest death a secret for a day at least. Within that time I hope to have your murderer for you!"

"Then we're going—"

"Yes, Watson, we're going to Silverschwantz's antique shop in Bond Street!"

I have often described the feeling of excitement Holmes felt when a case began to bring forth bits of evidence that he was able to piece together to move him dramatically towards a final solution. I must add to that my own excitement, not only in watching Holmes at work, but in his allowing me to help him in every way possible. It was just that same sort of feeling I held as our cab pulled up in front of Silverschwantz's antique store and we stepped inside.

The place was filled almost to the ceiling with furniture, toys, nicknacks and the most delightful music boxes I had ever seen. So delightful was all this, that I found myself being distracted from our purpose for being there.

"These music boxes are quite charming, aren't they Holmes?"

"Yes," he said, looking about, "but where's Mr. Silverschwantz?"

From a back room stepped an elderly man with a huge white mane of hair and a pair of pince-nez on his nose. He looked like a little gnome, and I could not help but smile as he came towards us.

"Mr. Silverschwantz?" asked Holmes.

"Yes, gentlemen. You are interested in musical boxes?"

"No, sir, in chairs. Particularly in the handsomely carved chair you delivered to Sir Edward Irvin a few days ago."

"Ach, yah, a magnificent specimen. He is pleased with it?"

"He was found dead in it, Mr. Silverschwantz," I said.

"And half an hour ago someone else was found dead in it, also," Holmes pressed on, "that chair was one of a pair, wasn't it?"

"Yah, but . . . ."

Suddenly Mr. Silverschwantz turned as white as a ghost.

"Gott in Himmel! That's impossible, I. . . . Gentlemen, please to follow me!"

Mr. Silverschwantz led us into the back where he had a small warehouse room filled with furniture.

"Look, gentlemen, look at this chair."

"It's exactly like the one at Sir Edward's house," I said.

"But my friend, there is such a difference," said the bespeckled old storekeeper.

"Fifteenth century Italian, isn't it?" Holmes asked.

"Yah, this is one of a pair of the famous Malapierri armchairs. There are only three pairs in the world, my friends. Of this pair, one, the one I delivered to Sir Edward, is simply a great specimen of the carver's art. This one, its mate, looks exactly like it, does it not?"

"Exactly," I said, "I can't see any difference, myself."

"You would if you sat in it, old chap."

"Precisely," said Silverschwantz, "that is why I have these cords stretched from one arm of the chair to the other. If anyone were to sit in it . . . well, sometimes nothing will happen. But sooner or later a hand will press on this hidden spring in the arm here, and death will strike."

"But nothing happened when you pressed the spring, Mr. Silverschwantz."

"I . . . I don't understand. . . ."

"I do," Holmes blurted out, "this is the harmless chair! The lethal one was sent to Sir Edward! He sat in it, accidentally pressed the spring, and drove the fatal needle into his brain!"

"I see it now, Holmes, it's just as that poor constable did today!"

"Sir Edward bought both chairs, I presume?"

"Yah, I would not sell the chairs separately."

"Then why didn't you deliver both at the same time?" I asked.

"He was afraid of the deadly one. He asked me to keep it here until he found a safe place for it in his home."

"It makes sense, Watson. Some devil switched the arm cord from the fatal chair to the harmless one so that you delivered death to Sir Edward! There is a subtlety in this crime worthy of the fiendish maker of the chairs, himself. Silverschwantz, didn't Malapierri die by being tricked into being seated in one of his own chairs?"

"Yes, he did."

"Now I think I know how to trap our killer!" exclaimed Holmes. "Please allow me to ask you some further questions, Mr. Silverschwantz. Then, Watson, we've much work ahead of us!"

We had found out how the murders had been committed, but not who had been responsible for them. Holmes spent a long time cross-examining Mr. Silverschwantz as to who might have had the opportunity of switching the tell-tale cord from the fatal chair. It transpired that four people might have been responsible. Sir Edward's daughter, and his secretary, Mr. Binyon, had been in the shop with him at various times. So had the butler, Travers. The fourth suspect was Sir Edward's brother, Peregren, who it appeared had dropped into the shop the day after the purchase had been made. With this last information, Holmes became very excited and launched into eager preparations to determine if Peregren Irvin was the guilty party.

"Holmes," I said in anger when we had returned to our lodgings, "I refuse to assume another disguise with you!"

"Come now, Watson, it's only for a short time, and it will be most fun assuming the roles of furniture removers."

"No! An emphatic no! I'm not an actor, confound it, I'm a doctor!"

Holmes looked at me with total exasperation. Then, as quickly, he cheered up and went back to clothing himself and making himself look like a typical furniture remover.

"All right, Watson, you can stay here. But you'll miss all the fun, I tell you!"

"Stay here? You mean I can't come along?"

"That's right. No need for you to help. I just thought that—"

"All right, Holmes, I'll do as you wish."

"I knew you'd see it my way. I will tell you what, Watson, instead of disguising yourself, just put some old clothes on and come along as a clerk who is there to see everything is going all right for the store. I'll do the talking and you just answer a bit when I speak to you. Here, these are some sales slips and orders I use for just such an occasion."

Mumbling angrily to myself, I slipped into some old clothes that I should have thrown out a long time ago. In no time at all we had rented a horse and van and were driving it along a quiet country lane near Dorking. We soon approached the house of Sir Edward's brother, Peregren.

"There's the house, Watson. Ramshackle looking place, isn't it?"

"Yes, extremely so."

"Why are you so morose, my dear chap?" he said laughingly. "You've hardly spoken a word on our drive down here."

"You never tell me anything," I said in a fit of depression. "Why are we trundling off into the wilds of the country disguised as furniture removers, and carrying the harmless chair with us?"

"Surely the reason is transparent, old chap. It's obvious we are up against an extremely cunning murderer. Now what advantage accrues to him in using the Malapierri chair?"

"An alibi, of course. He's nowhere near the place when it happens."

"Precisely. Apply your logic a little further. Three of the suspects, the daughter, Mr. Binyon, and Travers, the butler, live in the house and would almost certainly be present at the time of death. Therefore, who gains most by such an alibi?"

"Well, the brother, Peregren."

"Elementary, my dear Watson! Now you see why we trundled off into the wilds of Dorking."

"Look Holmes," I whispered as we came up to the house, "that must be Peregren standing up on the porch. He seems a funny looking fellow."

"Follow my lead, Watson. Good afternoon, G'vnor."

"You two fellows must have come to the wrong house," said Peregren, coming forward to our van.

"You are Mr. Peregrine Irvin, ain'tcha, G'vnor?"

"Yes."

"Then we come to the right house, all right, all right. Come on, Bertie, give us a hand." Holmes and I unloaded the harmless chair onto the porch.

"Jimminy crickets, ain't that a pretty chair, G'vnor? Bertie and me was admirin' it on our way down 'ere."

"Who told you to bring it here?" Peregren asked, quite puzzled by all this.

"Orders, G'vnor. A Mr. Silversnitch, or whatever his name is. Tells us your brother didn' want the chair and said as how we was to bring it to you," Holmes went on in the most dreadful accent.

"But my brother's dead!"

"Mr. Silversnitch said that your brother gave the order afore he died. Mind if I sit down in it, G'vnor?"

Without waiting for an answer, Holmes seated himself in the chair, laughing loudly.

"Core, wish me old trouble and strife could see me now!"

"Trouble and strife?" said Peregren.

"Trouble and strife, that's me wife, G'vnor. 'Ere, sit down yerself, sir, come on. Go on. Sit down, try it. Go on, go on, G'vnor. Take the weight off your plates of meat."

"What barbaric jargon do you speak? What on earth are plates and meat?"

"Plates of meat is feet, G'vnor. That's rhymin' slang. Go on, sit down in it. It's dast comfortable this chair!"

"Oh, very well," said Peregren reluctantly. He seated himself, resting his arms on the chair near the carved woodwork that would have contained the spring.

"Go on," insisted Holmes, "run your 'ands over the arms, G'vnor. Ain't that carvin' pretty? Ain't it just ducky?"

"Yes, yes it is, but I don't want the wretched thing. There's been some mistake, so you'd better take it back to London and tell him to sell it! I don't want anything of my brothers!"

"Jumpin' gehosaphat! Can't see why you don't want to sit in a nice chair like this, G'vnor.

But, you're the one as gives orders around here, so, come on Bertie, get your back into it. Back in the van it goes!"

"I don't know why you've made the trip for nothing but—"

"Aw, bless your heart," said Holmes, "we don't worry about that sort of thing, do we, Bertie?

"Course not. I'll just take these orders back along with the chair. That'll straighten things out," I said.

"Nice drive in the country, anyway. Good day, G'vnor!" yelled Holmes.

"Good day!" Peregren yelled back, shaking his head in disbelief.

In a moment we were off down the road, heading back to London.

"That was a false trail, Holmes. Obviously he knew nothing about the chair. He thought it was perfectly harmless."

"As indeed it was. But the murderer would have thought it fatal. I've slipped up in my reasoning somehow."

Holmes sat silently for a few minutes, baffled by this turn of events. Then, suddenly, he sat erect, his hands tight on the horse's reigns.

"But of course, Watson! Oh, what a fool I am! We must get back to London as fast as this tired nag can take us. Come on!"

"Holmes, I don't think I'll ever fully understand you. I haven't the slightest idea of what you are up to!"

"We must get back to Sir Edward's house and the staging of another little drama that I'm sure will give us the final answer to this problem!"

"Surely I don't have to continue acting in these dreadful clothes, Holmes!"

"No, we're finished with that, thank goodness."

Later, after returning to London, we cleaned up and went on to Sir Edward's house where Holmes spent a moment talking confidentially to Inspector Lestrade.

"I've made all the arrangements, Mr. Holmes, as you said. I've got Miss Irvin, young Binyon and the butler waiting outside. And no one knows we've switched the chairs."

"Splendid."

"You're sure this is the harmless chair, Holmes?" I said.

"Of course I am. Look here. I sit in it, so. Run my hands over the arms. Yes, this chair is harmless, as every person, save one, will know. Show them in, Lestrade."

"All at once, Mr. Holmes?"

"No, I think we'll take Miss Irvin and Mr. Binyon first."

Lestrade ushered in the two suspects as I stood nearby, watching intently, trying to deduce, as Holmes would do, whom the murderer might be. As Miss Irvin entered, she gasped.

"Oh, Mr. Holmes!"

"What's the matter, Miss Irvin?" he said.

"It's just so horrible seeing you there in the same chair where I saw father."

"Mr. Holmes," said young Binyon, "it's a trifle too macabre for you to assume the position of the corpse. Please get up!"

"But it seems the most comfortable chair in the room," said Holmes, dallying with these two suspects. "And I do like my comfort when I interrogate witnesses. However, it's hardly chivalrous, is it? Miss Irvin, please sit down, won't you. In this same chair."

"I . . . I don't like to sit down in the chair in which father died."

"Miss Irvin," I added, forcing the issue, "we couldn't bear to see you standing."

"Very well then."

"Don't sit down, Harriet!" yelled Binyon as he moved towards Miss Irvin. Holmes stopped his movement.

"Why not, Binyon? What's the matter? Isn't the chair safe?"

"No, no . . . I . . . " he began to stammer.

"Then perhaps you'd care to sit in it," said Holmes, forcibly moving young Binyon towards the chair, "to prove that the chair *is* safe. Sit down!"

"Very well," he said in resignation, "there."

"Splendid," said Holmes quietly, "it's a curious chair, isn't it, Mr. Binyon? I wonder about these carvings on the arms. They look almost as if they might activate concealed springs. I wonder what would happen if I—"

"No, for heavens sake, Mr. Holmes, are you trying to kill me?" said Binyon jumping up from the chair.

"Kill you?" I blurted out in anger. "Then you know how Sir Edward and the policeman were murdered!"

"I . . . I knew it must have something to do with the chair."

"You knew more than that, Robert," answered Miss Irvin. "You planned it. I remember now that when we went to the shop you—"

"Be quiet, Harriet!" yelled Binyon, as he grabbed Miss Irvin, turned and ran for the open door, pushing Lestrade aside.

"No, no, Watson, don't go after them. Lestrade will stop him. In any case the police are at the front door."

Holmes quietly pulled out his pipe, put it between his teeth and lit it.

"Oh, Watson, dear friend, I'm tired. I think I'll sit in this rather fateful armchair."

"So it was young Binyon all the time," I said.

"Yes, and he'd all but outsmarted me. I reasoned that somehow the murderer must have intended the device of this chair to clear him. And suddenly, after our incident with Peregren Irvin, I saw the real motivation. How better establish his innocence than seeming to be obviously guilty, and yet leaving a trail whereby an astute deduction could seem to clear him."

"I see it now, Holmes. It was his idea that Miss Irvin should come to you. He used you as a cat's paw."

"That's right, Watson. I'm afraid this whole case is a rather humiliating experience for me."

"Why do you say that?"

"Well, Lestrade had arrested the right man in the first place! Oh my," Holmes laughed, "no, my dear Watson, I shall never hear the end of this! Never!"

And, of course, he never did.

"I want you to raise your hands above your head, Miss Favisham. You, too, whatever your name is."

# 8

# THE CASE OF THE BACONIAN CIPHER

IN France, there was, at this time, a detective by the name of Francois Le Villard. Monsieur Le Villard was becoming a most popular figure in his own country due mostly to his having adopted similar techniques in crime detection as used by my good friend Sherlock Holmes. In the year 1889, to be exact, Le Villard had come over to London to discuss with Holmes the difficulties of translating some of his monographs into the French language. At this particular time I was in the early days of my marriage. This fact, combined with a busy medical practice, meant that I saw very little of my old friend. Of course, I missed Holmes greatly and, although he never admitted the fact, I am sure he missed me also.

One cloudless June afternoon, a day by London standards considered extraordinarily mild, I was on a house call and found myself in the neighborhood of Baker Street. It was a perfect opportunity to pay a visit to Sherlock Holmes. Mrs. Hudson was out, but having retained my old latchkey, I let myself in and mounted the familiar stairs. It gave me a strange feeling as I raised my hand to knock on what had once been my own living room door.

"Come in, come in!" I heard Holmes yell out.

When I opened the door I saw, seated near the fireplace, my old friend Holmes and another gentleman. They had obviously been in deep conversation when I knocked, but when Holmes saw me, he stood up, a look of utter delight on his face.

"Watson, my dear fellow," he said with glee, "how very nice to see you again."

"I'm glad to see you too, Holmes. I'm sorry I interrupted you. I didn't know that you had company."

"Not at all," Holmes insisted, "we're delighted, aren't we, Le Villard?"

"Mais oui," Le Villard said, standing and bowing slightly.

"Watson, this is Monsieur Le Villard."

"How do you do, sir," I returned with my own slight bow.

"I have often wished to see this Dr. Watson. Holmes has told me a great deal about you."

"That's very nice of you, Monsieur Le Villard," I said.

"Marriage suits you, Watson, you look in splendid shape. Gained a little weight, haven't you?"

"Yes, I have gained a few pounds," I admitted with a bit of embarrassment.

"It becomes you, dear fellow," Holmes added, "please sit down, won't you?"

"You're sure that I'm not interrupting you in some important discussion?"

"No, no, Monsieur doctor, we were having a good natured argument on the relative abilities of the French criminal compared to the English," Le Villard said, as I seated myself next to Holmes.

"You must lend me your support, Watson," Holmes said. "Le Villard is convinced that the English criminal is a very dull dog indeed."

"Well, we've met some far from dull ones in our time, I assure you."

"The exceptions rather than the rule, I fear, Monsieur doctor," Le Villard insisted.

"You are stubborn, aren't you, Le Villard?" Holmes said.

"Believe me, my dear friend," Le Villard went on, "I will yield to no one in my admiration of your knowledge and skill. That is why I wish I could persuade you to see my viewpoint on these matters. What could possibly interest you in this land of gray fogs, boiled potatoes and pots of tea?"

Holmes was laughing as I sat quite disturbed by Monsieur Le Villard's remark.

"Upon my soul, sir, you're not very flattering," I interjected, none too pleased by this observation.

"But I meant no offense, my friend."

"You say the English criminal is dull. Perhaps if you were to read a published story of mine called A STUDY IN SCARLET you'd think differently. It tells of a very exciting adventure that Holmes and I had together."

"I have read it," Le Villard returned.

"You have?" I said with surprise.

"An extremely gripping story, but surely you will admit that the crime was essentially of American origin."

"He's right, Watson, he's perfectly right," Holmes said, still laughing. "Dear me, what can I do to vindicate the 'dishonor' of the London criminal? Let me see."

Holmes placed his fingertips together for a moment in thought, while Le Villard sat patiently. I was about to again defend our position, when Holmes jumped up.

"I have it. A copy of today's Times. I shall introduce you to the section known as 'The Agony Column.'"

Holmes opened the paper and hurriedly found the advertisement pages.

"Yes, Le Villard, this should convince you of the color and variety of English life."

"'The Agony Column'? It sounds most painful. What is it, pray?"

"The personal columns," I said, "they are liable to contain anything from a lover's frantic appeal to his lady, to a ransom note."

"In my profession I've frequently found it invaluable as a medium for contacting the underworld," Holmes said, as he continued to peruse the columns. "Oh dear me, today's column seems rather uninspired, I'm afraid."

"May I examine it?"

"Yes, of course," Holmes replied, handing Le Villard the paper. It was but a moment before Le Villard found something and read it aloud.

"'If the lady who helped my little boy cross the road at the corner of Threadneedle Street last Wednesday at 4 P.M. will get in touch with Box 845, she will learn of something to her advantage.' It can be more colorful than that in Paris, my dear friends."

"I think we can do better than that, too," Holmes said, scanning the column again. "Here, look at this, will you?"

I glanced over as Le Villard and I read the notice, then, quite puzzled by the ad, I spoke.

"The printer must have been half asleep when he set up the type for this advertisement. 'Will any gentlemen interested in discussing cryptography and cipher writing please communicate with box XQL696. The Times.'"

"I fail to find this message any more stirring than the preceding one," Le Villard pointed out.

"You notice the execrable printing, don't you?" Holmes asked.

"Why indeed I do. It is all mixed up," Le Villard went on. "The first word 'Will' starts with a capital *W* and a capital *I*. The second word 'any' starts with a small *a*, and then has a capital *N* and *Y*. It is a shocking example of typography."

"And when it occurs in a paper noted for its excellence in typesetting, one realizes that this is no mistake!"

"What do you mean, Holmes?"

"This is undoubtedly a code message, Watson."

"Come now, my friend," Le Villard laughed cynically, "I defy even you to make a mystery out of a printer's negligence."

"I accept your challenge, my dear Le Villard," Holmes said excitedly. "If you recall, the Baconian bilateral cipher depends upon the use of two sizes of type. If we group the letters in units of five, the arrangements of small and capital letters within the groups should give us the message."

Holmes took the paper and placed it on a writing table. Pencil in hand, he began scribbling the cipher along the white border of the paper. Le Villard and I rose and quietly joined Holmes, our curiosity peaked by this intriguing problem my good friend had uncovered in the personal column.

"Let me see, now," Holmes went on, more to himself than to us, "two capital letters followed by three small, gives us the letter H, then two capitals, one small . . . yes, here you are, that gives us E."

"I still think you are trying to make an adventure out of a mere printing accident," Le Villard insisted.

"No mere printing accident could so readily fall into one of the great traditional ciphers," Holmes countered. "Now, let's go on with it. This message reads H . . . E . . . then L . . . H . . . E . . . L . . . P . . . Help; then Q . . . U . . . I . . . L . . . yes, Quilter! Help Quilter . . . E . . . L . . . M . . . Help Quilter Elms . . . . P . . . Penge. Here it is: Help Quilter Elms Penge!"

"Help Quilter Elms Penge. What does that mean?" Le Villard asked.

"If I may chance a guess," I said, "presumably that a man named Quilter who lives at a house called The Elms in the village of Penge, needs help."

"Ah, I see it now!" Le Villard said in amazement, "a helpless victim held prisoner. He smuggles out this message as a harmless personal with strict instructions that it be printed in this odd form. He knows that the amateurs of cryptography to whom it is addressed will decipher his call for help. Voila!"

"Monsieur Le Villard," I said with some smugness, "you seem ready to grant that adventure can exist in London, after all."

"The advantage, my dear Watson, of a more mercurial temperament than we Englishmen possess. Well, Le Villard, what about it? Should we set off for Penge and rescue the ingenious Mr. Quilter from whatever dire fate awaits him at The Elms?" Holmes said with marked amusement.

"I am all impatient!"

"Splendid!" Holmes exclaimed, then turned to me, "Watson, I suppose you are too busy to join us?"

"Too busy?"

"I mean, your practice," Holmes continued. "I'm sure you have patients to attend to."

"Yes, of course," I returned rather crestfallen, "I have two further visits to make today. One to a peppery old miser who has the gout, and the other to a wealthy society woman with an acute attack of hypochondria."

Holmes stood silently, a wry grin on his face, as he took one of his favorite pipes from the mantlepiece and lit it, obviously waiting for me to make a decision, and enjoying every difficult second I was in.

"To blazes with both of them! I'm coming with you, Holmes, if you want me."

"Excellent, Watson! Come on, let's grab our hats and coats. The game's afoot!"

It was down the stairs and out into Baker Street for the three of us. Monsieur Le Villard as excited by this venture as Holmes and I were. We hailed a cab and rode the half hour to The Elms, Penge, all the while Holmes and Le Villard talking about the comparative differences between police detection in France and England.

When we alighted from the cab, a gentle breeze greeted us on this most glorious summer afternoon. It was the kind of weather that begged one to take a slow walk about the city to enjoy this exceptional warmth.

"So this is the Elms, Holmes. It's quite a bit of land for such a modest neighborhood," I ventured to comment.

"To call it the Elms seems remarkably inapropos," Le Villard commented. "I cannot see an elm tree in sight."

"So you see, Le Villard, the English have more imagination than you give them credit for," Holmes said.

"Are you just going to walk up to the front door and knock, Holmes?"

"And why not, Watson? The direct approach is often the most satisfactory."

"You disappoint me," Le Villard said. "I had hoped that perhaps you would adapt one of the disguises in which you are so adept, I am told."

"Since it is unlikely that these people would know me by sight, that hardly seems necessary. However, I trust that this little problem may reward you with some colorful highlights before we are through with—" Holmes stopped abruptly, for the sound of three shots rang out. Le Villard and I were stunned, to say the least.

"Great Scott, Holmes," I exclaimed, "revolver shots. They came from the house!"

"We are too late. Monsieur Quilter has been murdered."

"I think not, Le Villard," Holmes went on calmly, "you will observe that the next door neighbor to the Elms was cutting his front lawn as we drove up. He's still engaged in the same occupation. Obviously revolver shots attract little attention in this vicinity."

"Mon dieu, you mean that violence and sudden death are so common that they do not even attract even a passing interest?"

"No, Le Villard," Holmes chuckled, "even the British are not that phlegmatic."

"Then what is the answer to those shots, Holmes?" I asked.

"That some member of this household is addicted to pistol practice. The fact that a shooting target is nailed to the back of the fence over there would further support the theory."

"That's rather ominous, in my opinion," I commented as Holmes stepped up to the front door, Le Villard and I behind him.

"It's best we keep our wits about us, anyway," Holmes said as he yanked the pull cord on the bell.

"Are you carrying a revolver, Dr. Watson?" Le Villard asked me.

"No, only a stethoscope. I'm afraid I was prepared for sickness when I left the house today, not for crime."

"I too am unarmed. How about you, Monsieur Holmes?"

"Only a magnifying glass, I'm afraid. Hardly a lethal weapon."

The door opened, revealing a well dressed woman with dark hair, pulled well back on her head. She seemed somewhat cold of attitude when she spoke.

"Yes, gentlemen?"

"My friends and I are calling on Mr. Quilter," Holmes said.

"Oh, who are you?"

"My name is Sherlock Holmes, and these are my friends, Dr. Watson and Monsieur Le Villard."

"Is Mr. Quilter expecting you?" she said coldly.

"I don't know," Holmes continued, "we read his advertisement in the Agony column of the Times today, and came down here at once. Are you a relation of his?"

"I'm his niece," she returned. "My name is Doris Favisham. Come in, won't you?"

We entered the house, which, to my surprise, looked far larger on the inside than I had expected. It was very richly decorated with exquisite furniture. As I glanced about I noticed a beautiful stairway that led to the upstairs floor.

"*Miss* Favisham, I suppose it is?"

"Yes, doctor, it's Miss Favisham."

"We heard three revolver shots as we were walking up the driveway. They gave us quite a start."

"Yes, Mademoiselle," Le Villard added, "we were afraid that we might have arrived at a time of tragedy."

"Tragedy?" she said in surprise, then laughed. "My hobby is revolver shooting. I was doing some target practice in the back garden as you arrived."

"Revolver shooting, Miss Favisham? That's very interesting. I flatter myself that I'm something of a marksman, myself," Holmes said.

"Really?" Miss Favisham returned, seeming to warm to us a little. "Perhaps we can have a match. Won't you sit down?"

"Your challenge intrigues me, Miss Favisham, but before I accept it, I'd like to see Mr. Quilter."

"Uncle George is paralyzed, you know. Spends all his time in a wheelchair. I'm not at all sure he'll see you."

"Well, at least you could ask him, can't you, Miss Favisham?" I said.

"It is his custom at this time of day to take a little nap. Perhaps tomorrow," she answered.

"Doris, Doris," came an elderly voice from upstairs, "who's in there?"

"It seems he is still awake," she said, then turned towards the stairway. "Some men have come to see you, Uncle."

"Well, bring them in, bring them in!" Mr. Quilter yelled down at us.

"Follow me, please, gentlemen."

Miss Favisham led the way as we went upstairs into a richly wood paneled room. There, seated in a wheelchair, a blanket lain neatly across his legs, was Mr. Quilter, gray of hair, and quite stooped in body; but his eyes were bright and revealed a great inquisitiveness for so old a man.

"Uncle, this is Mr. Sherlock Holmes, Dr. Watson and Monsieur Le Villard."

"Sherlock Holmes, eh?" he said, brushing aside the introduction. "Took you long enough to decipher my message and get here, didn't it? Your brother's a much faster worker, isn't he?'

"What makes you say that, Mr. Quilter?" Holmes said, quite chagrined by this news.

"I received this telegram from him at 11 o'clock this morning. Read it for yourself."

"What does it say, Holmes?" I asked.

"Most amusing. Listen to this: 'Suggest you consult my brother Sherlock.' And it's signed Mycroft Holmes. Yes, Mr. Quilter, my brother is a much faster worker. Or, shall we say that he suffers from the unfortunate habit of early rising. He undoubtedly read the Agony column three hours before I did."

"Don't know about that, but I've been expecting you all day. I imagine you know why I inserted that advertisement?"

"I had the impression that you were under some form of restraint, that you were in need of a rescue party, as it were."

"Rubbish!" Mr. Quilter declared, "my advertisement was a piece of subtle bait. The only person that could decipher the message would obviously be someone who knew the Baconian cipher."

"A very logical deduction, Mr. Quilter," Holmes said.

"Yes. I'm convinced, as any sensible man should be, that the so-called Shakespearean plays are written by Sir Francis Bacon. But I felt that it needed a clever man to prove the facts. I was sure that anyone who was able to decipher my message was the man I needed. What will you take to do the job? I'm a rich man; name your fee."

"You mean to say that you've inveigled Mr. Holmes down here just to do some research on the origin of Shakespeare's work?" I said, both annoyed and disappointed by Mr. Quilter's attitude.

"You needn't look so shocked, Dr. Watson," Miss Favisham added, "My uncle has offered to pay him a handsome fee."

"Well, what do you say, Mr. Sherlock Holmes?" Quilter said, pressing the point.

"It would be an interesting subject for research. I will concede that Ignatius Donnelly and others have proved, almost beyond doubt, that William Shakespeare of Stratford on Avon did not write the plays, but I doubt greatly that Lord Bacon did. I may devote my leisure in later years to some investigation on the subject, but, in the meanwhile Mr. Quilter, I'm afraid I am much too busy to take on such an assignment."

"Well, please yourself," Mr. Quilter said with disappointment. "Show the gentlemen out, Doris."

We bid our leave and followed Miss Favisham to the door.

"Too bad you had this long drive down here for nothing, gentlemen," she said.

"Yes, I'm afraid I quite agree," I spoke in disappointment.

"It would seem to me," Le Villard added, "that your uncle has a distinct talent for practical joking, mademoiselle."

"Uncle? Uncle never made a joke in his life. Mr. Holmes. Now that you're here, perhaps you'd like to indulge in a little shooting match?"

"Thank you, Miss Favisham, but as I told your uncle, I'm a busy man. Good evening to you."

"Goodbye, gentlemen," she returned, closing the door behind us. Holmes walked up the driveway, with Le Villard and I on either side. He seemed in deep thought as I spoke.

"Well, Holmes, old fellow, you're losing your touch. You'd never have made a blunder like this if I'd still been living with you."

"It is comforting for an aspiring detective like myself," Le Villard added, "to know that the great Sherlock Holmes is fallible."

Le Villard and I laughed in good humor at Holmes. Holmes stopped and turned to us.

"And am I to assume that I must continue the case alone?" he said in all seriousness, bringing us up short in our laughter.

"What do you mean continue the case? There isn't one. Quilter is in no danger," I said.

"He is in desperate danger," Holmes said, "I'm only afraid I may be too late to save him."

"But we have just spoken to the man," Le Villard insisted.

"Oh no," Holmes continued, "did neither of you notice the traces of fresh dirt on the boots of that supposedly paralyzed man? Gentlemen, I fear the Agony column has led us to murder!"

"Murder?" I said, quite stunned by my friend's most accusing words.

"There was fresh earth on the soles of his boots?" Le Villard questioned.

"Distinct traces, proving that the man in the wheelchair was not paralyzed."

"That man, whoever he is, is impersonating Quilter to put us off the track," I surmised.

"Then the real Quilter may have been killed."

"I'm afraid so, Le Villard. Let's stop here, shall we, now that we're far enough away from the house, and make our plans. This hedge will hide us from the house in case they're watching from the windows. Now, this isn't a hard picture to reconstruct," Holmes went on. "There undoubtedly is, or was, a paralyzed Baconian scholar named Quilter. He managed to smuggle out that ingenious plea for help, but Mycroft's unfortunate telegram gave the game away."

"Ah, I see it now," Le Villard said, "the people in there holding him prisoner forced him to reveal what he had done."

"And what they may have done to him, Heaven alone knows," I interjected.

"Let us continue our assumptions, gentlemen. One of the criminals, guessing from the telegram that I might appear on the case, posed as the crippled Quilter."

"What's our next move, Holmes?"

"Remember that singularly unattractive young lady skilled with a revolver, Watson? We must search the grounds as unobtrusively as we can."

"Search the grounds? For what?"

"I can answer that question, Monsieur doctor. To search for signs of the freshly turned earth of a grave."

Holmes quietly moved along the hedge, beckoning us to remain silent. A short distance past the house, we found an opening in the hedge that led to the grounds behind. Holmes pointed to the rear of the house.

"There, gentlemen. Notice how the rear windows have been curtained off completely. It's obvious our Miss Favisham and her accomplices do not wish anyone to see inside. Therein lies our chance to search the grounds. While no one can see in, those inside cannot see out. Come on."

The three of us forced our way through the hedge and methodically scoured the grounds for signs of freshly turned earth. It took but minutes for us to complete our task.

"Well," I said, "we didn't find any traces of the poor devil's corpse, thank Heavens."

"No. A great disappointment."

"You seem to be very blood thirsty, Le Villard," Holmes said with a cynical note in his voice. "Hello, look at the old fellow coming out of the servants' quarters. He's trimming the hedge over there."

"Must be the gardener," I said.

"Well, gentlemen, let's have a chat with him. He may be able to give us some information," Holmes proffered. We quietly walked to where the old man was working, while I occasionally glanced at the curtained windows to make sure that we were not seen.

"Good evening to you," Holmes said.

"Good evening to you, gentlemen," returned the gardener.

"Do you work for Mr. Quilter?"

"That I do, sir," he answered Holmes.

"And fine work, too. I've seldom seen a better kept garden."

"Thank ye, sir," said the man with a great smile, "I do pride myself at my work."

"I wonder if you can help me?" Holmes questioned.

"Be glad to, sir, if I can."

"Did you see a telegraph boy deliver a message here this morning?"

"That I did, sir. The boy came here about ten o'clock this mornin'. I was clippin' the front hedge at the time."

"And you've been working here on and off all day?" Holmes continued with his questions.

"Yes sir. Brought my lunch with me today, and ate it in the garden."

"Has anyone entered or left the house since that telegram was delivered?"

"No, sir. No one except yourselves. I saw you enter earlier, that I did."

"I suppose you run errands for Mr. Quilter?"

"Not much these days, sir. The poor old gentlemen keeps his chair in the house pretty much all the time, sir, he does. I did run a message for him yesterday, though."

"Oh you did, did you? Where to?" Holmes asked pointedly.

"Well, sir, I was prunin' the rose bushes under his study window, when the window opens and his hand comes out with a message. He told me to take it to the advert office of the Times, and to tell 'em to print it just the way it was, he did. He looked kind of worried when he gave me the message, and he whispered to me, just as if he was afraid in his own house."

"I'm greatly obliged to you, sir," Holmes said with glee. "Here's five shillings for your trouble."

"Oh, thank you sir, I'm much obliged to you, sir," he returned with surprise.

"Good evening. Come on, Watson. Le Villard."

"So that's how the message was smuggled out," I said, as we retreated back to our original hiding place.

"And no one has come to the house or left it since that telegram was delivered," Le Villard stated.

"Therefore Quilter, or his body, must still be inside that house."

"We are going to search the house, Monsieur Holmes?"

"Yes, we are."

"But Holmes, we're not armed," I exclaimed. "They certainly are. They probably won't even let us in."

"Yes they will, Watson. We have an infallible key to entry. A woman's vanity. Come on."

Quickly taking the initiative, Holmes walked straight up to the door and knocked, Le Villard and I behind him. When the door opened, it was Miss Favisham we saw once again standing before us.

"Oh," she said, "so you came back. I thought you wouldn't be able to resist my challenge to a pistol match, Mr. Holmes."

"Exactly, Miss Favisham. We had difficulty in finding a cab and decided to take a train back to London. The schedule meant an hour's wait, so I thought I'd accept your challenge."

"Good. Come in. We'll go into the back garden. Don't talk loudly, uncle is trying to sleep in the next room."

"Doris," came the familiar voice of Quilter, "don't bring anyone into my room. I want to sleep!"

"If your uncle wants to sleep, it seems an odd sort of lullaby, shooting pistols," I proffered.

"He's used to that, doctor. This way, gentlemen."

The four of us entered the garden, proving to me that, indeed, Miss Favisham and the man we had called Quilter had not seen us when we were searching the grounds only moments ago.

"Here we are," Miss Favisham said, "this is a fifty yard range, Mr. Holmes. Three shots. Best accurate score wins. How much do you want to bet?"

"You name the stakes, Miss Favisham."

"A sovereign?"

"Certainly. Now, won't you please take the first three shots?"

124

"Very well. There are six bullets in this revolver. All right, here I go."

Miss Favisham paused for a moment to steady herself, took careful aim, then slowly fired. One. Two. Three shots.

"Bravo, Miss Favisham, Bravo," I said. "A splendid job."

"A bull's eye and two inners. I could do better. Your turn, Mr. Holmes," she said.

The door to the study opened and a small man came forth, a stern look on his face.

"Doris," he said, "who are these men?"

"Friends of mine," she returned, "I'll introduce you in a minute, Jeffrey. We're in the middle of a match at the moment. Your turn, Mr. Holmes."

"Revolver, please."

"Here you are. You're sure you know how to handle a revolver?" she asked.

"Oh, quite sure, thank you."

"Then why are you pointing it at me?"

"Because I want you to raise your hands above your head, Miss Favisham. You too, whatever your name is!"

"Doris, who are these men?" said the man called Jeffrey.

"Put up your hands!" Holmes insisted with cold determination, "I shan't hesitate to shoot, I assure you!"

"What in Heavens name do you think you are up to?" said Miss Favisham in anger.

"Finding out what became of the real Mr. Quilter," Holmes replied. "Search the man, Watson. Le Villard, go in the house and check everything, please."

"Holmes," I exclaimed, "this man had a revolver on his hip!"

"Keep him covered with it. Now, sir, who are you? From your resemblance to the man in the wheelchair that we saw earlier, I should say you're a member of the same family."

"We're both relatives of Mr. Quilter," Miss Favisham said.

"That's right. My name's Davies. I'm from the Australian branch of the family."

"Relatives. Yes," Holmes said, "and doubtless you stood to inherit his estate in the event of Quilter's death. You moved in on this defenseless old man, terrorized him, lived off him and finally found it necessary to destroy him."

"You're . . . you're talking absolute rubbish," yelled Miss Favisham.

"He's telling the truth and you know it. I can tell by your expressions," I said, my anger rising.

"Move back into the house, both of you," Holmes demanded, pointing the gun squarely at Davies.

Slowly, deliberately, Holmes forced the two back into the house, never once taking his eyes from them.

"All right, lead the way to the study. The man posing as Quilter is still there. We heard him call out as we came in."

"Yes," I added, "we might as well confront the three of them together."

We entered the study, with Miss Favisham and Davies going on before us. There, in the wheelchair, was Mr. Quilter.

"He's still seated in the chair, Holmes. Though he seems to be asleep," I said.

"Le Villard!" Holmes yelled, "did you find anything?"

"Not a trace of the missing man, Monsieur Holmes," he returned, joining us in the study. Holmes turned his stony cold eyes on the conspirators.

"Davies, what did you do with Mr. Quilter?"

"I didn't do anything with him," Davies insisted.

"Of course not," Miss Favisham added, "he's sitting there in that chair!"

"It's no good lying to us. We know that man's an imposter," I said.

"But this is a fantastic situation," Holmes exclaimed in disbelief. "Nobody's left this house since the telegram arrived and nobody has entered it. And yet, Mr. Quilter has vanished."

"Good Lord," I said, quite perplexed, "how can that man sleep through all this talking. You'd think he'd been drugged."

"Le Villard! We're idiots!" Holmes exclaimed, "you are unquestionably the most promising detective in France, and some people have been kind enough to grant me a similar status in England, and yet my old friend Watson has just solved the case!"

"Really, Holmes? What are you talking about? How could I solve it? Explain yourself," I asked, completely dumbfounded by Holmes' words.

"Listen, Watson, listen to the breathing of that man in the chair. He *has* been drugged! There sits the real Mr. Quilter, the persecuted victim who sent a cipher message for help!"

"But Holmes," I said, "the man we spoke to earlier?"

"Was you, Mr. Davies, impersonating Quilter. After you had received us, you took off your disguise, adopted an Australian accent, and hid your drugged victim by placing him in his own wheelchair, knowing that would be the last place we'd look for him!"

"They would have kept him here until we'd gone, and then murdered him," Le Villard said.

"What a devilish plot, Holmes!" I exclaimed.

Suddenly, Miss Favisham, trembling and near to tears, spoke out.

"It was Jeffrey's idea, not mine," she said frantically. "I didn't have anything to do with it."

"That's a dirty lie! You're in this as much as I am," yelled Mr. Davies, his hands clenched in rage as if he were ready to strike her.

"Oh, that's splendid," Holmes managed with disgust. "Yes, it's really charming. Please continue the argument, won't you? It will make interesting evidence in court."

"You can't take us to court!" Miss Favisham yelled.

"Of course you can't," added Mr. Davies. "What's the charge? Quilter's still alive, isn't he?"

"When Mr. Quilter revives, under Dr. Watson's ministrations," Holmes said calmly, "you will be charged, I have no doubt, with attempted murder, abduction, duress, and probably several other counts. Monsieur Le Villard, if you'll find us a cab, we'll take these miscreants to Scotland Yard. Our work is done!"

"Listen to the organ peeling forth its madness. Come on, Watson! Something has gone horribly wrong!"

# 9

# THE ADVENTURE OF THE HEADLESS MONK

TOWARDS the end of November in the year of 1896, a dense yellow fog had settled over London. For almost a week it was impossible, from our rooms in Baker Street, to see the outline of the houses opposite. It was a most depressing time for Holmes and myself. Oftentimes, if I was not working upon a story about my friend Holmes, I would mull over the events in the *London Times*. It was as if the entire city had come to a standstill, the fog never lifting for a moment, day or night.

To me, it seemed especially hard on my friend Holmes, for he has always been of a restless, surging nature, and to be so trapped in his own lodgings was tantamount to being exiled from the world of crime detection that was so dear to his heart.

The first day of the fog Holmes spent at cross-indexing his huge books of criminal references. On the second and third days he tried to patiently occupy himself with a subject he had recently made his hobby, the music of the Middle Ages. But, on the fourth day when, pushing back his chair after breakfast, he saw the heavy fog, laced with factory soot swirling past him, Holmes' impatient and active nature could no longer endure this drab existence.

He paced restlessly about our sitting room, chaffing against the inaction. After several minutes of these perambulations, he turned to me and spoke.

"I take it there is nothing of interest in the paper, Watson?" he said nervously.

"There's news of a possible revolution, and an impending change in the government. Nothing to interest you, though. No crimes of any importance."

"It seems the London criminal is certainly a dull and unenterprising fellow these days. Look out of the window, Watson. See below, how the figures of people loom up, are dimly seen and then blend once more into the foggy depths. What a day for a thief or a murderer! He could roam London as the tiger does the jungle, unseen until he pounces, evident only to his victim."

"That's a cheerful thought," I said facetiously.

At that moment, Holmes and I could hear the doorbell below.

"Hello, I wonder who that is? You expecting someone, Holmes?"

"No. It's probably a visitor for Mrs. Hudson, or perhaps the local plumber has finally condescended to pay some attention to the faulty gas jet in our hallway."

"I don't think you're right on either count," I interjected. "I can hear Mrs. Hudson's footsteps on the stairs." In a moment Mrs. Hudson knocked on our door and then entered. She announced that there was a gentleman to see Holmes.

She handed him the man's card, which he quickly glanced at, a genuine smile of surprise crossing his face.

"Mortimer Harley, eh? Show him up, Mrs. Hudson."

"Very good, sir," she returned, then went to fetch Mr. Harley.

"Mortimer Harley, and who might that be, Holmes?"

"I've not had the pleasure of meeting him personally, but I'm quite familiar with his scientific reputation."

"Well, don't keep me in suspense, Holmes, tell me about him. In what does he specialize?"

"I suppose one might refer to him as one of the greatest authorities on all matters pertaining to the occult."

"You mean the fellow dabbles in supernatural stuff, and all that sort of thing?" I asked, my curiosity peaking.

"I mean, my dear Watson, that Mortimer Harley is an extremely intelligent man with a thoroughly comprehensive and scholarly knowledge of his field, and an intense belief in the existence of the supernatural force."

Holmes had just finished his words to me when Mr. Harley was ushered into our rooms. In the short moment it took for Mrs. Hudson to leave us alone with this prospective client, I had occasion to observe the man. He was of slight build, impeccably dressed and, although in his later years, seemed quite fit for his age.

"You are Mr. Sherlock Holmes?" he said, in a quiet and most cultured voice.

"Yes, and this is my colleague, Dr. Watson."

"How do you do, Mr. Harley, won't you sit down?" I said, gesturing to a chair.

He seated himself across from Holmes and I, carefully adjusting his clothing before turning to us.

"Well," he said, "you are probably wondering who I am and, and what's brought me here."

"We're not wondering who you are, Mr. Harley," I said. "My friend Holmes was just telling me of your scientific eminence."

"I am certainly flattered that you know of me, Mr. Holmes; just the same, you may be wondering why I am here."

"Please, be so kind as to inform us of your problem," Holmes said, leaning back in his favorite chair and casually lighting his pipe.

"Mr. Holmes, have you ever heard of the Headless Monk of Trevenice chapel?"

"Yes indeed, Mr. Harley. An apparition to be counted among our more 'intangible' national treasures," Holmes commented with a certain amount of sarcasm in his voice.

"I am sorry to appear stupid, gentlemen, but I have never heard of the Headless Monk of whatever-it-is chapel."

"Well, then, let me tell you about it, doctor. Trevenice manor, in Cornwall, was once an abbey.

"It was appropriated during the reign of Henry the Eighth, and several of the monks were killed in some of the 'minor difficulties' attendant on such an act. But one of the murdered monks, a certain Brother Hugh, the chapel organist, was persistent. He still haunts the chapel today, and still plays the organ. And since he was beheaded, he always appears headless."

"A charming little story, Mr. Harley," I said, quite amused, "but you don't expect us to believe it's anything but a legend, surely."

"Ah, a skeptic, eh? How about you, Mr. Holmes?"

"I'm extremely curious to know why you would come to see me, Mr. Harley."

"I'll tell you why. I have a rare opportunity to investigate the phenomena. You see, the son of an old friend of mine, a young fellow by the name of Leonard Miles, is secretary to the owner of Trevenice manor. It was he who asked me to stay there, and I find the invitation irresistible. Particularly since the phenomena have curiously increased of late, Mr. Holmes. Almost as though some, well, mortal agency was motivating the appearances."

"Now I see why you have come to me, Mr. Harley."

"I knew you would understand, Mr. Holmes. You see, I'm like my good friend and fellow investigator, Tarnacci. I believe in being prepared to meet phenomena on either the natural or the supernatural plane. If the phenomena are real, then they fall legitimately in my field—"

"Whereas," Holmes interrupted, "as I am sure you suspect, they are being contrived by human forces, then you think that is more in my department."

"Exactly."

"What do you say, Holmes," I broke in with excitement. "A little trip to Cornwall would make a nice few days. We'd probably escape this blasted fog down there!"

"To blazes with the weather, Watson, I'm much more concerned with the fog that surrounds the appearances of the Headless Monk of Trevenice Chapel. Mr. Harley, I accept your invitation, with pleasure! There's still time to catch the Cornish express, and we can be at Trevenice Manor before the moon is up!"

Allowing us no chance to reply, Holmes had already dashed into his bedroom and pulled down his Inverness cape and deerstalker cap.

"Watson, be sure to bring along your medical bag. We may find need for it. Hurry everyone, the game's afoot!"

Holmes knew that I relished the chance to get away from London at every opportunity, especially when on a case. I hardly had time to pack my bag before I found myself and Mr. Harley being pushed by Holmes out the door and down the stairs. A short few words to Mrs. Hudson explaining what we were up to, then out the front door as Holmes hailed a Hansom.

Within minutes we saw Victoria station loom up out of the swirling fog. The three of us had just enough time to purchase our tickets and board the express.

Holmes, of course, had been right. The moon was just making its appearance as the three of us walked up towards the manor house. Mr. Harley gestured for us to follow him as he turned towards the chapel.

"Don't you think that we should go to the manor house first, Mr. Harley?" I said, puzzled by his action.

"No I don't, doctor. We'll see enough of the others later. I simply can't resist taking a look at the chapel in moonlight. You understand, don't you Holmes?"

"Yes, perfectly. I must say it's a fascinating piece of architecture."

"It's practically a ruin though," I added. "I don't imagine it's been in use for some time."

"And yet it's been standing for well over four hundred years, I should say. Let's explore inside, shall we?" Harley said in excited tones.

I stopped suddenly at the foot of the great stone stairs leading into the chapel, for I saw what appeared to be a dark and massive figure moving towards us.

"Hello, what's this coming towards us?"

"If I hadn't heard the sound of his footsteps," said Harley, "I'd believe it was a psychic manifestation."

"He certainly looks as if he came from beyond the grave!"

"Who be ye, gentlemen?" said the man looming up before us. "Where be ye goin'?"

"Supposing you tell us who you are first, my good man," I said, somewhat taken aback by his size.

"Who be I? I be David Pendragon, sir, that's who I be! Stable hand here at the manor. Now I ask you gentlemen again, where you be goin'?"

"We're staying at the manor. We're just going to take a look at the chapel," Harley said reassuringly.

"Oh, don't ye do that, sir. People 'at go in there don't often come out the way they go in, sir. Don't ye do it, gentlemen!"

"What are you talking about, my good fellow?" I said.

"I be talking about the ghoulies, and the ghosties, and the organ music that comes out of the nowheres."

"You . . . you've heard it," Harley said excitedly.

"Course I heard it, sir. Just like I seen the poor monk walkin' around without his head on!"

"Take us into the chapel, will you, and show us where you saw the figure."

"Ah, that I will not, sir, not for all the gold in Porthcall will I go back and chance seeing the poor lost soul wandering about without his head on! If you gentlemen know what's good for ye, you'll not go in there either! Mark my words! Don't ye go in that chapel!"

He turned and walked away, his large and bulky frame casting a deep shadow across us. Night was fully upon us and a cold and cutting wind had risen.

"What an extraordinary chap. Seems really frightened of the place!"

"Yes," Harley said, "but it's more than blind superstition that accounts for his reluctance. Let's go inside, shall we, doctor?"

As we moved into the chapel, we found ourselves surrounded by deep and black shadows. Even though outside it was dark, in the chapel it was even darker, and it took a moment for our eyes to become accustomed to the meager light the moon cast through the stained glass windows. Suddenly, the sound of an organ filled the room, drawing me up short.

"Great Scott," I said, "listen to that! The ghost is playing the organ!"

"We're extremely fortunate. A psychic manifestation as soon as we entered the chapel!"

It was then, amidst the dim light, that I noticed the organ and the figure playing it.

"Psychic manifestation . . . rubbish!" I exclaimed, relaxing. "Look who's sitting at the keyboard. It's Holmes!"

We rushed forward until we stood by the organ, Holmes playing gently upon the keys.

"Holmes, you frightened us to death. Didn't he, Harley?"

"Speaking for myself, doctor, he disappointed me. I thought it was a genuine phenomenon."

"What do you think you're doing, Holmes? I was wondering where you were. I thought you were still behind us."

"I'm sorry if I frightened you, Watson. I was curious about this organ, so I slipped in by the side door ahead of you and tested the instrument. It's in astonishingly good condition for a disused chapel, don't you think, Harley?"

"Yes, I do, Holmes."

"One might reasonably presume that someone tends it with great care. In fact, I would go further and say—"

"Who are you? What are you doing in here!" came a woman's voice out of the darkness. Holmes turned towards where the voice had sounded, his eyes trying to pierce the black shadows for some sign of its owner.

"We are guests at the manor house, and we decided to pay a visit to the chapel before we paid our respects to our host."

"Oh," came the voice, as out of the shadows stepped a beautiful, well groomed young lady of slight build. "My father is your host. I'm Dorothy Brownlee."

"How do you do. My name is Holmes, and these gentlemen are Dr. Watson and Mr. Harley."

She curtsied to us, then turned back to Holmes.

"I heard the organ music and I was terribly frightened. You must have heard of the legend, I suppose?"

"You mean about the Headless Monk and the ghostly organ music, Miss Brownlee?" I said.

"Yes, doctor. And it's more than a legend, I assure you. That's why I rushed over here as soon as I heard the music. It must have frightened all the servants within hearing distance. Why were you playing the organ?"

"I was curious to see whether it was in good repair."

"Obviously it is, Mr. Holmes. Well, my father and his secretary, Mr. Miles, are expecting you, I know. Let's walk over to the house, shall we? I'm sure you've seen enough of the chapel tonight."

I was only too glad to get out of the cold and biting wind and into a warm house. Dorothy's father stood by the fireplace, his demeanor that of a strong man, proud of his station in life.

We were all introduced to Mr. Brownlee, who, in turn, introduced us to his secretary, Leonard Miles, a tall man of a quiet nature, and of looks, quite handsome. After the usual formalities, we relaxed and sat by the fire where we could rid ourselves of the awful cold that had penetrated to our very bones.

"I'm afraid Mr. Brownlee is rather angry with me. I hadn't told him that you were an expert on psychic phenomenon, Mr. Harley," said Mr. Miles, the first to start a conversation.

"I fail to see why the knowledge of that fact should make you angry, Mr. Brownlee."

"I don't want you ferreting about into this so-called ghost business. There's been enough trouble already! It's almost impossible to keep servants, and these Cornish people are incredibly superstitious."

I had been glancing at Holmes who was carefully observing the various members of our group. He turned to Mr. Brownlee with a smile, pulling his pipe from the Inverness cape.

"You haven't seen the ghost yourself, have you Mr. Brownlee?" Holmes asked.

"Of course not," he answered in irritation, "there isn't any ghost I tell you!"

"Then have you heard the mysterious organ playing?" Holmes went on.

"No, no I have not. And I don't want to talk about it anymore!"

One of the servants came in and told Mr. Brownlee that David Pendragon was at the door and wished to speak with him. I had pulled out my note pad and jotted down some comments concerning the nature of the entire business just before Pendragon was shown in. I was ready for any other pertinent information at hand.

"That's the fellow we met outside the chapel, isn't it?" I said to Harley.

"Yes, quite a colorful character."

"On the contrary," voiced Mr. Brownlee, "he's a superstitious old fool, if you ask me. But, I will admit, he is a good groom."

It was then Pendragon came to stand before his master.

"Begging your pardon, sir, but there be trouble at the chapel again tonight. I says to myself 'David, 'tis your duty to go to the master' and so I be here. As the moon was hangin' low tonight, sir, I hears the organ aplayin'."

"But that was Mr. Holmes, my good man," I interrupted.

"Aye, that's what he thinks, maybe. What I says to myself is 'What made him play the organ?' Then, this very night, I saw the Headless Monk. With my own eyes I saw that poor soul with his head off, wanderin' in the moonlight. I saw that, sir, with my own eyes I did!"

"Get out of here you blathering old fool!" yelled Mr. Brownlee. "And I'm warning you, if I hear any more nonsense about this ghost, you'll lose your job, you understand? Now be off with you!"

Cowed, old Pendragon, as big as he was, turned in fright and left hurriedly. Mr. Brownlee calmed himself as best he could and turned to us.

"Come, gentlemen, to the drawing room where I can at least offer you a drink."

Brownlee, with his daughter and Leonard Miles, moved to the drawing room ahead of us, giving me a chance to whisper to Holmes.

"Holmes, Mr. Brownlee seems absolutely rabid on the subject of the ghost."

"Yes, suspiciously so. I wonder what he's trying to hide?"

"Whatever it is, I don't think he'll be successful," Harley added. "In your profession, Holmes, you know that murder will out. It's true in my profession also. Try to suppress them as you may, gentlemen, ghosts will out!"

Nothing more was said of the incident as our host poured us drinks and entertained us until, warm and comfortable, we all retired for the night.

It was after breakfast, and Holmes and I, accompanied by Mr. Harley, found ourselves strolling casually along the grounds of the manor house. The wind had abated some, and, although the sky was filled with clouds, the sun managed to send its rays through here and there, dotting the land with a brightness that helped make the day a bit more cheerful.

"Well, Holmes, this place may be haunted, but I swear that I never spent a better night anywhere."

"And I've never eaten a better breakfast, Watson!"

"I heard you moving about quite late. Have you been out, Holmes?"

"Yes, gentlemen, I had another talk with David Pendragon," he said in whispered tones, "as well as some of the other servants. It was quite illuminating."

"I was up late, too, doctor," Harley said. "I decided to ignore the veiled threats of Mr. Brownlee, and so I did a little investigating in the chapel."

"And what were the results of your investigations, Mr. Harley?" questioned Holmes.

"Well, there was no psychic manifestation, you understand, but I'm sure of one thing . . . that chapel is evil. Evil to the heart of its stones. And I'll swear that evil does not stem from the hapless monk who was murdered there."

"You have confirmed certain suspicions aroused by my own investigations last night. There is evil here, Harley, and I think I know its nature. Unless I mistake every sign and reaction, someone has been initiating the local peasantry into the evils of the Black Mass!"

"Black Mass? Good Lord, what a shocking thought," I said, unnerved by this unexpected news.

"My own sensations last night confirm your theory, Holmes. There is a coven here, I swear it! Hiding its own obscene practices under cover of the haunting," Harley said.

"It sounds quite feasible," I added. "After all, the people are so superstitious that they'd keep as far away as possible from the chapel when they heard the organ playing."

"This problem falls into both our fields, Harley," Holmes replied with a smile. "The practice of black magic is a criminal offense."

"It's perhaps just as well the old laws against witchcraft are still in force."

"I imagine, Harley, that you have your own methods of combating such forces as we're up against?"

"Oh yes, Holmes. Though mine are not connected with the legal aspects of the case."

"May I ask what you plan to do, sir?" I wondered as we continued our quiet walk.

"Well, I have several rather elaborate preparations to make, doctor. It'll take most of the day, I'm afraid. However, I shall explain them to you all after dinner tonight."

There seemed no further reason to continue our talk at this point, and we put aside these unusual events in order to relax and enjoy the countryside. The day passed quickly and delightfully and it wasn't long before we sat at a table dining on quail and passing the time conversing about music, art, and the rising political unrest in our troubled world. In due time, the servants cleared the table, and we sat back to enjoy the evening.

"It's very pleasant to sit here," I said in quiet contentment, "after a good dinner with a superb brandy at one's elbow and listen to the piano being so charmingly played."

"You're very kind, doctor," said Dorothy.

"Won't you play something more, Miss Brownlee?" Holmes asked as he seated himself in a comfortable chair, pipe in hand.

"Are you enjoying your stay down here, Mr. Holmes?" asked Mr. Brownlee, himself comfortably seated near the fireplace.

"Very much, thank you. Both Mr. Harley and I have found the local folklore extremely interesting."

"I say," ventured young Leonard Miles, "you fellows haven't been investigating the haunted chapel business again, have you?"

Mr. Brownlee abruptly stood up, his fists clenched in anger.

"Now look here, if you have, I shall be very angry! It's abusing my hospitality! I told you distinctly I didn't want any more talk of ghosts!"

"Please seat yourself," Harley said, "for we are not talking of ghosts, Mr. Brownlee. I have something even more important that I must fight now. It's possibly a little hard to imagine me as a crusader; me, a little man beside the rest of you, as towering tall a group of men as I have ever faced. And yet, I am your Saint George."

"What on earth are you talking about, sir!" Mr. Brownlee said, his anger mounting each moment.

"I'll tell you in secrecy," Mr. Harley went on. "This mustn't reach the ears of the peasantry. I refer to myself as Saint George because I go to wipe out an evil that lives in your midst. A living, modern dragon."

Dorothy stopped playing the piano, turning to us in fright.

"Oh please, Mr. Harley, that sounds dreadful!"

"And to rid you all of this fiend," he went on, ignoring the frightened girl, "I must cleanse the chapel! Purify it! Exorcise it! Remove its residue of psychic evil. That, gentlemen, is my mission tonight!"

It was at that moment that Dorothy, unable to accept Harley's words, fainted. I was beside her in a moment.

"Get some smelling salts from my bag, somebody. Now!"

Holmes, unperturbed, still sat in his chair, puffing on his pipe.

"I'm afraid you were a little too graphic for the lady, Mr. Harley," he said with a casual air. Mr. Harley stood, straightened out his clothes, then bowed lightly to his host.

"I'm sorry if I frightened the young lady, but I am sure after tonight she will have no further grounds for fear in Trevenice chapel."

He turned and left for his room. Mr. Brownlee was beside himself with rage, glaring after this small man who spoke so boldly, while I and Leonard Miles tended to the distressed young lady. Holmes crossed his legs, took a great puff on his pipe and smiled at us all.

I had been asleep for quite some time when I was shaken to wakefulness by Holmes.

"Come, old chap, we've work to do," he said in gentle whispered tones. "Dress quickly and follow me."

"What . . . what time is it?"

"Nearing midnight. We must go to the chapel."

The cold penetrated even my heavy clothing as we crouched not far from the chapel. A thickening mist swirled about us, pushed forward by the wind. It seemed to crawl over the ground like long white fingers, rolling up over the steps and lingering against the chapel walls.

"Holmes," I whispered.

"Yes, old chap?"

"Did you hear anything?"

"Nothing but the owls and a clock in the manor striking midnight."

The silence seemed to go on unceasingly.

"I'm getting awfully jumpy. What do you suppose Harley's up to?"

"I can imagine his procedure," said Holmes. "Midnight, a crucial hour I suppose, in his endeavor. I wish him luck. My own plans are not nearly as clear, unfortunately. I sense a guiding force here that I—"

"There is something, Holmes! Listen!"

"Great heavens, it's the organ in the chapel!"

"And Harley's in there alone!" I exclaimed.

"Not alone! Listen to the organ peeling forth its madness. Come on, Watson! Something has gone horribly wrong!"

As soon as we heard that devilish organ music, Holmes and I rushed forward and raced down the path leading to the ruined chapel. By the time we reached the entrance, the organ music had ceased, and the tall, gangling figure of David Pendragon stepped forward, standing in our path.

"What would you gentlemen be wanting at this time of night?"

"Never mind that. What are you doing here?"

"I? I be here because the gentleman gave me five shillings to stand here and see that no one disturb him. That's why I be here. And nobody did come or go. He still be there, he be."

"When you heard that organ music, why the devil didn't you go in?"

"Organ music? I heard no organ music."

In disgust, Holmes forced the lumbering man aside.

"Come on, Watson!"

We rushed into the chapel, trying to see through the darkness that surrounded us.

"Great heavens, look at him!" I said when I saw Harley.

"We're too late, poor devil! A knife through his heart."

"It's obvious who did it, Holmes. That fellow Pendragon. I'll go and grab him before he gets away!"

Holmes stayed my movement.

"No, no, Watson. He's not our man. This murder was planned with devilish cunning."

"Curious thing. There's no sign of a struggle at all," I remarked as I examined the body of our friend, "Looks as if he just stood here and allowed himself to be stabbed."

"Observe these chalk marks with which the body is surrounded, Watson. It's known as a pentagram, often used to ward off evil. He thought it would protect him from the supernatural forces."

"Poor chap, for once his research went too far."

"Yes, because they touched not on the supernatural, but upon natural evil. And remember, Watson, that only three people besides ourselves and David Pendragon knew of this vigil."

"You mean Brownlee, his daughter and young Miles, his secretary."

"Exactly. Go back to the house, will you, and bring them here! Perhaps we can lay a ghost by trapping a murderer!"

It was not long before I woke the household and brought them to the chapel. Holmes began his questioning immediately, for now was as good a time as any to catch them off guard.

"But that's all I know, Mr. Holmes," said Leonard Miles.

"You've not established much so far, Holmes," I said, "the three of them all swear they were asleep and that they didn't hear the organ."

"Correct," added Mr. Brownlee, "and you can't prove otherwise, Holmes!"

"I think I can prove that not only one of you was awake, but also murdered Mortimer Harley!"

"But why should any of us want the poor man dead, Mr. Holmes?" Dorothy said in agitated tones.

"In your case, young lady, I confess that I find it hard to conceive a motive."

"Implying that Mr. Brownlee and I might have one?"

"Well Mr. Miles," I interjected, "you must admit that you are responsible for Mr. Harley coming here."

"And you, Mr. Brownlee, must admit that you did everything in your power to prevent the dead man from carrying out his investigations. Why? What are you trying to hide?"

"Nothing, Mr. Holmes, it's just that I wanted to sell the manor house. All this talk about ghosts was giving this place a bad name. And if it had gone on, I'd never have disposed of the property."

"Well, speculation can get us nowhere," Holmes said in grim determination. "Let's get down to facts. Is there any other entrance to this chapel besides the front and side doors?"

"None," came Mr. Brownlee's pointed answer.

"There was an old smuggler's cave which came out near the organ loft, but father had it bricked up some years ago."

"I had to, the tourists kept crawling in!"

"Go and examine it, will you, Watson?"

I did as Holmes asked, but I examined it quietly so that I might still hear the conversation as it echoed about the chapel walls.

"If you don't mind my saying so, Mr. Holmes," young Miles spoke up, "it seems obvious who did this murder."

"You've told us David Pendragon admitted that no one went in or out as he stood guard," added Mr. Brownlee. "He must have done it himself! You can tell the man's half-witted—"

"And superstitious. He might have killed Mr. Harley because he was attempting to interfere with the ghost."

"And then played the organ to celebrate the occasion?" Holmes said sarcastically. "I think you overestimate David Pendragon's capabilities, Miss Brownlee. Mr. Miles, Pendragon is waiting outside. Would you be kind enough to ask him to come here for a moment, please?"

"Certainly."

As Miles left to bring in Pendragon, I returned, brushing the dust and filth from my clothes.

"What did you find out, Watson?"

"Well, it's easy to see where it was bricked up. It's a solid wall now; no one could get in that way."

"But if no one came in or out," questioned Mr. Brownlee, "who else could have killed Harley except Pendragon?"

"The ghost," Holmes answered, "or rather the person disguised as a ghost. The dead man expected a psychic manifestation. When he saw the supposed ghost coming towards him, he offered no resistance. You can see there was no struggle if you carefully examine the dust on the floor here. Harley believed that the magical pentagram would protect him. . . . Ah, there you are, Pendragon."

"Aye, here I be, sir. But I don't know nothin' more than what I told ye."

"Don't be frightened, Pendragon," Holmes said reassuringly, "all we want is the truth."

"That's what I told ye, sir."

"When you said no one had entered the chapel tonight, you meant that NO MORTAL MAN had entered, didn't you?"

"That I did, sir. But how could I say I'd seen the ghost when Mr. Brownlee here told me I'd lose my job if I spoke of the ghost again."

"Now we're getting somewhere," I said. "So you did see the ghost?"

"That I did, sir. The poor soul walking through the moonlight with no head on his body!"

"You saw it quite clearly?" Holmes said pointedly.

"Just as clearly as I sees you now, sir."

"How tall was he?"

"He was . . . would you mind standing against the wall, sir?"

Holmes stood against the wall as Pendragon eyed him carefully before speaking.

"He was as tall as . . . well, his shoulders come to just where your shoulders come now, sir."

"A tall man, then. So we narrow it down to either you, Mr. Brownlee, or you, Mr. Miles," I said.

"This is utterly ridiculous!" shouted Mr. Brownlee.

"On the contrary, gentlemen, the case is solved!" Holmes said triumphantly as he lit his pipe.

"Which one was it, Holmes?" I said in expectation.

"Neither! Remember that the ghost is headless. That means the impostor must have built up fake shoulders covering the head. On either of these men it would have brought their shoulders to the level of my head."

"Holmes," I said in astonishment, "you're implying that—"

Suddenly the chapel filled with echoing laughter. We all turned to face Dorothy Brownlee, her face a mask of twisted anger and hate.

"Bravo, Mr. Holmes, I didn't think you'd catch me!"

"Miss Brownlee I must warn you that—"

"Keep back, don't anyone come near me! As you see, I have a revolver!"

"Dorothy," Mr. Brownlee yelled in astonishment, "for heaven's sake!"

"Don't speak to me of heaven! You thought I was a sweet little girl, didn't you father? You didn't know your dear, demure daughter could murder a man, did you!"

"Why did you kill Mortimer Harley?"

"Because he was a meddler, Mr. Holmes. For months I'd been practicing black magic here. For months I'd been building up the legend of the Headless Monk and the organ music. It made me so wonderfully alone, so gloriously free to practice the rites!"

I stood there in horror listening to this once quiet young lady now ranting and raving, her eyes burning with the fierce fires of madness. I couldn't move. Holmes stood beside me, his body tense, listening as intently as I.

"And then, Harley came here," she continued. "I let him live that first night because I thought he was a fool! But on the second night, when he said he was going to exorcise this chapel, to purify it he said, he signed his death warrant! If you could have seen his face. If you could have only seen his stupid, startled face as I plunged the knife into him. He bled so beautifully!"

"Holmes!" I yelled, "She's as mad as a hatter! What are we going to do?"

"Miss Brownlee, give me that revolver!"

"And let you take me to prison or an asylum, Mr. Holmes? NO! You'll never catch me!"

She began to ascend the stairs leading to the organ loft, her maniacal laughter ringing throughout the chapel.

"Dorothy, Dorothy, come back!" Mr. Brownlee screamed in agony as he watched his demented daughter withdraw.

"Look out . . . the railing behind you!" Holmes yelled, moving forward at last. Miss Brownlee raised the gun, aiming squarely at Holmes. He stopped abruptly.

"What, Mr. Holmes," she ranted, "and turn my head away from you so that you can attempt to stop me? No, I—"

She never finished her words as the weight of her body pushed against the railing, causing its rotting structure to collapse. With fear in her eyes, she went over screaming to crash heavily against the stone floor below. Even as she rolled to stillness, I could see from where I stood that she had broken her neck the instant she made contact.

In grief Mr. Brownlee ran forward to take his daughter in his arms. But it was too late. She had been mercifully killed in the very place where her black magic had reigned.

Holmes went to the sobbing Mr. Brownlee, standing over his crouched form.

"Mr. Brownlee," he said gently, "the powers of evil can be very frightening. You must come to realize and accept that your daughter has killed one man and might have killed more. She was insane. Hopelessly insane."

There was little any of us could do. Holmes gestured to me.

"Watson, be so kind as to help Mr. Brownlee to return to the manor house as soon as he is able. I shall send Pendragon to fetch the authorities so that we might clear up the remaining details of this case. When you are through, let me know. I think it is time we leave this sad place."

As we sat in our compartment on the Cornish express taking us back to London, both I and Holmes became acutely aware of the absence of Mortimer Harley. We sat quietly for a long time until, finally, Holmes broke the silence.

"I think it best, Watson, we leave this case unchronicled. Mortimer Harley would have wanted it to be that way."

"No Holmes, I disagree. Although you and he had different approaches to this case, he was not far off the mark. I think he would want the public to know that such beastly goings on exist in a world we hope and pray will be one of peace and caring. Harley was a gentle man. I'd like to do him justice by writing about this case so that his name will not be totally forgotten."

"Well, my dear Watson, do as you see fit," he said with a heavy sigh.

Holmes turned towards the window as dawn was just approaching over the countryside. I leaned back against the seat, exhausted by this adventure, determined to get some sleep before we reached London, when I heard Holmes speak in so soft a voice, it was almost below a whisper.

He said, "Rest in peace, Mortimer Harley, rest in peace."

"Aha!" Holmes said excitedly. "There's the answer, Watson!"

# 10

# THE CASE OF THE CAMBERWELL POISONERS

THE story I am about to reveal began in 1887, a rather busy time for both Holmes and myself. To be exact, it was the same year that Holmes solved the case of the AMATEUR MENDICANT SOCIETY, who held their meetings in a luxuriously furnished vault below a furniture warehouse. This particular case seemed to top off what I consider an unusually exciting year.

It was late in October and the equinoctial gales had set in with exceptional violence. All day the wind had howled and the rain beat against the windows of our Baker Street lodgings. It was around midnight, as best I remember, that the storm grew louder, and the wind in the chimney sobbed like a child. Our only solace came from the warmth of the fireplace and our comfortable lodgings. Much to our surprise, the door bell jangled, and, not wishing to disturb Mrs. Hudson, I ushered our midnight visitor in and he soon stood before us. He was a man of about forty-five years, pale of complexion, and trembling from, I felt quite sure, not only the cold of the storm, but from some inner fear that was written upon his face, like that of a man weighed down with great anxiety. And yet when he spoke, his tone was business like, and almost aggressive.

"I've come to you for advice, Mr. Holmes."

"That's easily obtained," said my illustrious friend.

"And help," the gentleman continued.

"That is *not* always so easy. Help the gentleman off with his coat, will you, Watson?"

I did so and offered the gentleman a seat which he gladly accepted. I continued my observations as he went on.

"I heard of you, Mr. Holmes, from Major Prendergast. He said that you could solve anything."

"I'm afraid he's said too much," returned Holmes, lighting his pipe.

"He also said you've never been beaten at crime detection."

"I've been beaten four times, sir. Three times by men and once by a woman. But suppose you introduce yourself. My friend here is Watson, Dr. Watson. I assure you he can be trusted in all matters discreet. Now, please continue."

"My name is Lovelace. Edmund Lovelace."

"And what, pray, brings you to me at this hour of the night, Mr. Lovelace?"

"I'm in terrible trouble, Mr. Holmes. You don't know anything about me, but if you'll accept my case, you can save four lives."

"I wouldn't say that I know nothing about you, sir," Holmes interrupted, "though it is true I know little beyond the somewhat obvious facts that you're single, you keep a dog, and that you are much preoccupied with your business which I take to be some form of insurance."

"What is this?" Mr. Lovelace questioned in total surprise.

"Nothing to worry about. But I'd wager that my friend is right, isn't he, Mr. Lovelace?" I said with some amusement.

"Perfectly. But I'll be hanged if I can see how he knows it."

Holmes smiled and leaned back in his chair, taking deep puffs on his pipe.

"It's the practical application of logic, sir. The briefcase that you carry might at first indicate a barrister or some other professional man, but your brisk, business-like manner counteracts that suggestion. An insurance broker who must visit clients at odd hours is the likeliest man to combine that manner with a briefcase at midnight."

I had seen Holmes do this many times, so I merely sat back and chuckled to myself, mostly out of my own astonishment that my friend never ceased to amaze me by his deductive logic.

"But the wife?" Mr. Lovelace asked in confusion, "and the fact that I am preoccupied with my business?"

"Your cuff links do not match, sir. Each is from a different pair. That would suggest preoccupation, and it's a mistake that neither a wife nor a man servant would have allowed to pass."

"How about the dog, Holmes?" I asked.

"Oh, surely that's obvious, Watson. I shall let you ponder on that matter while Mr. Lovelace tells us his problem."

"Mr. Holmes, are you as interested in preventing a murder as in solving one?"

"Naturally I am, Mr. Lovelace, even more so. But please tell me your story."

"I live with four cousins of mine in an old house in Camberwell. My grandfather left the house, and a sizeable fortune, to the five of us on condition that we live together and maintain the family unity. It probably won't surprise you to know that we've grown to get pretty much on each other's nerves."

"What happens if one of you dies?" I asked.

"His share is divided among the others, Dr. Watson."

"The wonder to me is, sir, not that a murder may take place, but that it has not happened long ago," Holmes said chagrined. "Who is responsible for the administration of the estate?"

"My cousin Gerald. He's much older than the rest of us and he's a thoroughly unpleasant, cantankerous man. He gets an extra share in the estate as administrator and in consequence he doesn't work. We feel, of course, that he lives off us and we're continually quarreling with him about it. There's going to be trouble, Mr. Holmes, I know it. Gerald hates us, and he's jealous of our share in the estate."

"You spoke of preventing murder just now," Holmes said, leaning forward in his chair, "yet I can see that you've selected your cousin Gerald as the potential murderer, am I right?"

"Yes, you are, Mr. Holmes, but don't think it's personal prejudice that makes me suspect him; I have good reason for doing so."

"What reason?"

"This evening, just before dinner, I helped Gerald off with his topcoat and went to hang it up for him. As I did so, I heard a strange metallic 'clink' in one of his pockets. I slipped my hand inside it and found a hypodermic syringe and a small vial of liquid, which I opened and smelled. Gentlemen, it reeked of bitter almonds."

"Cyanide," I said.

"And what did you do?" Holmes asked.

"I thought of destroying it, but I realized that would put him on his guard, so I replaced it in his pocket. Of course, I warned the others. And we decided that I'd come to you. I had to see a most important client tonight, or I would have been here earlier. Please forgive me for intruding on you at this unlikely hour, gentlemen."

"Perfectly all right, Mr. Lovelace," Holmes said. "Besides, you are already here and, quite frankly, I am intrigued by your problem. That's a most interesting stick you carry, sir. May I examine it?"

"Of course."

I laughed, for now I understood about the dog.

"I see now, Holmes, how you deduced that Mr. Lovelace has a dog. There are the marks of the dog's teeth on the stick."

"Yes, my dear Watson. But these marks, under scrutiny, give us even more specific information. He's a large dog, you've had him for some years, Mr. Lovelace, and he's now old and feeble."

"You are again perfectly right, but I simply cannot see how you can tell that from looking at a walking stick."

"This stick is covered with teeth marks," Holmes went on, "therefore it has been carried many times by the dog. Now it's a heavy stick so only a large dog could have carried it. And the teeth marks also indicate a large jaw. The older marks are deep, look here. The fresh ones, where the wood has not yet darkened, are shallow. Yes, it's obvious the jaws are losing their strength."

"That's very clever of you, Mr. Holmes," Mr. Lovelace said with somewhat obvious irritation, "but I don't see what it has to do with the case in hand."

"No? Surely it tells us that your story, Mr. Lovelace, may bear more implication than you think. On the other hand, its implication may be even more terrifying. I shall have to take the time to explain this later. Right now, though it's late at night, I feel that any further delay in this matter would be extremely dangerous. I suggest we get a cab and come to your house in Camberwell at once."

"What, Holmes?" I said. "In this weather?"

"Yes, Watson. We've been through weather such as this before. Come on, my dear fellow, grab your coat and hat. The game's afoot!"

The lashing rain beat against the cab as it hurried through the drenched and misted London streets. It was some of the foulest weather I had seen in years. Holmes sat beside me with Edmund Lovelace facing him, directly opposite. During the entire trip nothing was said, yet I had occasion to observe my dear friend as he contemplated quietly to himself. Mr. Lovelace seemed quite impatient to arrive home, and when we at last did so, he hurriedly ushered us into his house. As I gazed about, I could tell this was a moderately furnished house, speaking not of riches, but of the working man who had attained wealth by decent hard work. Mr. Lovelace's servant took our rain soaked coats and hats and placed them near the fireplace where they might dry. Seated in the living room were a woman and a man, who, upon our entrance, stood to greet us.

"Alice . . . Randolph," said Mr. Lovelace, "I'm glad you are still up. I was able to persuade Mr. Sherlock Holmes and Dr. Watson to come back with me. Gentlemen, this is my cousin Alice Harley and my cousin Randolph Lovelace. I told them about the whole business, Randolph, so we can all speak perfectly freely."

"Let's begin by sitting down, shall we?" said Alice Harley as she showed us two very comfortable chairs near the fireplace. "Randolph and I have just finished a little cold supper as we've been to the theatre tonight."

As we seated ourselves comfortably and the conversation began, I took the time to observe both Alice and Randolph. Alice Harley was of small build, but full, and bore little resemblance to Edmund Lovelace in facial appearance. Randolph Lovelace, on the other hand bore a striking resemblance to Edmund, but was much taller and thinner and seemed to possess a quiet nature. When he spoke his voice was even and measured in tone almost as that of a minister.

"Well, Mr. Holmes, I suppose Edmund told you about finding the hypodermic syringe, and the cyanide in Gerald's coat pocket?"

"Yes indeed," Holmes answered, "may I ask where your cousin Gerald Lovelace is now?"

"We left the house at seven, but I imagine Gerald went upstairs at eight as usual, didn't he Edmund?"

"That's right, on the stroke of eight, Alice. He's very fixed in his habits, Mr. Holmes. He goes up to his room every night at eight. There he reads, or works on his accounts and eventually goes to bed any time between ten and one."

"He might still be up," Randolph said.

"I should like to speak to him a little later. In the meanwhile may I ask you two young people to tell me, quite honestly, your feelings about your cousin Gerald?" Holmes asked.

"And you might as well be frank," Edmund said, "I've kept nothing back."

"All right," Alice said, sitting up stiffly in her chair, "Randolph and I hate him! First of all we're sure he is jealous of our shares in the estate and then we . . . we. . . . "

The young lady hesitated, then looked at Randolph.

"Alice and I want to get married, Mr. Holmes," Randolph said, "and Gerald won't hear of it."

"But you're cousins, aren't you?" I asked.

"Only second cousins, Dr. Watson. Gerald is dreadfully conventional. He's threatened us that if we do get married he'll go to court and try to have our shares in the estate annulled."

"And from the way the will is worded," Randolph added, "I wouldn't be surprised if he could do it. So you can see why we have no great love for him, and why we're afraid of him."

"You mentioned there were five cousins in the house, Edmund," Holmes said, "the three of you are here, and Mr. Gerald Lovelace is upstairs. Who and where is the fifth cousin?"

"The fifth cousin is my brother, Gilly. He's something of a tragedy, I'm afraid. You see, Gilly's twenty, but he never developed mentally beyond the age of eight. He had a bad fall in a hunting field when he was a young boy and has been like this ever since," Randolph offered.

"I'm sorry to hear that, sir," Holmes said.

"But he's the dearest and most gentle boy you've ever met," Alice said.

"And, incidentally," Edmund added, "the one person in this house who doesn't hate Gerald."

"The poor fellow doesn't understand the conditions of the will, I suppose?" I asked.

"No," returned Alice, "but if he did I don't think it would make any difference. I swear that Gilly loves every living thing, especially Gladstone. Gladstone is the name of his dog."

Holmes placed his hands together before he spoke, a thoughtful look on his face.

"His dog. Yes. The dog may be the key to this whole matter."

"The dog?" I asked, puzzled. "What makes you say that, Holmes?"

"When a man brings a quick and painless poison home to a household containing an old and feeble dog," Holmes continued, "it's more than possible that he has obtained that poison quite legitimately to give the dog a merciful death."

"To kill Gladstone," Alice said in surprise. "No, he wouldn't!"

"After all, Alice dear, he is old," Randolph said, "and he's almost blind now."

"But Mr. Holmes, if you think Gerald brought home the poison to put Gladstone out of the way, and I admit it sounds perfectly logical, what made you decide to come here tonight?" asked Edmund.

"Because I dare not even guess what you may have done by intruding the *thought* of murder in this situation. Where is your brother Gilly?"

"In his room, upstairs, asleep."

"I wonder if we might go up to him," Holmes asked, "I should like to talk to him if you don't mind. And after that I want a few words with your cousin Gerald Lovelace."

Holmes stood up, the others following suit as Randolph Lovelace led the way up a flight of stairs to the second story rooms. Quietly we entered Gilly's room where, in the dim light, I saw the young man sleeping peacefully in his bed. There on the bed was the dog, Gladstone, his head nestled gently on the pillow, with Gilly's arm around him.

"I'm afraid we'll have to waken the boy," Holmes whispered to the others. Alice leaned over, gently shaking the boy.

"Gilly, Gilly, wake up," she said softly. Gladstone began to growl.

"We're not going to hurt him," Alice said to the dog, petting him.

The young man stirred and looked up, rubbing his eyes.

"Who is it? Oh, hello, Alice," he said with a smile. He then noticed the rest of us standing behind Alice, and sat up quickly, a look of fright crossing his face.

"Who are these men? They've come to take Gladstone away, haven't they?"

"No, Gilly," Holmes said, "we've just come to admire him. Your brother has been telling us what a fine dog he is."

"Oh, that's different," Gilly said, smiling and petting Gladstone. "Isn't he beautiful? I just had a wonderful dream about Gladstone and me."

"What was it, Gilly?" Randolph asked as he tucked the young man back under the covers.

"Gladstone was young again and we ran through a field and we chased some rabbits, then we went down a rabbit hole. Gladstone was so beautiful. He was young again, you know. And we sat all 'round a table and had tea with the rabbits. It was so funny. They all had little green hats on, and with feathers. Then we went to sleep, just like now. I'm so sleepy. So sleepy. Come on, Gladstone, let's go back to the tea party."

Gilly placed his arm around the dog again and soon they were asleep. It was a peaceful but sad sight.

"Poor boy," I said, shaking my head.

"His world may be a great deal more pleasant than ours, Watson," Holmes said in whispered tones.

"That's what I'd like to think, Mr. Holmes," Randolph added.

"And now," Holmes continued, "I'd like to have a few words with your cousin Gerald."

We left the room as quietly as we entered, as Randolph Lovelace led us down to the end of the hallway where Gerald's room was located.

"I'm afraid Gilly wasn't much help to you, Mr. Holmes," said Alice before we entered Gerald's room.

"On the contrary, young lady, he told me exactly what I wanted to know."

"Look, Holmes," I said, "there's no light under the door. He must have gone to sleep."

"I'm afraid we must waken him, too," Holmes said.

Randolph knocked on the door, and we waited, but there was no answer. Again he knocked, and still no answer.

"He must be a heavy sleeper," I said.

"But he isn't," Randolph said, "he's a remarkably light one."

This time Randolph knocked very hard and loud on the door, and still there was no reply. I looked at Holmes whose eyes had narrowed, a look of curiosity on his face.

"Come, let's go in," he said, opening the door. "Strike a match, will you, Watson?"

I did so, but the light of the match was too dim to make out anything but a figure in bed.

"The gas mantle is at the head of his bed, Dr. Watson," Alice said.

I moved forward until I could discern the gas mantle clearly; I lit it and stood back as the light filled the room.

"Why he's lying on the covers," young Randolph said. "He must be . . . there's blood on the pillow!"

"Great Scott, Holmes!" I exclaimed. "The back of his skull is smashed in! He's been murdered!"

Alice Harley backed away, frightened and trembling. Randolph quickly comforted her as Holmes examined the body.

"Yes, murdered, Watson, but not by the blows on his head. Look here on the table by his bed," he said.

"A hypodermic syringe and a broken vial!"

"Yes, a broken vial," Holmes said, lifting it to his nose, "with the pungent odor of bitter almond!"

"Poor devil," Randolph said. "Though I won't pretend I liked him, it is a ghastly way to die."

"'All they that take the sword, shall perish with the sword,' so the scriptures say, Mr. Lovelace. The very suspicion of the killing has brought murder to pass. Well, it's too late to prevent it. Our job now is to find the killer and see that he's brought to justice!"

Alice Harley and Edmund Lovelace wanted to immediately call the police, but Holmes prevailed upon them to give him the opportunity of examining the scene of the crime carefully before they were sent for. Reluctantly the household agreed to Holmes' wishes. And so, a few minutes before 1 A.M. that October night, with the rest of the household retired to the living room, Holmes and I stood alone in the room of death.

"Watson, turn the gas up a little higher and examine the body."

As I did so, Holmes made a methodical and very thorough examination of everything within the room. When I was through examining Gerald Lovelace, I stood watching, as I had done many times before, constantly amazed at Holmes' methods as he would pick up a bit of information here and a bit there from all that he could survey.

"You know, Holmes," I couldn't help saying, "I think you should have sent for the police straight away."

"In a case like this, Watson, I prefer to be my own police. When I have spun the web, they may take the flies, but not before. What are the results of your medical examination, old chap?"

"From what I can tell, he was first beaten on the head with that poker lying on the floor, then he had the full vial of cyanide injected into his left wrist."

"Can you estimate the time of death at all accurately, Watson?"

"No. This room's confoundedly hot which makes an accurate placement of time difficult, Holmes. He might have died anytime from one to five hours ago."

Holmes began to pace slowly about the room giving the problem much thought as I patiently waited for him to speak. He halted before the incriminating vial, raised it and looked at it once more, then turned to me.

"It is now one o'clock," Holmes said, "and we know that he was alive at eight. Mr. Edmund Lovelace saw him leave for his room at that hour."

"Yes, *if* he was telling the truth," I added.

"One thing we do know for a fact, Watson, is that this man was murdered at the exact moment he was going to bed. He's wearing his nightgown and nightcap but his bed has not been slept in."

"Is it possible the murderer might have killed him shortly after eight, then dressed him in his nightclothes to confuse us?"

"No, my dear chap," he said, "you will notice that the hypodermic needle passed through the sleeve of his nightshirt, here. Also the nightcap is crushed and bloodstained from the blows of the poker. No, Gerald Lovelace had prepared for bed."

"It seems that way, Holmes. Look at the glass of water on the night table, the prayer book, and the watch."

"Signs of a prosperous and meticulous man," he mused. "Very fine gold watch, and in excellent condition." Holmes picked the watch up and, turning it about in his hands, made note of the fine engraving on the case. Casually he laid his fingers on the stem and began to wind the watch. I could hear its mechanism clicking.

"Ah ha!" Holmes said excitedly, "there's the answer, Watson!"

"What do you mean 'There's the answer, Watson?'" I said somewhat cynically.

"I just wound this watch one turn and then it was fully wound. That provides us with the time schedule for our murder. Come on, Watson. We'll send the servant for the police and, while they are on the way, I should like to put a few more questions to this family."

In short order everything was done as Holmes asked and we were once again gathered in the living room with Edmund Lovelace and his cousins.

"Before the police arrive," Holmes said, "I should like to hear your statements again very carefully. Mr. Edmund Lovelace, what were your exact movements tonight?"

"I left here shortly before ten. From ten o'clock until the time I came to Baker Street I was with my client."

"His name and address, please."

"Derrick Waterlow. 39 Onslow Square, South Kensington."

"Thank you. Make a note of these, Watson. Now, you, Miss Harley, and you, Mr. Randolph Lovelace, went to the theatre together. Can any independent witness testify as to your movements?"

"Yes, Mr. Holmes," Alice Harley said, "we went with friends; the Grant Morseby's. They live at the Clarington Hotel off Charing Cross."

"What time did you leave this house?" Holmes pressed on.

"Well, it was about a quarter to eight, wasn't it Alice?" Randolph added.

"Yes, and after the play we went to the Cafe Royal for a little refreshment with our friends, and then came back here."

"I see. And what time did you arrive back at this house?"

"Just a few minutes before midnight," Randolph said, "I remember the grandfather clock in the hall striking just as we went into the drawing room."

"And your brother Gilly, sir. I hate to waken him again. Have you any idea of his movements tonight?"

"He never goes out after dark, Mr. Holmes. But I spoke to the cook as we came in tonight and she said he played cards with her until just after ten o'clock."

"He was fast asleep when I looked in on him shortly after midnight," Alice said.

"Thank you both. You've made a note of all these facts, Watson?"

"Yes, I've written them down."

"Good, then let's be on our way to Baker Street."

"But the police, Mr. Holmes, they will be here soon!" Edmund said in surprise.

"I know," Holmes said with a restrained smile. "Please give them my regards, will you? Apologize for my informality and tell them that I shall have the answer to this matter probably in a little over 24 hours. Good night to you all."

With that, a bemused Sherlock Holmes grabbed his coat and hat and, with me close on his heel, left the Lovelace family to ponder at what appeared my friend's quick and moody action.

Wearily I climbed the stairs to our lodgings, threw my coat and hat down and fell into a chair near the fireplace. I was cold, wet and quite tired by now and the fire had dwindled to a mere glow, throwing off little heat to comfort me. Holmes had followed me up and, after hanging his coat and hat up, went and stoked the fire.

"Thank you, Holmes."

"That should warm us a bit."

Holmes crossed to me and, pulling Gerald Lovelace's watch from his pocket, held it aloft where I could see it glistening in the light of the fire.

"Watson, dear chap, I place the watch thus on the table beside your chair. Don't touch it or move it. Just keep an eye on it, will you? I shall be in my room for a while working on some notes for a monograph."

Holmes left me there in my state of exhaustion, but I did as he told me, periodically checking to see if it was still running. I shook off the tiredness I felt by checking the alibis of the Lovelace household against each other. They seemed correct.

Before I knew it, night had turned into day and then again night. Holmes occasionally came out of his room and, fiddling with his chemical bottles or his microscope, would take notes on some exotic and unusual experiments he was involved in, then as quickly return to his room. I placed my dispatch box to one side and, glancing at the watch, slowly closed my eyelids, for they were now quite heavy with sleep. Suddenly I was startled by Holmes' figure standing before me.

"Is the watch still running?" he asked.

"Yes. And that's another thing, Holmes. What will the police say when they find that you took the dead man's watch?"

"I have no idea."

"Why did you take it, anyway?" I asked.

"You sound sleepy, old chap," was Holmes' reply.

"I'm confoundedly sleepy."

"Then why don't you go to bed?" he said.

"What are you going to do?"

"Continue my vigil, with my pipe and the watch of a dead man."

I rose and walked heavily to my room, turning only to say goodnight to Holmes, which he acknowledged with a nod of his head. Somehow, without my remembering, I slipped beneath the covers and fell into a deep sleep. It seemed like only minutes had gone by when I heard a distant voice calling. I stirred as it grew louder gradually realizing Holmes was seated on my bed beside me.

"Watson! Watson! Wake up!"

"What time is it, Holmes?" I said, yawning.

"Five o'clock in the morning."

"What are you doing up at this hour?"

"The watch has just stopped. I'm about to rewind it," he said, expectation in his voice.

"What are you rewinding it for, Holmes?" I asked. "Especially since you've waited over 24 hours for it to unwind."

"When I know how many turns it takes to wind it fully, I shall have the answer to this whole business!"

He continued winding the watch as I sat up in bed, brushed the sleep from my eyes, and watched him intently.

"Ten, eleven. . . . "

"You're being confoundedly mysterious, as usual, Holmes," I said in puzzlement over Holmes' reason for this whole watch thing.

"Fourteen! Fourteen turns and the watch is fully wound. Get your clothes on, old chap."

"For Heavens sake, Holmes, where are we going at this hour?" I said, quite annoyed.

"To the house in Camberwell. Now I know who murdered Gerald Lovelace!"

Mumbling to myself because of Holmes' irritating habit of plunging into matters at a moments' notice, I dressed and joined him downstairs where he was impatiently waiting with a Hansom.

It took me almost the entire trip to the Camberwell house for me to be sufficiently awake to gather my wits about me. It was Edmund Lovelace who opened the door for us.

"Ah, I'm glad it is you that let us in, Mr. Lovelace. Please take us up to your young cousin's room at once," Holmes said.

"Gilly," Edmund Lovelace said, quite puzzled, "what do you want with him?"

"I'll explain in a moment. Please take us up to him."

"Of course, but what brings you here at this hour of the morning?"

"Mr. Holmes knows who murdered your cousin," I said.

"Well, I'm glad to hear it. It's more than the police seem to know. They were here half the night cross-examining us."

We climbed the staircase and went the short distance to Gilly's room. Holmes was about to take the liberty of knocking, when Edmund spoke up.

"I don't think we need knock, Mr. Holmes."

Edmund opened the door and we entered. Edmund stood by Gilly's bedside and gently shook the boy.

"Gilly."

"I'm awake," came Gilly's immediate reply. "We heard you coming up the stairs, didn't we Gladstone?"

Gilly looked up and saw Holmes and I standing behind Edmund. He clutched at Gladstone, pulling back from us.

"It's the same men again. You're not going to take Gladstone away, are you? Please don't take him away."

Holmes seated himself on the bed alongside Gilly and Gladstone, a gentle smile on his face. He ran his hand along Gladstone's body, petting him softly.

"Don't worry, Gilly, we're not going to take him. Gilly, you really love that dog, don't you?" Holmes said.

"Of course I do. More than anything or anybody."

"I believe," Holmes went on, "you'd even kill a man who'd try to hurt Gladstone, wouldn't you?"

"Oh yes, sir. I would."

"Gilly! No!" exclaimed Edmund in total disbelief.

I too stood in astonishment at this revelation and was about to speak, when Holmes gestured to us to remain silent. He turned back to the boy.

"Gilly, I don't think you'd really kill a man. I don't think you could," Holmes said.

"Couldn't I, though."

"Tell me then, how would you kill him?"

"I'd hit him first," Gilly said as he sat up in bed. "I'd take a poker and hit him on the head so he couldn't fight back. And then I'd take the nasty needle he told me he was going to stick in Gladstone, and I'd fill it full of that water he showed me, and I'd stick it in him! That's what I'd do. Then he'd be dead, and . . . and he couldn't hurt my Gladstone any more. Not ever!"

A deathly silence filled the room as Edmund Lovelace and I stood sadly by. Holmes scratched the sleeping dog behind its ears, then gently laid his hand on Gilly's arm.

"Goodbye, Gilly," Holmes said, "pleasant dreams."

"Goodbye, sir," Gilly said smiling, then turned to his dog, pulling the creature's head closer to him so it would nestle in his arm.

We left quietly, shutting the door behind us. Holmes turned to Edmund with one of the saddest looks I had ever seen on his face.

"Are you satisfied, sir?" Holmes sighed.

"Yes. Poor Gilly. There's no doubt about it, of course," he said in great sorrow.

"How can there be," I added, "no one had described the murder to him, and yet he's just given an exact description of its method."

"What will happen to him? They won't try him, will they?" Edmund said with great anxiety.

"No, no, no. A little pressure in the right places and he'll be released to a private nursing home. I'll do everything I can, Mr. Lovelace."

"Thank you, Mr. Holmes, thank you very much."

"I'll notify the police," Holmes went on, "and make sure everything is taken care of. Please tell the others what has transpired here, while Watson and I take our leave. It has been a long and tiring journey for all of us."

We left that sad and depressing house and hailed a cab to take us back to Baker Street. As the Hansom made its way through the still rain drenched streets, I turned to Holmes, who had lit his pipe and now sat back, the first signs of fatigue filling his tall, thin body.

"Now that the whole depressing case is finished with, Holmes, perhaps you'll tell me how you knew that Gilly committed the murder?"

"Consider the time schedules, old fellow. You checked the alibis of the other cousins and found them satisfactory. That meant that Alice Harley and Randolph Lovelace could have committed the crime only at midnight. Edmund, only before ten. Gilly, only around eleven. You said that the time of death could have been at any of those hours."

"Yes I did, but how could you pin it down to eleven?"

"The watch gave me the specific answer. When I picked it up I unthinkingly wound it, made one turn, and it was then fully wound. Now when does a methodical, precise man like Gerald Lovelace wind his watch?"

"Just as he's going to bed," I replied.

"Exactly, Watson. So it was obvious to me that he was killed precisely one watch stem turn before I wound his watch."

"Now I'm beginning to see daylight, Holmes. That's why you let the watch run down."

"That's what I did, and it took twenty-eight hours, from one o'clock the night before last until five this morning. Now how many turns did it take to rewind it?"

"Fourteen, wasn't it?"

"That's right," Holmes continued, "therefore one turn of the watch stem equaled two hours, proving that Gerald Lovelace had been murdered two hours before one o'clock. At eleven P.M."

"When Gilly was the only one who could have done it!" I said. "You know, Holmes, I still find it hard to believe that boy was capable of such a ghastly crime. He seemed so gentle."

"Oh, he is, he is, my dear fellow. Except when his beloved dog's life was at stake. Probably out of some mistaken notion of kindness Gerald Lovelace warned the boy of his intentions regarding the dog. Ah, it's a sad business, Watson, a sad business."

"I hate to think of that boy spending the rest of his life in a mental home."

"I have one prayer for his future," Holmes said. "The dog Gladstone can't live very long. I pray that Gilly does not long outlive him."

We searched on, the flicker of the bobbing lanterns and scurrying figures in the frosty moonlight forming a weird and fantastic pattern.

# *11*

# THE ADVENTURE OF
# THE IRON BOX

RECENTLY, after a joyous Thanksgiving and Christmas spent quietly at home, a small package came by post, addressed to me. When I opened it I found, much to my pleasure, a most expensive pipe, a small pouch of my favorite tobacco, and a beautifully stitched wallet of Moroccan leather. I opened the note that was tucked inside the wallet and read this:

"To Dr. Watson, for his help in enlisting his dear friend Sherlock Holmes to put to rest the problems of the Dunbar clan. A Joyous Christmas. Signed, Sir Ian Dunbar."

The receiving of this gift brought back, vividly to my memory, an adventure that Holmes and I had, and in which Sir Ian played a prominent part. The adventure I am about to relate took place the day before New Year's Eve in 1899.

Sherlock Holmes and I sat in opposite corners of a first-class railway carriage as we sped towards Edinburgh in the Flying Scotsman. This adventure actually started off as a holiday visit after my old friend Sir Walter Dunbar had asked Holmes and I to spend a few days with him on holiday at Dunbar Castle, some twenty miles outside Edinburgh. After we left Kings Cross station Holmes, his sharp, eager face framed in his deerstalking cap, dipped into the bundle of fresh papers he had brought with him. We left Bedford far behind us before he thrust the last ones back into their pouch and placed it on the seat beside his tall, gaunt frame. He leaned across the aisle and offered me his cigar case.

"Care for a cigar, Watson?"

"No, thanks old fellow, but I'll stick to my pipe. What papers were you working on, Holmes?" I asked.

"Just some notes for a monograph I intend to write on snake venom, its various antidotes and uses in medical science."

He glanced out the window for a moment, quickly perused his pocket watch, then turned back to me.

"The Flying Scotsman is living up to its name," he said. "We're going splendidly. Our present rate is fifty-three-and-a-half miles per hour."

"Oh," I commented, "I hadn't noticed the quarter mile posts."

"Nor have I, but the telegraph posts from this line are sixty yards apart. With the aid of a watch the calculation is a simple one. Watson, my dear fellow, we have several hours ahead of us. Tell me more about Sir Walter Dunbar. I have a feeling he is in some kind of trouble, and that you haven't wanted to talk about it."

"Well, it's not exactly trouble, Holmes, but there is a strange problem that confronts the Dunbars. A problem that will be settled at midnight tomorrow."

"Indeed. The night of New Year's Eve?"

"Exactly. But to really appreciate the story, Holmes," I continued, "I have to begin by telling you of the death of old Sir Thomas Dunbar, the father of Sir Walter Dunbar. Sir Thomas was severely wounded at Waterloo though he managed to last long enough to get back to Dunbar Castle. The story goes that, as he lay on his death bed, he told his wife of their plans for their unborn son, gently holding his wife's hands in his as she continued to weep for him. He tried to comfort her as best he could and managed to make her understand that he was not afraid of his soon to come death. His deepest pain was that he would not have a chance to see the child his wife would bear him. Sir Walter Scott, the great poet and novelist, was Sir Thomas' closest friend, yet he had not come to pay his last respects. This too bothered the dying man. There was a knock on the door and in came another friend of Sir Thomas. It was Sandy Murdock, the lawyer and executor of Sir Thomas' estate. Seating himself beside the dying man, he listened intently as Sir Thomas told both he and his wife that the best part of his wealth was in the form of gold in a large iron box placed under the bed. It was essential that Sandy Murdock keep the iron box in trust for Sir Thomas. He was to turn the box over to his as yet unborn son, on the New Year's Eve before his twenty-first birthday. Sandy Murdock protested, for the child could turn out to be a girl. Sir Thomas would hear none of this, for he knew the child would be a boy and insisted that the young lad be named Walter, after his good friend Sir Walter Scott. No amount of insistence on the part of Sandy Murdock would change Sir Thomas' mind. It was to be a boy, Sir Thomas said, he was sure of it. With these words, the dying man watched as Sandy Murdock wrote up the legal document that would make his last wish binding. He then asked Sandy Murdock to pull out the iron box that he might add something to the gold for a rainy day. It was his way of making quite sure his son would not want for money. Shortly afterward, Sir Thomas Dunbar died peacefully. As it happened, much to the surprise of Sandy Murdock, it was a boy that was born to the Dunbar family."

"A very interesting story, Watson," Holmes said as he lit a cigar, "and that child is, of course, the gentleman we are going to see now, Sir Walter Dunbar."

"Exactly."

"And the first baronet, Sir Thomas Dunbar, was a friend of Sir Walter Scott, while his son can boast of your acquaintance. Why it's a family singularly rich in literary friendships," Holmes said with a touch of sarcasm in his voice.

"That's not very funny, Holmes," I said, "but let me continue, for in Sir Walter Dunbar lies the irony of this whole matter. Remember I said that the iron box was to be turned over to Sir Walter on the New Year's Eve before his twenty-first birthday. And the poor child was born on February the 29th. It was a leap year."

Holmes laughed and I chuckled with him.

"So poor Sir Walter is still waiting for his iron box full of gold," Holmes said with glee.

"He'll be eighty four next year and yet, with only one birthday every four years in the eyes of the law, he will at last be twenty one!"

"A most amusing situation," Holmes added, "though I'm afraid Sir Walter finds it far from entertaining. The lawyers must have been extremely scrupulous in abiding by the letter of the document."

"Old Sandy Murdock is dead now, of course, but he too has a great grandson, William Murdock, who still handles the Dunbar estate. He'll be at the castle tonight to formally hand over the iron box."

"Under these circumstances, Watson, I am delighted you accepted the holiday invitation of Sir Walter. I've needed a rest, but I've always loathed too strict a one. This situation may pose a nice little problem for me."

"Problem?" I asked, quite puzzled.

"Yes, I'm reasonably certain that the aged Sir Walter Dunbar will not get his iron box full of gold on this New Year's Eve, either. But we shall see, old fellow, we shall see."

I settled back in my seat, staring at the wry smile on Holmes' face. Once again, in his mysterious way, he made comment on this situation that left me completely in the dark. It was times such as these that I wanted to shake my head in disgust for not knowing what was going on in the mind of my good friend. But I merely sat there, knowing full well that, if I waited long enough, I would understand fully Holmes' oft said cryptic words.

After the long journey, we hired a horse and carriage and rode quietly through the countryside, taking in its beauty until we arrived at Dunbar Castle, to be greeted by Ian Dunbar who, with a broad grin on his face, shook my hand most fiercely.

"Dr. Watson, it's a pleasure to see you and Mr. Holmes here at the castle."

"Thank you, my boy. Holmes, this is Ian Dunbar, Sir Walter's grandson."

"I'm very proud to meet you Mister Holmes. I've heard a lot about you from Dr. Watson and I've also had the pleasure of reading about some of your cases in stories the doctor has written. Our grandfather will be down to meet you in a few moments. I'll have my man servant take your things to your room. In the meantime, let's go into the library."

We followed Ian into the castle, its majestic arched rooms looming over us in ancient splendor, its walls of stone and wood holding history that, if they could talk, would reveal much of the calm as well as troubled times of Scotland. In the library Ian poured us some drinks and we made ourselves comfortable awaiting the arrival of Sir Walter.

"I imagine Sir Walter is quite excited about tonight's ceremony, isn't he?" I said.

"Wouldn't you be if you waited sixty-three years too long for an inheritance." Ian returned. "Thank the Lord I had the foresight to be born on the prosaic date of August the twenty-first."

"In the event of your grandfather's death, you would be the next baronet, I take it," Holmes asked.

"Yes, Mr. Holmes. You see, my father was killed two months ago in an accident."

"Yes, I read about it in the papers, my boy," I said, "I'm very sorry."

"Thank you, doctor," Ian returned, a look of sadness in his young eyes, which vanished as he continued to speak. "The opening of the box isn't going to be the only ceremony at midnight. Dorothy and I are announcing our engagement."

"Dorothy?" I asked, not familiar with the lady mentioned.

"You don't know her, doctor. Dorothy Small. She and her father are staying here, too."

"My congratulations," Holmes proffered, "and that of the good doctor also, I'm sure."

"Thank you both. It's been quite a battle with her father, though. He's a business man and isn't impressed with titles when they aren't accompanied by a suitable income. But, when we told him about the inheritance, he relented and gave his consent."

The door to the library opened and I expected to see Sir Walter enter, but it was a young and beautiful woman that greeted us. Holmes and I stood as she entered.

"Dorothy, darling," Ian said, "I want you to meet two friends of mine, Mr. Sherlock Holmes and Dr. Watson."

"How do you do, gentlemen."

"Well, from what this young man's been telling us, I gather that congratulations are in order," I said.

"Thank you, doctor. I finally persuaded father that Ian would make a worthy son-in-law. For a while I was afraid we would have to elope to Gretney Green and live in a cottage on bread and cheese and love and brave the parental wrath, just as they do in the story books."

What a bright and amusing young girl she was as Holmes and I chuckled at her vibrant attitude. We were all about to seat ourselves and have a warm chat when the door opened again and in came Sir Walter, his great white beard and heavy sideburns surrounding his face like a giant bush, seeming to set his mellow face off in sharp relief. A man most fit for his years, proud of his life, his castle and his lands. Beside him stood another man of lesser build, whom I did not recognize, with the stern look of a business man, impeccably over-dressed for such a casual atmosphere as existed in my friend's castle.

"Watson, me dear boy, 'tis good to see you again," Sir Walter said, a bright smile crossing his face. "And this must be your friend, Sherlock Holmes."

"How do you do, Sir Walter," Holmes said.

"Very well, for a young nipper who'll be twenty-one at midnight. Oh, gentlemen, I almost forgot. May I introduce Mr. Herbert Small."

"I believe we should congratulate you on the engagement of your daughter," I said after the usual introductions.

"That was supposed to remain a secret until midnight," Mr. Small said with irritation, "when the Dunbar box was finally opened."

"Ah, donna be grouchy, Herbert," Sir Walter chided, "the children are in love, and I'm going to settle money on Ian. It's New Year's Eve, so let's enter into the spirit of the occasion. Bring out the glasses, Ian. I've had some bottles of my special pride put out and it's the finest port in Scotland. The Creme of Dunbar. Aye, my father laid the first bottle down the year before I was born. And the drink of the brew will surely warm the cockles of your heart."

Even though Sir Walter tried to make it a festive evening, in view of the coming ceremony, I could see that Herbert Small was still nervous and irritated and seemed somewhat relentless about the events at hand, though he tried to keep patient.

"When is this lawyer fellow, young Murdock, getting here?" he said.

"Any moment, Herbert," Sir Walter answered, "as soon as he arrives we'll have dinner and then we'll be ready for the evening's ceremonies."

"He's bringing the famous iron box with him, Sir Walter?" Holmes asked with great curiosity.

"If he doesn't he won't get any dinner, Holmes! Ian, pass the glasses around, me boy."

As we received our drinks and chatted, the door opened for a third time and a young man entered, carrying with him the famous iron box. Sir Walter introduced young Murdock to us then helped Ian pour him a drink. I turned to Holmes, warmed by the coming events my friend Sir Walter had waited for, low these many years.

"I must say that this is rather exciting, Holmes. The famous iron box with its inheritance of gold to finally be opened."

"Yes, Watson, and from the size of the box, at a rough guess, I should estimate its cubic content in gold to be around five thousand pounds. Not a vast sum, perhaps, to a business man like Mr. Small, but a windfall to an impecunious Scottish baronet."

"Yes, I suppose it is," I returned.

"A strong young man, Mr. Murdock," Holmes continued.

"How do you mean strong, Holmes?"

"A box that size full of golden sovereigns would weigh a considerable amount, and yet the lawyer carried it in single handed."

"Gentlemen, and lady," Sir Walter said loudly to everyone assembled, "let us retire to the dining room where I have a bonnie supper for us all to mark this great occasion."

Amidst bright conversation, we seated ourselves at the designated places at table and prepared for the meal at hand. Sir Walter rose from his seat, a great smile on his face, raising a glass of his famous and well deserved Creme of Dunbar before him.

"Now that we're all assembled, I am going to propose a toast. Though it is still some hours off yet, let us drink to the New Year. That means a lot to some of us. To 1900!"

Surrounded by good cheer and good food we all touched our glasses together, one to another, around the table. The last was Miss Small, who turned to Sir Walter and spoke.

"We should toast more than just 1900, Sir Walter, we should drink to the new century that is about to begin."

"I'm afraid that wouldn't be quite appropriate, Miss Small," I commented. "To be accurate, the 20th century won't begin until January the first, 1901, and not 1900."

"Of course," Mr. Small added, a wry smile on his face, "that's it. Dorothy, I'm afraid your wedding can't take place for some time yet."

"Father, what are you talking about?"

"I read an article in the *Guardian* the other day that said just the same thing as you, Doctor Watson. And what's more, it said something even more important. It said that 1900 is not a Leap Year!"

"Rubbish!" Sir Walter exclaimed. "Leap year comes every four years. There was one in eighteen and ninety-six, and obviously 1900 is also a leap year."

I think Mr. Small may be right, now that I think of it. What do you say, Mr. Holmes, do you know?" Ian asked.

"Well," Holmes answered rather bemused, "I had hoped no one would bring up this point. It's the little 'problem' I referred to on the train, my dear Watson."

"Holmes, for Heavens sake, answer!" Sir Walter said, his face draining of all its color. "Is 1900 a Leap Year or no?"

"I'm afraid it is not, Sir Walter," Holmes answered firmly, "because of a slight imbalance that would otherwise be produced in the calendar. Of the even century years, only those divisible by 400 are Leap Years. In other words, 1600 was a Leap Year, the year 2000 will be a Leap Year, but 1800 and 1900 are not Leap Years."

"Then you have no birthday next year, Sir Walter, and I'm afraid I can't open the box tonight," young Murdock added.

"And the Dunbars won't get their inheritance," Dorothy Small said, quite visibly shaken by the news.

"And you, my dear," said her father, "don't marry for a few more years. I won't allow you to marry a pauper!"

"Mr. Holmes, are you sure of your facts?" Ian asked.

"I'm very much afraid that I am, young man."

Sir Walter slumped back in his chair at the head of the table, a complete look of desolation written on his face.

"This is terrible. I canna stand any more!"

"Now, now, don't take it too badly, Sir Walter," I said, leaning forward with a drink in my hand. "Here, drink this."

With trembling hands, Sir Walter drank from the glass, then once again fell back into his chair.

"After all," I continued, "you only have to wait another four years."

"Another four years! At my age, young man, at my age! Oh no, I shall never live that long."

A deathly pall lay over us and we ate our meal fitfully when it should have instead been one of great delight. Sir Walter hardly touched his food, his despondency so overwhelming that it affected all about him. When it was over, everyone quietly excused themselves, with Sir Walter the last to leave. His steps were heavy as he ascended the staircase to his rooms, leaving Holmes and I alone at the table. We rose and went back into the library where we sat quietly, facing each other in comfortable chairs. Holmes pulled his pipe out, stuffed some tobacco in the bowl and lit it while I sat, quite dejected over my friend Sir Walter's bitter plight. Nothing was said for quite some time until I turned to Holmes, who was sitting with his fingertips together, a contemplative look on his face.

"What a miserable meal, Holmes. Sir Walter has gone to his rooms, the young lovers are nearly in tears and Small and the lawyer Murdock seem to be positively gloating."

"Yes, a most depressing atmosphere in which to welcome the new year. But let us, at least, make the best of it. I think I'll go and have a talk with Sir Walter and you, my dear chap, might try to cheer up the young folks. Some of your experiences in India may get their minds off their troubles."

"A good idea. Where are the young couple?"

"I saw them enter the living room," he said, rising from his chair and leaving the room. I followed suit and, as I walked towards the living room, Holmes ascended the stairs to Sir Walter's rooms.

"I'll meet you back in the library. Call me if you want me, Holmes."

I quietly entered the great living room and there, seated before the great fireplace were the young lovers. They were talking in low voices, their silhouettes dancing on the back wall as the nearly spent fire flickered and cast a warm red glow on everything. They looked up and saw me as I entered.

"There you are, my dears," I said, trying to be as cheerful as I could. "All alone in front of the fire, aye?"

"I'm afraid we're not in very good spirits, sir," came Ian's reply.

"Nevertheless, I'll sit down here and join you, if you don't mind. Misery loves company, you know."

"You're very kind, doctor. I was just trying to persuade Ian to elope with me. but he's being most ungallant. He won't even consider it."

"How can I, darling." Ian pleaded. "I've got under two hundred pounds a year in my own right. How could we live on that? I was counting on the money that grandfather was going to give us to get me started."

"Don't fret, the both of you. Miss Small, a little earlier you talked of Gretney Green, and bread and cheese and love in a cottage. There's a lot to be said for that, you know."

"A lot to be said for it, yes, doctor," Ian returned, "but have you ever tried it?"

I pulled a chair up beside them, these two gentle and young creatures, still filled with wonder and hope. And when I spoke, I meant every word I said.

"Not literally, my boy, but I must tell you that when Mary, my wife, and I were first married, I had very little money. In fact my income was just about the sum that you mentioned. And, I am glad to say, we were very happy."

"But you had a profession, doctor," Ian went on. "Look at me. I've been trained for nothing except to be Lord of Dunbar Castle. I can't support a wife on tradition."

"But you're young, Ian," Dorothy insisted. "You can get some kind of position, I'm sure."

"Yes, of course, of course you can. As a matter of fact I think that—"

The door to the living room was suddenly flung open and there, standing in the center of the room, his long shadow cast eerily across the room by the dying flames, stood Holmes, tense and as high strung as a bow.

"Holmes, what is it? What's wrong?"

"There's devil's work afoot, Watson. Come with me, old fellow. And you, Mr. Dunbar!"

"Mr. Holmes, what's happened?" asked a frightened Dorothy.

"It's Sir Walter. I went to his rooms. They were in darkness, but in the moonlight I saw two figures struggling by the open casement. One of them was Sir Walter. As I entered he disappeared from sight. His attacker had pushed him out of the window, into the moat! The other man got away in the darkness. We must get lanterns and go out to the moat at once, though I'm very much afraid, Mr. Dunbar, that your grandfather is beyond our help!"

Holmes' entrance was so sudden and the news so shattering that each of us felt confused shock. Following the lead of my friend Holmes, we grabbed lanterns and rushed outside, but it was a hopeless task. The water was eight or ten feet deep, and it seemed obvious that the elderly Sir Walter would not have the slightest chance of saving himself, but we searched on, the flicker of the bobbing lanterns and scurrying figures in the frosty moonlight forming a weird and fantastic pattern. By now the entire household had been aroused and quickly joined us in the search. The night was cold and a biting wind had risen up from the now mist covered hills, making attempts at rescue all the harder for us. All credit must go to Ian Dunbar for taking the lead in the search, directing the servants and the others in their efforts. Holmes, too, was frantically looking, his lantern casting its yellow light across the waters of the moat in an unearthly pattern. Mr. Small and I were searching the edges of the moat in hopes that Sir Walter may have swum to safety, clinging to the grass for his life. I must say that Mr. Small, to my great irritation, seemed of little help.

"I don't see why your friend doesn't call the police, Dr. Watson. He's accomplishing nothing."

"Because there might be a chance of finding the old man alive, Mr. Small," I said with irritation. "He wants to avoid a scandal, if possible, for your sake, sir, as well as the Dunbars."

"A scandal can't touch me, or Dorothy over this. Her engagement was never announced, thank Heavens."

"It's a great pity, sir. I should think that some new blood in your family would be a great improvement."

"You're being confoundedly impertinent," he said.

"And you are being confoundedly heartless, sir!" I returned with anger, then moved away in disgust. Holmes came towards me, out of breath and perspiring profusely.

"Well, Holmes," I said, "have you given up hope?"

"I'm afraid we'll never find him without dragnets and grappling hooks. We'll have to call the police. What time is it? Sir Ian, do you know the time?"

"What did you call me, Mr. Holmes?" Ian said as he approached us.

"Sir Ian."

"By Jove, yes," I said excitedly. "It does seem a bit premature, Holmes, but of course you are right! If your poor grandfather is dead, Mr. Dunbar, then you are the baronet now."

"And the time, Sir Ian?" Holmes again asked.

"It's a quarter to twelve, Mr. Holmes."

"A quarter of an hour to the new year, Sir Ian. Doesn't that fact suggest something to you?"

"Yes, it does, Mr. Holmes. So I'm the new baronet, am I? Very well, then, there will be no more talk of the police for fifteen minutes."

Sir Ian turned to the rest of the household who were still searching for Sir Walter.

"I want all of you to come back to the castle with me!" he shouted. "As the last chime of midnight rings out, I shall have a statement to make, a statement that I want you all to hear!"

Slowly we turned away from the moat and returned to the castle, gathering in the living room. I stood next to Holmes, quite perplexed, while he, in his confounded way, seemed very pleased.

"What's he brought us all back here for, Holmes?" I asked. "There's something very funny going on. I tell you, I don't like the look of it."

"And I, Watson, like the look of it very much."

"I wish you wouldn't be so dashed mysterious. What are you up to? You haven't taken a step yet towards finding the murderer."

"Haven't I? Then I wonder what causes the beads of perspiration on Mr. Small's brow. And I wonder what causes the singular look of apprehension on the face of Murdock, the young lawyer. You remember, of course, on my remarking how easily he carried the large iron box?"

"Great Scott, yes. And it would have taken a strong man to throw Sir Walter out of the window."

"Quiet, Watson. Do you hear the clock chiming? The new year is approaching."

I listened, and counted the chimes until the last chime of midnight sounded. Sir Ian stood in the center of the living room, tall and straight, no longer the gentle young man I had grown to like, but the new lord of the castle, surrounded now by his servants and all the guests.

"Ladies and gentlemen," he began, "in view of our recent tragedy, this is one New Year's

Eve when none of us feels like song and jollity. But there still remains a ritual duty for me to perform. Mr. Murdock, open the iron box, please."

"But, but I can't do that. It was only to be opened for your grandfather."

"No, Mr. Murdock. The phrase was that it was to be opened 'on the New Year's Eve before the baronet's twenty-first birthday. I am now the baronet, and I shall be twenty-one next year on August twenty-first. Open the box please, Mr. Murdock."

"Ian, darling, how frightfully clever of you," Dorothy said.

"Good lad," Holmes added, "I hoped he'd think of it."

"But, Sir Ian . . . " Murdock said nervously.

"Murdock, open that box!"

"Very well, Sir Ian, but I'm afraid you're in for something of a shock."

Murdock pulled a large key from his pocket and unlocked the box, forcing the lid back on its rusty hinges.

"Great Scott," I exclaimed, "the box is empty!"

"Except for a sheet of note paper in the bottom!" Holmes said.

"What's the meaning of this, Murdock?"

"Read that paper, Sir Ian, and you'll understand," Murdock replied.

"'I.O.U. four thousand sovereigns.' And it's signed Alexander Murdock, on behalf of Murdock and Murdock, lawyers. You'd better explain this."

"It's the family skeleton, Sir Ian," Murdock said. "That note is signed by my great grandfather, the one that witnessed the original deed concerning the box. As soon as Sir Walter was born on that February the twenty-ninth, my great grandfather realized the money wouldn't have to be produced for eighty-four years."

"And so he stole it!" Sir Ian said in anger.

"He borrowed it. He always intended to pay it back, but he was never able to. When he died he told my father of his secret, and my father in turn told me. We've always planned to put back the money, Sir Ian, but we've never been able to."

"But this is daylight robbery," Mr. Small added. "You should prosecute them, Ian; the firm is still in business. You can ruin them, you can sue them for every penny they have."

"Mr. Small," Sir Ian said in disgust, "you've already shown a marked aversion to my family. I suggest you allow me to handle this affair."

"Bravo, Ian," Dorothy said with outright glee.

"How dare you, Dorothy. Go to your room!"

"No one is going to their room, Mr. Small. No one is leaving here until the police arrive. I'm convinced that one of you murdered my grandfather tonight."

"And if you ask me, it's obvious who that someone is."

"Who, Dr. Watson?" Sir Ian asked.

"You, Mr. Murdock." I continued. "You came here planning to kill poor old Sir Walter because you never intended to open that box. You felt that your secret would die with him."

"That's a lie! I was going to tell Sir Walter everything and then ask for time to pay the money back. I didn't kill him."

"Of course he didn't," Mr. Small said, "there's your murderer, you yourself, Sir Ian."

"Father, what are you saying?"

"I'm saying that Ian's the murderer. He saw that the box wasn't going to be opened for another four years. He realized that without the money he couldn't marry Dorothy, so he killed his grandfather and then ordered the box opened."

"You're trying to cover yourself!" Sir Ian yelled. "You pushed grandfather out of that window tonight. You thought that if he died the box would never be opened, so Dorothy couldn't marry me."

Mr. Small was beside himself in rage. The entire night had turned itself into a series of invectives as Murdock, Small and Sir Ian battled with each other, their rage increasing at each accusation. It was then Holmes stepped forward into the fray, his tall figure commanding attention. I turned to him and spoke.

"Upon my soul, Holmes, you seem remarkably calm."

"Do I, my dear Watson?" Holmes said with a tinge of sarcasm, "I must say I'm absolutely fascinated by listening to three people accusing each other of murder. And each of them producing perfectly sound motives. It's a remarkable example of the dangers of reasoning from motive alone. We should profit by experience, Watson."

"Mr. Holmes," said young Dorothy in anguish, "how can you be so calm? There's a murderer in this room."

"I suppose this game of charades is getting a little out of hand, Miss Small. Let's conclude it. You'd better come out now!" Holmes yelled at the conclusion of his statement.

From behind a nearby tapestry emerged Sir Walter Dunbar. It seemed beyond belief as our small group stood motionless watching the old man come forth, glee written on his face like that of a young child. It was Mr. Small who found enough voice to speak first.

"What kind of game have you been playing, Sir Walter?"

"'Tis a bonnie game that Holmes and I invented. You might call it forcing the issue. I was determined to have the box opened before the next four years were out, whilst I was still alive to look inside it. But the trickery of your family, Murdock, has made me a very unhappy man."

"Sir Walter, I shall pay back the money in a few years. I swear I will."

"It'll be too late to do me any good," Sir Walter said sternly, "but I'll take care that Ian gets it. I've half a mind to prosecute you."

"Grandfather, the money isn't important, now that you are all right."

"Aye, but you were counting on it just the same, me boy, so that you could marry Dorothy; I know that."

"She'll never marry a pauper," Mr. Small said with biting words, "I won't allow it!"

"When I'm twenty-one, you can't stop me, father. And I am going to marry Ian."

THE LOST ADVENTURES OF SHERLOCK HOLMES

"Be quiet!" Mr. Small yelled in exasperation. "And you, Sir Walter, have created a very unsavory business. I think that you owe us an explanation of your behavior tonight."

"You tell him, Holmes," Sir Walter said with unabashed glee, "I fancy a wee drop of Creme of Dunbar. Watching you all search for my body in the moat has made me thirsty."

"The explanation is a very simple one, ladies and gentlemen," Holmes said laughingly. "When you arrived here tonight, Mr. Murdock, I knew from the way you handled the box that it could not contain the sum of gold it was supposed to."

"And so you suspected fraud," I said, "and devised a plan to force the opening of the box."

"Yes, and Sir Walter was an eager conspirator."

"Of course I was. Ian is twenty-one next August. Suppose I had died after he came of age and before my next birthday four years hence? The box would never have been opened."

"And so we invented the fake murder story." Holmes added, "By the way, Ian, I must congratulate you for grasping the possibilities of the situation so speedily. If you hadn't demanded the opening of the box, the Murdock secret might still be a secret."

"It's a clever plan, Holmes. Too bad that it had to have such a miserable ending," I said.

"I'm not sure that we've finished with the matter, Watson. Mr. Murdock, you say that your family took four thousand pounds from that box?"

"Yes, Mr. Holmes."

"Curious. I would have sworn from its size that it would hold closer to five thousand. And in your account of the legend, Watson, you told me that Sir Thomas Dunbar stated on his death bed that he had put something else in the box. Something for a rainy day, is that it?"

"Quite right, Holmes."

"Did the Murdocks find that extra something?"

"No, Mr. Holmes, they found nothing but the gold," Murdock answered.

"That's very odd. I think I'll take a closer look at that box, if you don't mind."

Everyone watched as Holmes closely inspected the box.

Dorothy Small turned to her father, determination written on her face.

"Since this seems to be a night of telling secrets, I think you might as well know, father, that if you don't give your consent, I shall elope with Ian."

"Bravo, my dear, bravo," I said with pleasure.

"I admire your resolution towards your father, young lady, but I hardly think it will be necessary," Holmes said. "Permit me to show you all the treasure of the Dunbars."

"What have you found, Holmes?" Sir Walter asked in surprise.

"The 'something for a rainy day' that old Sir Thomas spoke of. You see, since the cubic contents of the box obviously differed from my calculations, I deduced the existence of a false bottom. I was correct. And in that space I found this!"

Holmes thrust forth a large sheath of yellowing papers.

"It's a manuscript," I declared.

170

"Quite so," Holmes continued, "the manuscript of a book. Look at the title page and see the author's name."

"*The History of the Dunbar Family* by Sir Walter Scott!" I read aloud.

"I think, Sir Walter, that an original and unpublished manuscript by your distinguished namesake will prove worth several times the gold that is missing from that box."

"You've saved the day for us, Holmes, me boy! God bless you. Aye, this has been as strange a new year as ever I knew, but it's turned out to be a bonnie one, thanks to you, Holmes."

It seemed to me there was a tear in old Sir Walter's eyes, but he quickly raised his arms and shouted with joy, his mood so bright that I was not sure if I saw correctly.

"Come, everyone, fill up your glasses! We're going to drink a toast to the New Year!"

"By Jove, yes, Sir Walter, this is now a truly happy occasion," I said, overjoyed at my old friend's good fortune.

"And let's complete it," Holmes added, "by singing the traditional song of the season, 'Auld Lang Syne.' In this case, when we sing 'Should old acquaintance be forgot,' I feel that in our hearts we should be thinking of Sir Walter Scott. Though he died over sixty years ago, he's made us all very happy here tonight."

We raised our glasses high and began to sing. Dorothy and Ian pressed their hands together, and even Mr. Small, a man I had come to detest, seemed the better for it. Holmes even exhibited a fairly good singing voice, which surprised me. And my friend, Sir Walter? Not only was he the happiest man among us, but now, I knew for sure that I had seen a tear in his eyes. A tear of joy for a man celebrating his twenty-first birthday.

"Wonderful, Dr. Watson. Just the story we need to round out the book."

# *12*

# THE ADVENTURE OF
# THE NOTORIOUS
# CANARY TRAINER

IT was my general practice, when finishing one of my numerous stories about my good friend Sherlock Holmes, to dispatch the manuscript by post to my literary agent, Arthur Conan Doyle.

But there was one occasion when I received a telegram from Mr. Doyle requesting my presence to discuss publication matters. Holmes had recently come to London to purchase some rare books on alchemy and was, at the same time, all too happy to share a weekend with me at my lodgings. As I stood reading the note from Mr. Doyle, Holmes was preoccupied at the time playing his violin, which he had brought with him. As I was in no need at the time to concentrate on my writing, I took the opportunity of excusing myself.

"Going to see your agent, Mr. Doyle?" Holmes said, his bow poised above the violin.

"How the devil did you guess, Holmes?"

"Watson, look down at your side," he commented, pointing the bow at me. I gazed down at myself, but saw nothing unusual. He saw my puzzlement and, with a chiding look, put his violin and bow aside, then walked over to me.

"This, my dear fellow, is what told me," he said gently touching the box tucked tightly under my arm.

"My dispatch box! Of course," I replied with a look of embarrassment on my face.

"Who, except you, Watson, would bother to drag his dispatch box with him. A dispatch box that has for years been the sole repository of every exaggerated tale you have written about my various criminal cases?"

"Holmes," I said, cut to the quick by his displeasure over my work, "possibly you are right! And now, no longer wishing to be insulted for the many hours I have devoted to relating your unusual cases, I will take my leave. Good day!"

I had reached the front door, thoroughly disgruntled by Holmes' attitude, when I heard him shouting to me from my study.

"Watson! I meant no harm. It is merely the view of a man whose occupational endeavors have instilled in him a cynicism that, even to my dearest friend, manifests itself quite often. I am truly sorry."

"Thank you, Holmes," I returned, feeling much the better for his apology, "I must hurry now."

"And I, dear chap, must hurry back to my violin and another bout with Mozart. Have a good meeting, Watson!"

It was not long before I had made my way across town by cab to find myself seated before Mr. Doyle, a man of enormous size and strength, a large moustache covering his face and the rugged good looks of a well traveled, well educated individual.

"Dr. Watson, the publication of your previous Sherlock Holmes stories has been most successful and, for us both, most gratifying. I called you here because I feel it is time to gather your unpublished stories together and organize them in book form. It'll mean good profits for you."

"That's splendid, Doyle, absolutely splendid!" I said quite pleased by his words.

"That is why I asked you to bring along your dispatch box, your notes, and all your newly completed stories. I propose we take some time to look over your work, have some lunch, and return to finalize the arrangement of the stories in some proper order. I'd like to read everything while you are here so that we may discuss which stories to use for the book. Does this appeal to you?"

"Perfectly. It isn't often an author is given time to work closely with his agent on such matters. And I would invite the chance to have some say on how the book be put together."

We spent the entire day going over every detail of every story I had as yet unpublished. It was long work and difficult, with some of my stories, such as THE GIANT RAT OF SUMATRA, being rejected due to its extreme length.

It was almost midnight when, at last, Mr. Doyle pushed aside the last remaining story.

"Well, doctor, I believe we almost have a book here."

"Almost?" I said in dismay.

"It lacks but one story to give us enough for a good sized book. Have you anything else we may look at?"

"I do have some notes here," I said, quite fatigued now by the long day, as I reached for my note pad in my inside coat pocket, "but they are sketchy at best."

I handed them over and Doyle sat for a moment reading them. There was a look of excitement on his face as he turned to me, his moustache turning up in a great smile.

"That's the ticket! This one will make a perfect ending for the book. Can you fill in the details so I may have a better idea of what the story is all about?"

"If you'll just hand me my note pad so I can make reference to it, I believe I can."

He sat back, folding his great arms across his stomach, waiting for me to begin. At first I was a bit hesitant, having to rely on my brief notes, but the story soon came along as my memory brought back each vivid detail. This then, is how the adventure transpired:

Holmes had been working on his book "The Practical Handbook of Bee Culture, with some observations on the segregation of the Queen." He had been engaged in writing it when the adventure of which I speak took place. It was in the summer of 1908, I remember. I had managed to persuade Holmes to leave his Sussex bee farm for a few weeks and to join me for a holiday in the little fishing village of Kingsgate, in Kent. We were staying at a charming little inn called The Fisherman's Arms, and for the first few days our holiday was a delightful one. One afternoon, when we had finished a late tea, we had decided to sit outside on the lawn sunning ourselves, and enjoying our pipes. Holmes sat back in his chair, his long thin fingers pressed together, gazing thoughtfully at the multi-colored fishing boats bobbing at anchor in the harbor. We sat quietly for some time like this in the pleasantness of the warm sun, the sea air invigorating, the sound of birds singing their tuneful melodies, and a gentle breeze touching us. Holmes finally turned to me and spoke.

"Watson, you're really a splendid companion. I can't think of anyone else who would let me smoke my pipe in silence for half an hour without asking me what I'm thinking about."

"That's not very surprising, Holmes, after all the years we had been together."

"Well, nevertheless," he returned, "the gift is a rare one, old chap, and I appreciate it."

"Thank you, Holmes. By the way, since the half hour is up, what have you been thinking about?"

Holmes laughed, his eyes twinkling.

"If you must know, Watson, I've been thinking about the lack of enterprise in the modern criminal. Audacity and romance seems to have passed forever from the criminal world. Read this note I received this morning while you were bathing. See for yourself how low I have sunk."

I took the note and immediately became aware of the strong scent of perfume. Holmes relit his pipe, waiting for me to read the note, which said:

"'Mr. Holmes, I am staying in the same inn as yourself and as I have had a very frightening experience I thought perhaps you would help me please do. Mary Victor.'"

"Unusual sentence structure, Holmes. No commas."

"An exciting document, isn't it?" Holmes said, his voice tinged with sarcasm, "written on Lavender note paper, reeking of perfume and the handwriting obviously that of an adolescent girl."

"You haven't bothered to answer this note, of course."

"Oh yes I have, Watson. While you were still bathing I sent a message back by our good landlord that I would be glad to see her."

"Whatever for, Holmes? You came down here to complete your handbook on bee farming."

Holmes didn't reply at first, but leaned forward in his chair, a look of annoyance crossing his countenance.

"Confound it. You hear that constant chirping? It's coming from those two wretched canaries getting their sun bath on the window sill above us."

"I think it's rather jolly to hear the little fellows singing away up there," I said.

"I find the sound most distracting. Let's go inside, Watson."

We rose and began our walk the short distance to the inn. I had wanted to stay a bit longer and continue my enjoyment of the outdoors, but I also did not mind deferring to Holmes' wish.

"You know, those birds are owned by a charming couple I met in the dining room yesterday; a Mr. and Mrs. Wainright. I had quite a nice chat with them."

"I'm afraid their charm will escape me as long as their pets continue to tweet in that irritating manner. You've spoken of the peace and quiet of the country inn, Watson, and yet I find that the incessant chirping of canaries put me off on my concentration and, therefore, on continuing my writing."

Once back in our room, Holmes slammed shut the windows to lessen the sound of the canaries. He seated himself at the table to continue his work on bee farming while I perused one of the local newspapers. It was not long, though, when we heard a knock on our door.

"Come in!" Holmes said, putting his work aside. When the door opened a young girl entered, very beautiful, but shy, and seemingly quite disturbed.

"Ah, Miss Mary Victor, I presume?"

"Yes, Mr. Holmes."

"Please come in and shut the door. This is my old friend, Dr. Watson. You may speak quite freely in front of him. Now, sit down, young lady, and tell me what's troubling you."

She curtsied to me and I nodded back as she seated herself. She held a folded piece of paper in her hands and constantly pulled at it as she spoke, directly indicating her nervousness.

"Mr. Holmes, I came down here from London to get away from someone, but I've been followed. I've been afraid to leave the inn until last night when I felt I couldn't stand being cooped up any longer. So I went for a walk on the seashore. Someone followed me, Mr. Holmes. I ran back here as fast as I could, but by doing so, he now knows where I live, and I'm frightened. Please help me."

"My dear Miss Victor," Holmes said coldly, "I'm afraid you must be much more specific before I can help you. Who has followed you down here and why are you afraid of him?"

"I'll tell you the whole story," she continued, "it will sound strange to you, but, I swear it's. . . ."

She paused for a moment as she looked out the window, then quite suddenly stood up.

"There he is again! Down by the gate! I'm going to my room!"

"Now, now, don't you be frightened, Miss Victor," I said, trying to calm her, "I'm sure we'll be able—"

Without waiting for me to finish, she rushed from our room, slamming the door behind her.

"Bless my soul, what an extraordinary thing!" I remarked in bewilderment. Holmes had gone to the window to see who had frightened the young girl.

"I don't see anyone outside who might have frightened her," he said with curiosity. "There are two or three fishermen loitering about, but. . . . Wait a minute. There's a young fellow walking up the path. Come on, Watson, let's see who he is."

"Good gracious me, here we go again!" I said, greatly annoyed by these constant interruptions to our vacation.

"I think we'll take the liberty of accosting him."

Holmes rushed down the stairs and out the front door, I in quick step behind him.

"Excuse me, sir," Holmes shouted at the young man, "are you looking for Miss Mary Victor?"

"Is she young and pretty?" he returned.

"Yes sir, she is, and extremely so," I said.

"Then I'm looking for her. Where can I find her?"

"I can see you're being facetious, sir," Holmes commented.

"Well, there's no harm in that, is there? By the way, who are you gentlemen, may I ask?"

"My name is Holmes, and this is my friend, Dr. Watson."

"I'm Basil Carter. You're not Sherlock Holmes, are you?"

"That is my name."

"I thought you seemed familiar. I know your brother, Mycroft."

"Oh, indeed," Holmes laughed. "Then I presume you are connected with the foreign office."

"Yes, I'm in the consular service."

"Are you staying at the inn, young man?" I asked.

"For a few days. It's funny that I should run into the great Sherlock Holmes."

"Why, may I ask?" Holmes ventured.

"I was planning a murder. But with you gentlemen here, I see that I shall have to be very discreet."

"Who is your intended victim, may I inquire?" Holmes asked.

"There are two of them. The two canaries in the room next to mine. The wretched creatures have been driving me mad."

Holmes and I laughed heartily.

"I quite sympathize with you, sir," Holmes proffered. "I've been thinking of committing a slight case of mayhem on them myself."

"We can take one apiece, Mr. Holmes. Well, I'm glad to have met you both. I'll probably see you again. Goodbye."

The young man turned and, whistling loudly to himself, walked jauntily down the path.

"I don't like that fellow, Holmes," I said, suspicion in my voice. "If you ask me, he's the man who has been frightening the poor girl that came to us. There was a peculiar look on his face when you asked him if he was looking for Mary Victor."

"There's only one person who can settle the question, and that's the young lady herself. Come on, Watson, let's go back inside."

"Wait Holmes," I interrupted, "here comes Wainwright, the owner of the canaries." He was of small stature, and yet his clothes seemed to fit him much too snugly. His large head of graying hair was tossed to and fro by the swift breeze that had come up from the sea.

"Good evening, Mr. Wainwright!" I yelled at him as he came up to us.

"Good evening, gentlemen."

"This is my friend, Mr. Sherlock Holmes, the man I told you about yesterday."

"I'm honored to meet you, sir. Beautiful evening, isn't it? I just took a stroll down to the store to get some more bird seed. By the way, Mr. Holmes, I hope our canaries don't bother you. The little fellows are such a comfort to my wife and me."

"No, no, not at all, sir," Holmes said. "I find their chirping very soothing."

I looked at Holmes in astonishment over this outright deceit, but kept my thoughts to myself.

"I'm so glad," Mr. Wainwright said. "Good night, gentlemen."

"Good night, Mr. Wilson," Holmes returned.

"Not Wilson, Mr. Holmes. It's Wainwright."

"Oh, I beg your pardon, I'm so sorry. I thought you said Wilson. Good night."

Mr. Wainwright looked suspiciously at Holmes, but turned away and went into the inn.

"That's not like you to mix up names, Holmes."

"I didn't mix them up, Watson. I never forget a face. Mr. Wainwright is in reality Wilson, the notorious canary trainer, whom I had the pleasure of sending to prison for a seven year stretch in 1895. Some years later he made one of the most spectacular escapes from prison in the history of crime, and has since managed to evade all efforts to recapture him!"

"Great Scott!" I exclaimed, "and he seemed like such a gentle old man."

"Possibly he has reformed, but I doubt it. Our stage is set for an intriguing problem, old chap, and our cast is an interesting one. A frightened young girl, a diplomat of uncertain integrity, and a noted criminal. Watson, I have a feeling that once again the game's afoot!"

"But Holmes, you've come here to rest and work on your handbook," I said in exasperation. "Now you want to plunge right in to investigate some young girl's problems."

"Watson, you amuse me. Vacation or not, I am at my best when I can use my mind to solve some crime or, of more interest, some murder. It is even better if I can prevent a crime from happening. The handbook be damned, I'll finish it later. It's getting late. I shall go to our rooms and make some notes on the scant information I have so far, then do some thinking on it over a good pipe. Coming?"

"No. I want to walk about a while. This sea air is invigorating. I shall join you presently."

I walked for some time, my thoughts tumbling through my mind in no particular fashion as the gentle breeze coming off the sea continued to refresh me. I was disgruntled that Holmes would prefer a pipe in a small room rather than enjoy the evening outdoors as I was doing now. I stood on the path near the sand and watched as the sun slowly set, filling the sky with a red glow that was magnificently reflected off the clouds. I soon became aware it was cold out and quickly returned to the inn. On my way to our rooms, I stopped for a moment and knocked at Mary Victor's door, but there was no answer. I returned to find Holmes sitting by the window, gazing at the harbor in the last of the sunlight, his pipe still lit.

"Well, goodnight, Holmes. Still thinking about Mary Victor and her problem?"

"No. Just relaxing a bit before bed. Goodnight, Watson."

I slept deeply that night, waking totally refreshed to find that Holmes was already at breakfast. I joined him as quickly as I could, then, after a very good meal, we strolled down to the pier, not far from our lodgings.

"Holmes," I said with curiosity, "why are we strolling along the pier instead of staying at the inn? I thought you said that you were expecting trouble?"

"I am, old chap," he said cheerily, "and I'm sure it will find us out."

"You know, Holmes, I'm still completely mystified by the behavior of that girl Mary Victor. I knocked at her door last evening and again this morning just before I joined you for breakfast. I couldn't get any answer."

"And the landlord told me that she was not seen anytime last night, nor this morning, and yet her room has not been vacated. Curious." Holmes added.

As we walked along, both Holmes and I noticed the village constable sunning himself on the pier.

"Good morning, Sergeant Blake!" Holmes called out.

"Mr. Holmes, Doctor Watson, how are you, gentlemen?"

"Splendid," I said, "and very appreciative of the weather that you've provided for us."

"Think nothing of it, sir. We always arrange that for our really distinguished visitors," he said laughing. We all joined in.

"Holmes, look there," I said pointing, "that figure standing by itself at the end of the pier."

"Well, our friend Wilson, the canary trainer."

"He's got a revolver," I added excitedly.

"We don't want any of these goings on in Kingsgate," Sergeant Blake said nervously. Almost by instinct the three of us hurried towards Wilson.

"Here you!" Sergeant Blake shouted. "What are you doing waving that revolver about!"

"Keep back, the three of you!" Wilson yelled, as he brandished the revolver at us. We stopped not more than ten feet from him.

"I'm the law here," Sergeant Blake continued, "don't you tell me what to do!"

"Keep back, I say. I'm not afraid to fire!"

"Better do as he says, Sergeant, he's not one to trifle with. Just exactly what are you up to, Wilson?" Holmes asked.

"You've caught up with me once again, Sherlock Holmes, but this time you're not going to send me back to prison, and maybe the gallows! If I can't escape you, then I'll take my own way out with this revolver!"

"Wilson? What in thunder are you talking about?"

"The murder at the inn last night. I did it! I'm confessing in front of the three of you, so you leave my wife alone. She didn't know anything about it. And now, I hope you're satisfied, Mr. Sherlock Holmes!"

Wilson raised the revolver and placed the barrel to his temple.

"Wilson!" Holmes shouted, suddenly running forward. "You fool, stop it!"

But it was too late. A shot rang out and Wilson went limp, as his body fell over the side of the pier and into the water.

"Strike me pink, he done it!" Sergeant Blake exclaimed in amazement.

"Get help, Sergeant, it's possible he isn't dead!"

"Holmes," I said, "let me help. I can look at the body."

"No, Watson, the Sergeant will take care of Wilson. I want you with me. We have a lot to do, come on!"

"What the devil do you have up your sleeve, Holmes?"

"First, Watson, we must go to the telegraph office down the street, and then, back to the inn."

With a determined air about him, Holmes strode before me, his keen senses alerted, his mind working at full power. The game was more than afoot, for Holmes and I had actually been witness to a suicide. I had not encountered an actual death by gunshot since my days in India during the Second Afghan war, and I must confess I was quite shaken by the suddenness of the event.

We entered the telegraph office where Holmes quickly wrote out a message to be sent, and as quickly, we were again on our way to the inn.

"Holmes," I asked, "what was the telegram you sent off just now?"

"A message to my brother, Mycroft. The innkeeper informed me just before breakfast that Basil Carter, the young diplomat we met yesterday, left the inn rather hurriedly in the early hours of this morning. I expect Mycroft will fill me in shortly on some details about our mysterious Mr. Carter. Come on, let's go upstairs."

"We'll have to break the news to Mrs. Wainwright, I suppose," I said as we entered the inn.

"Before we do that I think we'll see if Miss Victor is in her room. Which one is it?"

"Here, at the top of the stairs."

Holmes knocked on the door, but there was no answer.

"I think we'll take the liberty of looking in. Ah ha, as I suspected, the door is unlocked."

We entered the room to discover it was completely disheveled.

"Good Lord, what a mess," I said, "clothes strewn all over the place, open suitcases, and no Miss Victor."

"Looks as if the young lady planned for an immediate departure."

"But Holmes, where can she be? No one has seen her since last night."

"Is that you, Mary?" came a voice from the hall. Holmes and I turned to see a stately woman enter. I recognized her instantly as Mrs. Wainwright.

"Hello, doctor. I beg your pardon, gentlemen, I thought I heard Mary Victor come in. You must be Mr. Holmes. I'm Mrs. Wainwright."

"Mrs. Wainwright, I'm afraid we have some rather bad news for you," I said.

"Your husband shot himself a short while ago at the end of the pier, and his body fell into the sea," Holmes said quietly.

"Is he dead?"

"We must presume so, madam," Holmes continued. "I had the police sergeant bring help and I suspect they are searching for him now. Sergeant Blake should be back here at any moment now."

"So he did it, after all."

"You don't seem very surprised, madam," I said.

"He threatened to do it," she said, a look of disgust on her face.

"Mrs. Wainwright, before your husband shot himself, he confessed to committing a murder in this inn last night."

"A murder? Whose murder?"

"At the moment, we're not quite sure," I said.

"He must have been out of his mind," she replied.

"Mrs. Wainwright, I'm afraid I must ask you some rather painful questions. Are you aware that your husband was a criminal, that he served a prison sentence under the name of Wilson?"

"Yes, I knew that, Mr. Holmes. He told me when we were married two years ago, but he said that he'd changed his ways ever since he came out of prison. That's why he changed his name. He was trying to make a fresh start."

"You know no reason for his planning to kill anyone at this inn?" I asked.

"None. And unless you find someone murdered, I wouldn't give much thought to it."

"Yes, if you'll forgive my saying so, madam," Holmes said coldly, "you seem remarkably unmoved by your husband's tragedy."

"Why should I pretend. We were very unhappy together. This might be the best way out of it for both of us. My husband carried quite a large amount of life insurance. In the event of suicide, would that be payable?"

"That depends on the policy, madam, but from your attitude, I begin to doubt that your husband is dead."

"What do you mean?"

"I mean that if Mr. Wilson," Holmes said with a touch of disgust in his voice, "or if you prefer it, Mr. Wainwright, wished to disappear in spectacular style, what could be simpler than to pretend to shoot himself, drop into the sea and—"

Holmes was cut short as Sergeant Blake came rushing up the stairs to join us.

"We found him, Mr. Holmes," the Sergeant said, quite out of breath. "We fished him out straight away. Dead as a doornail. Shot himself right through the head, he did."

"Well, that disposes of your last theory, Holmes!" I exclaimed.

"Did you find the revolver, Sergeant?" Mrs. Wainwright asked.

"Yes, madam, got it right here with me. One bullet missing. Mr. Holmes, have you found out if anyone here's been murdered?"

"I found out very little, as yet. Wait a moment, listen."

The four of us stood there, but it was deathly quiet.

"I don't hear anything," I said.

"Exactly," Holmes added, "you hear nothing, and yet we're within a few feet of the Wainwright's room. There is one sound we should be hearing very clearly at the moment. The sound of the canaries, chirping. We've heard little else for days. Come on, Watson!"

"Where are you going?" Mrs. Wainwright asked.

"To your room, madam. I'm afraid I must dispense with asking your permission."

We entered Mrs. Wainwright's room, followed by the lady and Sergeant Blake.

"There's the bird cage, on the window sill, but the birds are gone."

"No," Holmes proffered, "if you look more closely, Watson, you'll see them on the bottom of the cage."

Holmes was right, as I reached into the cage and pulled the birds out. They lay limply in my hand.

"By Jove, Holmes, they're dead."

"And yet, when we entered the inn a few minutes ago, they were still chirping."

"Who on earth would want to kill a couple of birds?" I asked.

"That, my dear fellow, is one of the things we have to find out. So far, I must admit, I'm puzzled by this whole affair. We have a self-confessed murderer, and the nearest thing we can find to a corpse is a pair of dead canaries!"

Mrs. Wainwright looked at us with disdain as I placed the two dead birds back in their cage. It was a most perplexing problem and I could see Holmes was deeply troubled by the incidents of Mr. Wilson's suicide and the poor birds.

"Gentlemen, if you don't mind, I'd like to be left alone," Mrs. Wainwright spoke up. We excused ourselves as she rudely slammed the door behind us.

"An extremely hard woman, Watson. I pity poor Wilson for what, I imagine, he must have endured with her. Sergeant, if you'll excuse us, Dr. Watson and I have work to do. I shall be in touch with you shortly."

"Right you are, Mr. Holmes," Sergeant Blake answered.

"Watson," Holmes said turning to me, "back to Miss Victor's room. I've not fully examined it yet."

We returned to Miss Victor's room where Holmes quietly and efficiently examined everything. I watched for a while as he carefully examined various articles with his magnifying glass. Finally, with thoughts of my own, I spoke.

"You know, Holmes, the murder that Wilson confessed to before he committed suicide might have been the killing of those two canaries."

"I think not, old chap. Wilson obviously loved the creatures and kept them in spite of the fact that they were dangerously up to identifying him with his criminal past. Ah, this is interesting, very interesting."

"Oh, what have you found?"

"This note lying on Miss Victor's dressing table, partially covered by a paperweight. It's the same note she held in her hand when she visited us in our rooms. See where she pulled at it while she spoke to me? It reads: 'You think you can hide from me, Mary, but you can't. Wherever you go, I shall follow you, so why not get wise to yourself and stop running away.'"

"Sounds as if the poor girl was in danger, all right."

"Possibly, Watson, but the writer of that note was certainly obliging. Though the letter is unsigned, he at least gives us a clue to his identity."

"What clue?" I said, puzzled.

"The phrase 'get wise to yourself' is very un-English; it's American. Come on, old chap."

"Where are we going now?"

"The envelope to this letter has the Kingsgate postmark on it. I should be surprised if that fount of all knowledge, the village postmaster, can't help us find an American visitor."

And off down the street to the center of town we went, with Holmes fairly leaping on ahead as I protested to him that this supposed period of rest for the two of us had turned into a nightmare. Holmes laughed, for he knew, as well as I, that no matter how much I might complain about his running about or being mysterious over some aspect of a case, I was, in truth, enjoying every minute of my involvement with my best of all friends. When we arrived, it was but a few minutes before Holmes obtained the necessary information he wished. The postmaster was most cooperative, once he obtained a guinea from Holmes. We discovered the "author" of the threatening note was a Walter C. Bunker who was rooming at 15 Laburnum Grove, a small hotel just the other side of the inn. Holmes thanked the postmaster for his information and we left to meet this Mr. Bunker face to face. Upon arrival, the owner of the hotel, a kindly woman, told us the young man had left for the nearby cemetery. Once we were directed as to where this cemetery was, we were off again on this wild goose chase.

As we entered the cemetery, Holmes finally spoke.

"Well, Watson, the cemetery seems deserted. Wait, do you hear that?"

"Music, Holmes."

"Yes, and coming from the chapel."

"Good Lord," I said, "it's a funeral."

"Or a wedding. Come on. We'll soon get to the bottom of this."

Slowly and carefully we walked to the crest of the hill and, as we entered the chapel, the music changed to a bright and cheery tune.

"By Jove, it is a wedding, Holmes."

"I'm afraid we're on a false trail, Watson, but we best make sure."

"Pardon me, sir," Holmes whispered to a man standing at the back of the chapel, "just one question. Can you tell me the names of the couple who are getting married?"

"Miss Mary Victor and a young American by the name of Bunker."

Holmes and I made our way out of the chapel until we were at a safe distance where normal talking would in no way interrupt the ceremony.

"Yes, we have been following a false trail, confound it," said a bemused Holmes. "The frightened young lady was merely frightened by her persistent American fiancee."

"But the threatening letter he sent her?" I asked.

"Ambiguously worded, when I come to think of it. In any case, we can cease to worry about Miss Victor. As she is now Mrs. Bunker, I think we can assume she is out of all danger."

"Now you've got to start all over again, Holmes."

"Oh no, no, my dear fellow, the field is narrowing. We'll head back for the inn, and I have a feeling now that we're on the last lap of our strange adventure."

"But Holmes, I can't understand any of this. I'm completely in the dark about Wilson's suicide and this so-called murder he's committed," I said as we made our way back to the inn.

"Patience, Watson, patience. We'll have the answer to this intriguing puzzle in due time."

When we arrived at the inn, we met Sergeant Blake, who had been waiting for us, and the landlord, who handed Holmes a telegram. He opened it quickly to read its contents.

"What's it say, Holmes?" I asked impatiently.

"Here's another suspect eliminated. This telegram is the answer from my brother Mycroft. It concerns my inquiry about the movements of Basil Carter, the young man who left the inn so mysteriously in the early hours of this morning. His answer informs me that the gentleman in question was recalled to the foreign office suddenly, and arrived in London quite safely a few hours ago."

"Now I'm completely puzzled," I said in total frustration.

"And I, old fellow, at last see daylight! Sergeant, go upstairs and get the dead man's widow and bring her to my rooms, please, and then I think I can give you the solution to this problem."

# THE ADVENTURE OF THE NOTORIOUS CANARY TRAINER

As the sergeant went to fetch Mrs. Wainwright, we returned to our rooms where, lighting his pipe, Holmes stood waiting, his eyes twinkling with excitement. I, on the other hand, merely sat dejected, unable to fathom this entire case. In a few moments Sergeant Blake ushered Mrs. Wainwright into our rooms. She stood before us, as stony cold as ever.

"What do you want of me, Mr. Holmes?" she asked.

"Please sit down, madam. You and Sergeant Blake make yourselves comfortable. Now, in the first place, the murder occurred this morning and not last night."

"I know what you're hinting at," Mrs. Wainwright said. "The canaries. I admit I killed them. You can't do anything to me for that."

"Why did you kill those birds?" Holmes said pointedly.

"I hated them as much as my husband loved them! And when I knew he was dead, their singing drove me mad. And so I killed them."

"Then they must have been already dead when we told you of your husband's suicide."

"True, Watson, but the lady was fully aware that her husband was dead when we informed her of the fact. You see, she murdered him!"

"You're talking rubbish!" Mrs. Wainwright spat back at Holmes.

"Yes, Mr. Holmes, how could she have murdered him? We saw him shoot himself before our eyes," Sergeant Blake added.

"Because, when Wilson raised that revolver to his head, he was convinced that it contained blank cartridges. Unfortunately for him his wife had deliberately replaced the blanks with live cartridges."

"Great Heavens, why? How?" I exclaimed.

"Let me reconstruct the case for you," Holmes continued. "Wilson, with the connivance of his wife here, had contrived a disappearance plot. He knew that I had spotted his real identity, so he planned this rather dramatic exit, confessed to a non-existent murder and then, had his plan materialized, he was to shoot himself with a blank. All from the pier, an apparent suicide."

"What a fantastic scheme," I said. "How did he plan to get away?"

"He would have swum under the water a safe distance, and so made his escape."

"But Holmes, his plan couldn't have possibly worked."

"Perhaps, Watson, but at least it was ingenious. If it had succeeded, he would have destroyed his true identity and have had his revenge on me by making me search for a murder that had never been committed! Unfortunately for him, his wife was his accomplice, and saw in the scheme an excellent way of killing her husband."

"You think you're so very clever, Mr. Holmes, but even if it were true, how could you prove it?" Mrs. Wainwright asked.

"Observe this revolver, Mrs. Wilson. It's the one your husband shot himself with."

"What can you prove from that?" she asked, a worried look crossing her face for the first time since I met her.

"Ever hear of fingerprint tests?" Holmes asked.

"I've heard of them. But that revolver has been under water."

"True," Holmes continued, "quite true. But, thanks to the researches of my excellent friend Dr. John Thorndike, an infallible test has been discovered for recording fingerprints even after immersion in sea water. I applied the test to the prints on the revolver and the bullets, and compared them with some that we found on the water glass in your room. They are the same, Mrs. Wilson! Now, does a man let his wife load his suicide weapon? Sergeant Blake, I think it is obvious that the time has come for you to take over the case!"

Mrs. Wainwright, or shall I say Mrs. Wilson, turned pale, grasping at the door to support her, lest she faint. For a moment I suspected she might indeed faint and I was about to rise from my chair to help her, when she stood up, straight and tall, that same cold expression returning to her face.

"All right! So I did change the bullets," she said in anger. "I hated him. I'm glad he's dead. And what's more, I'd do it again!"

Sergeant Blake and I were perplexed by this sudden revelation of truth, for we least expected this turn of events. Blake secured Mrs. Wilson by the arm and was about to escort the lady to the police station when he turned to Holmes, a quizzical look on his face.

"Mr. Holmes, before I take Mrs. Wilson to the station and book her on a murder charge, I wonder if you wouldn't mind answering a question?"

"With pleasure, Sergeant."

"This finger print test. I'd like to know about that. I've never heard of being able to take prints after a revolver has been handled two or three times and soaked in salt water."

"Yes, Holmes," I added, "and I'd like to know when you performed the test and took the prints off the glass in her room. Except when I was taking my morning bath, I thought that I was with you all the time."

"You were, my dear fellow," Holmes laughed. "I can give you the answer in one word: BLUFF! Yes, Mrs. Wilson, bluff. There is no such test. It would be almost impossible to expect clear prints after so much handling and totally impossible after submersion. Fortunately for us, Watson, Mrs. Wilson was gullible enough to believe me and give us her confession. You may take her away, Sergeant."

When Mrs. Wilson realized what my friend Holmes had done to trick her, she began screaming invectives at him and it was under great duress that Sergeant Blake managed to drag her away.

"What a strong headed and repulsive woman she is, Watson. I'm certainly glad this matter is over."

"But what about Dr. John Thorndike? There's no such person, is there?"

"Yes indeed there is, Watson. He helped me with some important fingerprints in my great success last year on the case of the Red Thumb mark."

"You didn't tell me about that case, Holmes?" I said.

"No I didn't. It was deliberate, old chap. With your taste for writing sensational stories about me, I was afraid you might publish the affair."

"Would it have mattered if I had?" I asked, somewhat disappointed by his lack of trust in me.

"Oh yes, it would have mattered. You'd have given away . . . what shall I say . . . professional secrets? You would have provided the public, and in particular the criminal public, with a complete education on fingerprints. And when that happens, my dear Watson, we shall have no tricks left. That will be a sad day for detectives!"

"Wonderful, Dr. Watson. Just the story we need to round out the book. May I suggest you go home and write it up. You may post it to me as soon as you are finished and I will inform you as to when the publication date has been set."

I agreed and we shook hands on it. As I rode my way across town in a Hansom, I was thrilled that my as yet unpublished stories would first become a book. Far better for me, I thought, than to publish each story, one at a time, in the *Strand* magazine, even though Mr. Doyle, as well as myself, constantly received letters from the magazine asking me to submit more stories.

When I reached home, I found Holmes still up, although it was well after midnight. He was at my desk, pipe in mouth, pouring through various books and copious notes he had taken while I was away. As I entered, he looked up, put his work aside for the moment and spoke.

"Well, Watson, I'd just about given you up for lost. Welcome back to, if I might say so, a most comfortable home only you could have established."

"Holmes, I'm most delighted by the proceedings of this entire day," I said in excitement. "Let me tell you about what happened."

I sat down and told him the entire story of my encounter with my agent, Arthur Conan Doyle. He listened attentively, his face expressing various moods as I jumped from detail to detail. When I had finished, it was as if I had relived the entire day once again, and I found myself no longer tired.

"Watson, you delight me and depress me all in one stroke," he said.

"How so, Holmes?"

"I am, of course, delighted that your writings have found a marketplace and that you will profit from all this. I am depressed became I have always felt you have done far too much elaborating on the cases I have undertaken."

"Oh, Holmes," I said, quite annoyed, "do be reasonable."

"You are right, Watson, I am being unreasonable. This is your night, or rather, your day, as it is almost three in the morning. Congratulations!"

"Here. Just a moment, Holmes, I'll get out that bottle of sherry I keep for such occasions and we can drink to a most successful enterprise; my new book."

I quickly poured two drinks and handed one to Holmes. He was smiling profusely and, in a delightful gesture, raised his glass high. I followed suit and we drank in silence, enjoying not only the wine, but our friendship which has lasted all these long years. It was then I noticed, more closely, the books and papers on which Holmes had been working. The books were so ancient the pages were coming out of the spine, and were all handwritten on parchment. Next to them were Holmes' own notes, with cryptic coding and strange symbols along with his quite recognizable handwriting.

"What the devil are you working on?" I asked.

"These books, my dear Watson, are ancient alchemist diaries that are quite rare. I have been spending the better part of this evening deciphering the very odd and strange code methods used in those bygone days. I have finally cracked some of the most difficult ciphers I have ever encountered."

"What do they tell you?"

"This one," he said, holding up one page of writing that was absolutely foreign to me, with odd looking characters and pictures, "is a formula for an elixir of life. As I suspected in my preliminary work to uncover these diaries, there is a direct link between various alchemy formulas and a precious substance produced by the common bee, royal jelly."

"A fountain of youth?" I said, laughing.

"Quite right, Watson, an elixir that will sustain life for hundreds of years and prolong a human being's physical structure from the moment he drinks it."

"In other words, a formula that will stop your aging, leaving you in the exact state you are in now, correct?"

"Exactly."

"Are you going to make up this elixir, Holmes?"

He smiled at me, but said nothing.

"Are you?" I asked again.

"Well . . . ," he returned, leaning back in his chair and touching his fingertips together, a wry smile on his face. I sat down quickly, and stared at Holmes, this incredible man who never ceased to work, never ceased asking questions to seek out answers. I began to chuckle, then laugh.

"I see nothing funny about what I said, Watson."

"It's not that, Holmes, it is simply that you will never die. Especially now that I have published so many stories about your various cases. As long as people continue to read even one story I have written about you, you shall live forever. So you see, Holmes, your elixir of life is already working."

Holmes threw his head back and laughed uproariously.

"Watson, my dear, dear Watson. Whatever shall I do without you?"

"And I with you, Holmes. Without you, there would have been no cases for me to write about, and we would not be sitting here, sherry in hand, to celebrate our friendship."

The room grew silent now, as my words finished. There was no more need of talk. Holmes and I sat a long time in silence, he at his work and I with my dispatch box beside me and, pen in hand, jotting down more notes on other adventures we had experienced. There was no need for sleep that night and, although this was not 221 B Baker Street, we were at home as before, in the latter years of our life.

Good friends forever.

"Now, now, Sir," I cautioned. "Put that knife down. Holmes, help me grab him!"

# 13

# THE CASE OF THE GIRL WITH THE GAZELLE

HOLMES has always, in my estimation, been a man not only of action but of great depths that, sad to say, I will never come to understand completely. Perhaps it is best left that way. Having lived with him for many years, I did come to understand this moody and intense man beyond that of many around him. Inspector Lestrade never understood Holmes. Gregson, on the other hand, with slight reserve, admired my friend for his keen abilities in crime detection. But few people had the pleasure, and sometimes the irritation, of knowing Holmes in all aspects of his life. He has always been an intense man, and this has helped him not only in solving the many crimes I have been witness to, but allowed him a flexibility to change his mind as well as his manner. But there is one thing Holmes has never changed: His outright hatred of the most dreaded criminal of our time, Professor Moriarty.

Ever since their first meeting, which I have described earlier in THE CASE OF THE APRIL FOOL'S ADVENTURE, Holmes and Moriarty have tried to best each other. Such an adventure, as the one I am about to tell, occurred in the Autumn of 1887, I remember. Holmes and I were seated on either side of the fireplace in our Baker Street lodgings. The great man, his eyes half closed, his long thin fingers pressed together, lay back in his chair, pipe lit, filling the room with large blue clouds of tobacco smoke, and discoursing on one of his favorite subjects, Professor Moriarty.

"Moriarty is the Napoleon of crime, Watson. He is the organizer of half that is evil, and nearly all that is undetected in this great metropolis."

"Surely that is a great exaggeration, my dear Holmes."

"No it isn't, my dear fellow. He has a brain of the first order and his agents are numerous and splendidly organized. He himself sits motionless like a spider in the center of his web. But that web has a thousand radiations, and he knows every quiver of each one of them. It's fortunate for me that there is only one Moriarty! If every criminal were equally astute, I'd be in bankruptcy within the year."

"I don't think you need to worry about bankruptcy, Holmes," I said. "As I came in just now, I picked these letters up from the hall table and slipped them into my pocket. Here you are. They don't look like bills to me. I observed the crest of the Duke of Carlyle on the top envelope."

I handed the letters to Holmes who methodically opened each one.

"Oh, dear me, 500 guineas! His grace is extremely generous in his evaluation of my services," Holmes said.

"I don't agree. After all, you did save him from a shocking scandal."

"Listen to this letter, Watson: 'I seen you yesterday, when you come to the cricket match. You wasn't watching the cricket. If you value your life, keep your filthy long nose to yourself!' And it's signed, Joe the Butcher."

"Who on earth is Joe the Butcher?"

"A minor criminal that I was instrumental in sending to prison for a short term," he laughed. "He flatters himself, though. I was watching the cricket. I had no idea that Joe was back in practice again. I must get my Baker Street Irregulars to keep an eye on him."

Holmes continued to open the letters, some of which were unimportant. He stopped at one, his curiosity peaked.

"Hello, here's a letter on Carlton Hotel stationery, Watson. I say, this is interesting. Very interesting: 'Dear Mr. Holmes, I have been informed that you are a man of ability and discretion. My life is in grave danger and I need your help. Upon receipt of this letter, please come to my hotel at once. I shall be expecting you.' And it's signed Francois Dulac."

"Who is this Dulac, anyway, Holmes?"

"Watson, old fellow," Holmes said, his facial expression turning hard, "we were talking of Moriarty just now. I have a notion that this letter may lead us to him. Francois Dulac, the writer of this letter, is recognized in France as the one indisputable authority on the paintings of Jean Baptiste Greuze."

"I still don't see the connection with Moriarty," I said, quite puzzled.

"If there is one thing Moriarty loves more than the dazzling abstractions of mathematics, and the even more dazzling achievements of crime, it is the paintings of Greuze! The suggested combination of impending danger and a Greuze expert spells Moriarty to me. Get your hat and coat, old fellow, we're off to the Carlton Hotel to see Monsieur Dulac at once!"

Before Holmes had given me a chance to fully absorb the portent of his words, he was up and putting on his Inverness cape and deerstalker cap. I followed hurriedly as we left our Baker Street lodgings and hailed a cab. Enroute, Holmes took the time to explain in greater detail the history of Dulac as well as Moriarty's uncompromising interest in the paintings of Greuze. It was not long before we stood at Monsieur Dulac's very door.

Holmes knocked on the door and we waited, but there was no answer. He knocked again.

"Should I go and get someone to unlock the door?" I said.

"No, no, old chap. I don't want to attract attention to our prospective client. A hotel lock shouldn't be very hard to pick."

Holmes pulled various implements from his pocket.

"I think a skeleton key should do the trick quite easily."

Holmes carefully placed the key in the lock and began adjusting it in his attempt to open the door.

"Well, the man at the desk downstairs said that Monsieur Dulac was in his room."

"No, Watson. He said he *thought* he was in his room. Ah, there it is. Easier than I had anticipated. Come on, let's go in."

Holmes entered the room cautiously, I behind him.

"It doesn't look as if anyone's occupied this room, Holmes. No signs of any personal belongings."

"Very observant, Watson. See here, no clothes hanging in the wardrobe, and no luggage."

"Yet, he's still registered here. I don't understand."

"Hello. What's this stain on the carpet by the bed here, Watson?"

"Great Scott, could he have been murdered?"

"It's a blood stain, Watson, and the blood is still damp. I'm afraid we're too late. Come on, we can do no more good here."

"You're not giving up, Holmes?"

"Of course not, my dear fellow. Let's see what we can find out from the hotel manager. I refuse to believe that in the 19th century a distinguished foreigner can vanish into thin air!"

Holmes and I quickly descended to the main floor and approached the desk. He asked for the manager and shortly a very thin and well dressed man came forward. Holmes, now intense and completely motivated by the events that had so far transpired, quite bluntly asked about the whereabouts of Monsieur Dulac. I could see that old excitement return to his eyes as I observed and listened to everything that was said.

"Yes," the manager spoke, "Monsieur Dulac did have a visitor early on today, Mr. Holmes."

"Do you remember his name?"

"I think it was Perkins, or Parsons, but I'm not sure."

"Can you describe his appearance?" Holmes said.

"I think so, Mr. Holmes. He was a very tall gentleman. Tall and thin, with deep sunk eyes."

"Clean shaven?" Holmes pressed on with his questions.

"Oh yes, sir. He had a high forehead, and a funny way of moving his head from side to side."

"By Jove, Holmes," I said in astonishment, "that's almost an exact description of Moriarty!"

"Exactly, Watson. Have you seen Monsieur Dulac since this Mr. Perkins or Parsons called on him?"

"No I haven't, sir, but his visitor came back only an hour ago. He had some men with him and they carried some large packages out of the hotel."

"Packages," Holmes said with curiosity, "but not luggage?"

"No. Packages, Mr. Holmes."

"Has Monsieur Dulac received any other visitors since he arrived here?"

"None that have been here to see him, sir. But I understand that Sir Henry Davenant has been most anxious to get in touch with him."

"Sir Henry Davenant!" Holmes exclaimed, "thank you! I'm extremely obliged to you. Come on, Watson!"

As we left, Holmes must have seen how completely in the dark I was about all the answers he had received.

"The plot begins to clear, Watson. Sir Henry Davenant is a millionaire whose art collection is world famous. A year ago the papers were full of his latest acquisition, the gem of his collection. And what do you suppose it was? Jean Baptiste Greuze' painting called 'Young Girl with the Gazelle.' And now it would appear that for some reason Moriarty wishes to prevent a meeting between Sir Henry Davenant and Monsieur Dulac. Now do you see why the plot begins to clear, Watson?"

"Yes, of course. It seems quite logical, Holmes, but what are you going to do?"

"Davenant is said to be somewhat of a hermit. He won't have anything to do with officials, interviewers and people of that sort, but we know that he wishes to consult an expert on the paintings of Jean Baptiste Greuze. The next move should be obvious, old chap!"

"Gracious me, you mean that you'll impersonate one!"

"Certainly. If a Greuze expert is what he wants, than a Greuze expert is what he is going to get!"

It was back to Baker Street where I sat quite fascinated, as usual, by Holmes' adept hand at makeup.

There, Watson, I am now an expert on Greuze paintings!"

"Holmes," I said, quite amused, "your disguise is amazingly effective."

"Monsieur," Holmes said with a French accent, "you do me the great honor. If I appear convincing to the astute Dr. Watson, how can I fail to convince Sir Henry Davenant?"

"My dear fellow, it's marvelous. Appallingly good!"

"Come, Watson. It's off to Sir Henry's home with us."

Like a whirlwind, the entire evening so far had been spent mostly in traveling back and forth from our lodgings in Baker Street. It was just such events that lifted me to the state of excitement as I knew it always did for my good friend Holmes. No sooner had Holmes transformed himself, than we were again off in a Hansom, to find ourselves before the home of Sir Henry Davenant. Once again Holmes knocked upon a door, but this time that of one of the most elegant mansions I had ever seen, its large front facade made up of the most exotic, and beautiful woods.

"I only hope that I can be equally convincing in the role of a patron of the arts," I said, as Holmes and I waited for someone to come.

"Watson, you are fine dressed just as you are in your own clothes. Well tailored and, if I may say so, quite neat. I would venture to say that the clothes of a doctor and that of an art patron are not unsimilar. Ah, here comes someone now."

Holmes introduced himself as Andre Vernet, art expert and protege of Monsieur Dulac, and I as an art patron by the name of Mr. Watson. Although Sir Henry's servant was quite reluctant to grant us an interview with his master, Holmes, in his inimitable way, managed to convince the servant to at least have our presence made aware to Davenant. He ushered us into the hallway where I was quite awed by the elegant and very expensive tapestries, furniture and objet d'art, to say the least.

"Well, Holmes, we got into the house. Now let's hope that you can impress the master of it."

"Not as easy a task I fear, old fellow. I have to match opinions on the paintings of Greuze with an expert. My own knowledge of the subject is somewhat sketchy, I'm afraid."

"Yes. But mine is absolutely nil," I said rather bemused.

"Greuze was a naturalistic painter who flourished at the close of the 18th century. Though his paintings command a fabulous fee in this day and age, he himself died in great poverty."

A door opened at the other end of the hallway and a young lady stepped forward. She was petite in appearance with long and beautiful hair, handsomely dressed and bore herself with some elegance.

"Monsieur Vernet," she said, "will you and Mr. Watson come with me, please. Sir Henry is most anxious to meet you."

"Merci, Mademoiselle," said Holmes bowing.

"My name is Violet Jackson. I look after Sir Henry's art collection."

"Indeed," I said, "a very pleasurable job, I am sure, my dear. From what I hear he has a magnificent gallery."

"He has one of the finest in the world."

Miss Jackson led us down another hallway, this one of shorter length, and opened a door to a large room that I could only surmise was Sir Henry's den. There, standing in the middle of the room was a man of medium height, slightly balding white hair, dressed in the most expensive silk suit I had ever seen. This, then, was the famous millionaire, Sir Henry Davenant.

"You may go, Violet," he said, then waited until the lady had left the room. He spent a moment looking at the both of us. I felt uneasy, but I could tell Holmes was quite in his element with his outrageous disguise.

"You must be Vernet, I'm sure, and this is Mr. Watson?"

"That's correct, Sir Henry. Mr. Vernet is staying with me at my home."

"I see. Well, sit down, won't you? Look Vernet, you are a friend of Dulac's, aren't you?"

"I think I may claim that honor, monsieur."

"Then why in thunder can't I get in touch with him? He's staying at the Carlton Hotel, isn't he?" said Sir Henry in anger.

"He was, or has been staying there, oui," Holmes said.

"I've left half a dozen messages for him asking him to come and see me, and he hasn't answered one of them. I can't understand it. It's most important that I see him!"

"Monsieur is in some trouble, perhaps?"

"Perhaps," Sir Henry said. "Now you fellows are familiar with the painting by Greuze called 'Young Lady with the Gazelle' aren't you?"

"Yes, Sir Henry," I said, "yes, indeed."

"Ah, you are, aye? Well then, what do you think of it?" Sir Henry was looking directly to me for an answer, but never having seen the painting, I did not know what to say. As I fumbled for the proper words, Holmes spotted my nervousness and, thank heavens, plunged right in.

"It is one of the greatest works in my humble opinion," Holmes said. "Of course, I have only seen a reproduction, but it seemed to me to have a freshness and vigor in the flesh tints, and a great firmness and brilliance of line. You are indeed fortunate to own it, Monsieur."

"Don't know about fortunate," Sir Henry said in caustic tones, "thing cost me 40,000 pounds!"

"Would you grant me the honor to examine the original?" Holmes said.

"Well, I don't know whether I ought to. I've had to guard it very carefully ever since . . . well, perhaps in your case I can make an exception."

"Are you implying you've received threats regarding the painting, Sir Henry?"

"Yes I have, Mr. Watson, and they worry me so much that I've even thought of engaging the services of a private detective. The Duke of Carlyle strongly recommended a fellow by the name of Sherlock Holmes. I was seriously thinking of going to him."

"Instead of which, he has come to you, Sir Henry," Holmes said, changing his voice from that of the Frenchman to that of his own. "A fact that will save us all a lot of time, I'm sure."

"What kind of horse play is this, sir? Who the devil are you!" Sir Henry said, puzzled and suspicious. Holmes pulled off the Vandyke beard he had so carefully put on earlier.

"My name is Sherlock Holmes."

"Why do you come here masquerading as a French art expert?"

"Because I've heard of your aversion to giving interviews and I wanted to see you urgently. I felt that in the character of a supposed Greuze expert I was most likely to gain immediate admission. And this is not Mr. Watson, but Doctor Watson, my colleague."

"It's all turned out for the best, Sir Henry," I said. "You wanted to consult Mr. Holmes and he was most anxious to see you."

"Yes, yes," Sir Henry said rather reluctantly. "Well, I'm glad you fellows are here. You see, I'm devilish worried about that Greuze of mine."

"Why, Sir Henry?" Holmes asked.

"I bought it at an auction. There was another man bidding against me all the time, and when it was finally knocked down in my name, he became most insulting. He seemed unable to bear not owning the picture himself. He told me bluntly that I wouldn't enjoy it long. Well, I didn't think much about it at the time, but lately I've been receiving postcards repeating the threat. And I don't like it, that's a fact."

"You've kept those postcards I hope, Sir Henry?" I said.

"No. I threw them in the fire where they belong."

"That's a pity, Sir," Holmes ventured. "Do you recall the name of this bidder at the auction who threatened you?"

"No. Didn't know his name."

"Then perhaps you can describe his appearance?"

"Let me see . . . he was tall, clean shaven. Oh yes, had a curious habit of moving his head from side to side."

"Moriarty again!" I exclaimed.

"Yes, old chap," Holmes said, "my supposition was correct. Tell me, Sir Henry, is the painting safely guarded?"

"I'd say that it was impregnable, Holmes. It's not in my regular galleries. I've had a special strong room build for it when I started to receive these threats. It has a lock to which only I know the combination, and a special clockwork device that so controls the room even I can only enter it during certain daytime hours."

"And yet, Sir Henry, with such thorough precautions you appear to be frightened. Why?" Holmes questioned.

"Well, I hardly dare trust my own shadow, Holmes. As you possibly know, one of Greuze' pupils, a certain Madame Ledue, imitated his paintings most successfully. Several of the experts were fooled. I confess that I've been frightened lately, since I received the threats, that a clever man might try and substitute a fake painting for the original, if indeed he hasn't already done so! That's why I was so anxious to get in touch with Dulac. He'd know a fraud at once."

"But Sir Henry," I asked, "surely a substitution would be impossible if you're the only one that knows the combination to the lock of the strong room."

"Well, that's what my logic tells me, doctor," Sir Henry replied, "and yet I'm very uneasy, I must confess."

"Sir Henry, would it be possible to examine the painting now?" Holmes asked.

"Certainly. By the way, Mr. Holmes, what happened to Francois Dulac? Did he leave the Carlton Hotel?"

"He did, sir, though the circumstances of his departure made us distinctly uneasy," Holmes said.

"In what way?"

"His room was empty. There were no signs of luggage, and yet there was a—"

Holmes paused in his explanation, for Sir Henry's secretary, Violet Jackson, at that moment entered the room.

"Yes Violet, what is it?" Sir Henry asked.

"This note was just left for you, Sir Henry. I was asked to deliver it at once."

"Who left it, Violet?"

"He didn't give his name, Sir Henry."

Sir Henry opened the note as I looked at Holmes, who acknowledged me with a nod of his head. We both suspected it was from Moriarty himself.

"Why, it's the same fellow again," he said in disbelief. "Listen to this: 'I told you you wouldn't enjoy the painting for long. You didn't, did you?'"

"Holmes, it *was* Moriarty who delivered the note!" I exclaimed. Holmes burst into laughter, surprising us all.

"I don't see anything funny about this! What makes you laugh? It's obvious my painting has been stolen!" Sir Henry said indignantly.

"Forgive me. I find nothing funny about it either, Sir Henry. But I must admit a certain pleasure. You see, once again I'm crossing swords with an adversary who is more than worthy of my steel! And now, shall we look at your famous, but suspect painting?"

Disgruntled by the entire affair, Sir Henry led the way as, together with Miss Violet Jackson, we descended a flight of stairs. Doors opened where I least expected a door to exist. Finally, after walking down a narrow stone staircase that brought us to the lowest depths of the mansion, we came up against what appeared to be a blank wall. It seemed that we could go no further. Sir Henry pressed against a panel adjacent to the wall, and a small door opened, revealing a time clock. He adjusted a combination of numbers, and suddenly a hidden door in the wall slid back. We now stood in the interior of a small room. A room with no windows and very little light. An oil painting stood on an easel in the center of the room before us. It was the incomparable Greuze painting 'Young Girl with the Gazelle.' It was magnificent even in that dim light. We stood looking at it in fascination for a moment, and then Sir Henry spoke.

"Thank Heaven the painting is still safe!" he said with much relief.

"Yes, Sir Henry," Holmes said rather bemused, "if it still is the same painting."

"It looks the same, Mr. Holmes," Miss Jackson said.

"The fact remains that only Francois Dulac could tell us if it is the same, or a brilliant copy."

"But he isn't here to tell us," Sir Henry added.

"Of course we could ask the experts at the British Museum to pass judgment."

"But how could it have been stolen? It would be impossible to smuggle it out of here and replace it with a copy!" Sir Henry stated.

"There is only one way of being absolutely certain," Holmes said. "With your permission, Sir Henry, I should like to make a test."

"Are you going to take a sample of the paint, Mr. Holmes?" asked Miss Jackson.

"Yes. That should give us certain proof."

"Very well. You had better do it, Violet. You're more adept at this sort of thing than I. But be careful. Remember the painting cost me 40,000 pounds!"

"A minute fragment of the paint will be sufficient for the test, won't it, Mr. Holmes?" Miss Jackson asked.

"Yes indeed. No need to worry, Sir Henry."

"With my fingernail, Sir Henry, I'll scratch off a tiny sample. There you are, Mr. Holmes. Is that enough paint for you?"

' Splendid, Miss Jackson, splendid." Holmes returned.

Carefully she placed the tiny sample in the center of Holmes' handkerchief, which he tied with a knot and quickly pocketed.

"And now, Sir Henry, I shall return to Baker Street and analyze this paint. Within an hour I shall be able to tell you whether the painting is worth 40,000 pounds or a plug farthing!"

Once again we caught a cab and found ourselves back in Baker Street where Holmes immediately set to work. I simply sat back and watched as my illustrious friend tinkered away with various chemicals and mixtures in the small corner he had set aside for such work. I had almost dosed off when Holmes was again ready to return to Sir Henry Davenant's home. Another cab and we were on our way. I was about to ask Holmes what he had found, but he had anticipated my words and asked me to patiently wait until we had arrived so that everyone would know the answer.

When we arrived, we were again ushered into Sir Henry's study where he and Miss Jackson were awaiting us with, what I would assume, was unnerving anticipation.

"Well Holmes," Sir Henry said anxiously, "what is the result of your tests?"

"I'm afraid there is no doubt that your painting is a fraud."

Sir Henry almost collapsed into a nearby chair. Stunned by this news, he first seemed terribly dejected, but that mood quickly changed to bitter anger.

"A fraud. I can't believe it!" he said.

"The sample of paint that I examined," Holmes went on, "was manufactured not more than 25 years ago, and Greuze died in 1805."

"Well I still say that it's a fine painting whoever did it. I wouldn't mind having it myself."

"I agree with you, Doctor Watson," Miss Jackson added. "In fact, I'd be glad to buy it. It's a brilliant copy. And more than likely it was done by Madame Ledue."

"You're remarkably quiet, Sir Henry," Holmes said.

"40,000 pounds. 40,000 pounds!" yelled Sir Henry suddenly rising from his chair. He reached over and grabbed a knife from his desk.

"Now, now, sir," I cautioned, "put that knife down. Holmes, help me grab him!"

Holmes and I moved forward, but Sir Henry raised the knife in a gesture of defiance.

"Don't worry, gentlemen. I'm not about to commit suicide in despair if that's what you're thinking."

"Then why are you grasping that knife, sir?" Holmes asked on his guard, ready to leap forward at the slightest provocation.

"Because I have work to do in my strong room. I'm going to use this knife to slash that lying canvas into 40,000 pieces!"

Sir Henry turned and swiftly walked to his strong room where the painting stood. Miss Jackson hurried after him, followed by Holmes and myself. All the way down to the room Miss Jackson pleaded with Sir Henry. Holmes and I did likewise, backing up Miss Jackson's statements, trying to dissuade Sir Henry from destroying the painting, even if it was a fraud.

By the time we had come to once again stand before the painting, Sir Henry had calmed down. He was breathing heavily as his anger subsided. I was much relieved to see he had come to his senses.

"Yes, well, I suppose you're right, Violet. It is childish to mutilate this fraud," Sir Henry said as he placed the knife in his coat pocket.

"It's a brilliant fraud, Sir Henry," Miss Jackson continued in her pleading, "I'd like to have. I'll buy it from you, gladly."

"Buy it from me? Hah, you can have it! Go and make arrangements to have the wretched thing taken away at once. I don't want any frauds in my collection."

"Yes, Sir Henry, and thank you."

Miss Jackson quietly left. Holmes and I stood silently as we watched Sir Henry staring at the painting. He sighed deeply, then quickly gathered his strength, turning to us, revealing once again, that anger he had shown before.

"Now, Mr. Sherlock Holmes," Sir Henry said with slow deliberation, "I'll pay you any fee you name if you can tell me how the original painting was stolen!"

"Well, Sir Henry, the how must here precede the who. And the how I must confess, seems impossible."

"Yes," I chimed in, "I quite agree. This is a sealed, metal room, the only entrance being through this one door. And it has a combination that only you know, Sir Henry."

"Perfectly true. It's impossible for anyone to enter this room without my being present. Or I would have sworn it was."

As Sir Henry and I had spoken, Holmes was already inspecting the walls for some clue as to the theft.

"Come on, Watson, help me examine this room. There is the possibility of a secret panel. Here's a ventilator, though it's not large enough for a human being to get in, let alone drag out such a large canvas painting."

"Well, you'll find no flaws, I'm sure," Sir Henry said with great cynicism. "This room was built like a giant safe. And the time lock on the door is equally solid."

"Is the time lock working now?" Holmes asked.

"Yes," Sir Henry said, "it started five minutes ago when we opened the door, but don't worry, it's perfectly safe with the door open."

"When the door is closed it couldn't be re-opened again, I take it, Sir Henry?"

"Not until the morning, doctor. I had the lock specially designed."

"Very ingenious," Holmes quickly added, "this presents as pretty a problem as ever I've tackled, Sir Henry. A large painting stolen, and a fake one substituted, in a sealed room to which only you have access. I must confess the *how* seems utterly impossible."

"Remember what you always say, Holmes: 'Throw out the impossible, and whatever remains, no matter how improbable, must be the possible.' "

"Thank you, Watson. Let's consider the *who* for a moment. Is your butler absolutely reliable?"

"Absolutely," Sir Henry replied.

"How about Miss Jackson?"

"Completely trustworthy. Brought letters of recommendation from most of the leading art galleries in London. Intelligent, too. And serious minded. She's made a deep study of mathematics as well as her knowledge of painting."

"Mathematics?" Holmes said, his keen eyes widening. "How do you know that, Sir Henry?"

"She had a book with her the other day. I was surprised at the title. Could have been a novel, but no, it was called *The Dynamics of an Asteroid,* and it was inscribed to her by the author."

"Hah! Now we have something," Holmes shouted, *"The Dynamics of an Asteroid",* and inscribed to her by the author. Thank heavens for your memory, Sir Henry! That book was written by Professor Moriarty, the same man who bid against you at the auction and has been sending you the threatening postcards. I suspect Violet Jackson is an accomplice of his!"

"Violet Jackson?" said an astonished Sir Henry.

Suddenly the door to the room was slammed shut.

"Holmes, we're trapped. The door! Someone slammed it shut!"

"Yes," Holmes said with a smile, "and it's not very hard to guess who that someone is."

"But I . . . I can't believe that Violet is a criminal," Sir Henry said.

"Look, Holmes, there's a note being pushed under the door."

"Strike a match, will you old fellow?"

"I did so as Holmes retrieved the note and opened it. I held the match over the note as he read it.

" 'Forgive my unlady-like eavesdropping, but with Mr. Sherlock Holmes as near the truth as he is, I'm afraid it would be unwise for me to remain here any longer. On the other hand, you are in no danger of smothering in the strong room, but your imprisonment should delay my pursuit till morning. Violet Jackson.' "

"She's escaped us, Holmes!"

"Don't worry, Watson. Miss Jackson's failure to procure the painting for Moriarty will land her in a far worse dilemma than anything we could subject her to. Moriarty has never tolerated failure on the part of his minions. A brilliant plot, old fellow, a brilliant plot! Moriarty is at the zenith of his powers! How fortunate that we were able to foil him."

"What do you mean, foil him? My painting's been stolen!"

"Your painting, Sir Henry?" Holmes said with a hint of amusement in his voice. "Oh no, no. It's here in this room."

"What on earth are you talking about, Holmes?" I said with my usual inability to keep up with my friend's logic.

"You reminded me of my own dictum, Watson. I discarded the impossible. It was impossible that the painting had been stolen, therefore it had NOT been stolen."

"You mean that this painting is the original Greuze?" Sir Henry asked.

"Yes, of course, sir. Surely the whole plot is crystal clear now."

"Just about as clear as porridge to me," I said in absolute frustration.

"Well then, let me explain," Holmes went on. "The whole episode of Francois Dulac, the note asking me to meet him, the empty hotel room, the significant bloodstain, and the apparent disappearance of Dulac were all part of Moriarty's plot. The real Dulac, I now believe, never left France. Moriarty created him in England to lure me into the case."

"Why in thunder should he want to do that, Holmes?"

"Yes," Sir Henry added, "I should think you're the last person he'd want on the scene."

"On the contrary, sir," Holmes laughed, "he knew that I'd grab at his bait. The apparent murder of a Greuze expert would make it seem likely that your painting had been substituted, Sir Henry. He wanted me to test the painting, which I did. I fell into his trap very neatly."

"But the paint, Holmes, you said that it was no more than 25 years old."

"Yes, my dear fellow, and therein lies the answer."

"I see it," Sir Henry said, "Violet, as his accomplice, had prepared the painting before hand, and carefully scraped off a piece of modern paint!"

"Exactly, Sir Henry! And Moriarty had assumed, quite correctly as it turned out, that as soon as you thought your painting was a fraud, you'd want to get rid of it."

"And that girl was going to take it out of this house with your full approval, and turn it over to Moriarty. What a fantastic scheme!" I exclaimed.

"A devilishly clever one, Watson. If it hadn't been for your chance remark about the book on mathematics, Sir Henry, I'm very much afraid 'Young Lady with the Gazelle' might even now be on its way out of your house."

"Holmes, I can't tell you how grateful I am," Sir Henry said, "and I'm going to express that gratitude in a very material manner, I assure you."

"Thank you, Sir Henry, but I wouldn't dream of accepting a fee for this case. I've been shockingly obtuse. I might easily have let them walk away with your treasure right under our noses."

"Are we locked in here for the night, Sir Henry?" I asked.

"I'm very much afraid so, Doctor Watson. Though I shouldn't be surprised if my butler notices our disappearance and comes looking for us. But he won't be able to open the door. It'll need a professional locksmith to get us out of here."

I was crestfallen, but Holmes placed his hand upon my shoulder, a smile on his face.

"Don't be gloomy, my dear fellow. You are locked in with one of the loveliest girls in history, and she's genuine at that!"

I couldn't help seeing the humor of Holmes' statement and soon all of us were laughing, forced by circumstances wrought by Professor Moriarty, to spend the night in conversation. As it turned out, that night, as well as the entire adventure, proved to be most satisfying after all.

# BIOGRAPHIES

## DENIS GREEN

Born in England, Denis Green began his career
as an actor on the British stage, appearing in
various productions and working closely as actor
and production manager to his friend Leslie
Howard. He came to America with Howard to
perform on Broadway and decided to stay. His
acting and his occasional writing brought him to
the west coast where he appeared in various
feature films. He was soon hired as head writer
of *The New Adventures of Sherlock Holmes* radio
series and worked closely with Leslie Charteris
on the Holmes radio scripts. When Charteris
decided to leave the show, Green hired Anthony
Boucher to take his place. The talents of both
men brought the radio series to a new height.
They went on to write other mystery series for
radio. With the advent of television, Denis
continued to write, but returned to acting and
appeared on such shows as *Rawhide, Wagon Train*
and others, up until his death in the 1960's.

## ANTHONY BOUCHER

Anthony Boucher excelled in the writing of
science-fiction, fantasy and mystery stories. For
years he was the *New York Times* Mystery Book
Critic. He was hired by Denis Green to work on
the Sherlock Holmes radio series where Denis
set the tone of Victorian England and wrote
most of the dialogue, while Anthony wrote the
plots and the twist endings to the radio shows.
Boucher also wrote the novel *The Case of the
Baker Street Irregulars,* in honor of Sherlock
Holmes, and established one of the first Sherlock
Holmes scions in San Francisco. He went on to
write *The Adventures of Ellery Queen* radio series.
A prolific writer, he continued to write fiction

and later became editor of *The Magazine of Science Fiction and Fantasy*. After his death, the Mystery Writers of America named their annual writers convention after him: The Boucher Convention. An honor that has continued for over twenty years.

## KEN GREENWALD
Born and raised in Los Angeles, California, Ken was influenced first by dramatic radio in the 1940's, and later by films. Multi-faceted, he became an actor and comedian and appeared in two television series in the 1960's before going on to write and direct a number of short film comedies, one of which was nominated for an Academy Award. His love of radio drew him to the Pacific Pioneer Broadcasters radio archives where he became a member. He continues to work in film and television and, as author of this book, works closely with, and is part of The Baker Street Associates.

## ALFREDO ALCALA
Born in the Philippines on August 23, 1925, Alfredo Alcala has had, since childhood, a natural talent as an artist and illustrator. He was deeply influenced by American comic strips and by such great American illustrators as Dean Cornwell and J.C. Leyendecker. During the Second World War he worked with the underground as an artist, memorizing the location of Japanese military camps and bunkers, then drawing special maps for the resistance movement. He has never had any formal training or studied at any art school, yet, over the years his ability at composition, rendering figures and illustrating comic books have made him a much sought after artist. Alfredo Alcala now resides and works in Los Angeles, California.